‘THE MAN WHO BROKE IN … will take your breath away.’

…sa (Spain)

‘This memoir i… chapter in history.’

Daily Express (UK)

‘Avey is a natural rac… maintains a sense of proportion in describing his story … journey from civilisation to the most horrific place on earth.’

Sunday Herald (UK)

‘What starts as an act of reportage then becomes a moving and ultimately triumphant story of survival.’

Belfast Telegraph (UK)

‘Exceptional’.

Morgenpost (Germany)

‘An astonishing heroic tale of a steady character.’

Jüdische Zeitung (Germany)

‘An admirable story’.

Periodista digital (Spain)

‘A remarkable story’.

De Telegraaf (Holland)

‘This is the most amazing Holocaust memoir it’s been my good fortune to read . . . this is a beautiful, uplifting book about a real ben adom, a mensch, who saw evil and, instead of averting his eyes, did what he could to help the victims.’

Washington Jewish Week (USA)

‘A brave and bracing story’.

Canberra Times (Australia)

Denis Avey was born in Essex in 1919. He fought in the desert during the Second World War and was captured and held as a Prisoner of War in a camp near Auschwitz III. In 2010 he received a British Hero of the Holocaust award.

Rob Broomby is a British Affairs correspondent for the BBC World Service. He was formerly the BBC Berlin correspondent and has worked as a broadcast journalist mainly with BBC Radio for more than twenty years.

THE MAN WHO BROKE INTO AUSCHWITZ

DENIS AVEY with Rob Broomby

HODDER

First published in Great Britain in 2011 by Hodder & Stoughton
An Hachette UK company

First published in paperback in 2011
Reissued in paperback in 2019

32

A CIP catalogue record for this title is available from the British Library

ISBN 978 1 444 71419 7

Typeset in Sabon MT by Hewer Text UK Ltd, Edinburgh

Printed and bound in Great Britain by Clays Ltd, Elcograf S.p.A.

Hodder & Stoughton Ltd
Carmelite House
50 Victoria Embankment
London EC4Y 0DZ

www.hodder.co.uk

To the memory of Ernie Lobet,
and a man I knew only as Hans.

Foreword

This is a most important book, and a timely reminder of the dangers that face any society once intolerance and racism take hold. Denis Avey, who is now ninety-three, wants his book to be a reminder that Fascism and genocide have not disappeared – as he has said, 'It could happen here'. It could indeed happen anywhere where the veneer of civilization is allowed to wear off, or is torn off by ill will and destructive urges.

It is good that Denis Avey now feels able to tell his story. Many of those who went through the traumas of the war years, including Jewish survivors of the Holocaust, found, as he did, that in 1945 'no one wanted to listen'. Sixty-five years later, a British prime minister, Gordon Brown, welcomed him to 10 Downing Street to hear his story, to commend his courage, and to give him a medal inscribed 'In Service of Humanity'.

It takes courage to be a witness. To this day, Denis Avey recalls with horror, among so many other horrors, a Jewish boy 'standing to attention, drenched in blood, being beaten around the head.' This book should be read by all those who want an eyewitness account of the nightmare that was the slave labour camp at Buna-Monowitz, just outside Auschwitz, where the Jewish prisoners in particular were subjected to the harshest of treatments, and killed once they were too weak to work for their SS taskmasters.

Denis Avey's experiences of the Nazi treatment of the Jews are disturbing – as they should be, for the human mind finds it hard to enter into a world dominated by cruelty, and where a small gesture like that of Denis Avey towards a Dutch Jewish prisoner is a rare shaft of light and comfort. He also tells us of his time before being made a prisoner of war: fighting in the Western Desert. Here too he tells a powerful tale without flinching from the horrors, and the death of his friend Les, 'blasted to kingdom come' next to him. 'Les was the chap with twinkling eyes. I had come all the way from Liverpool with him, I had danced with his sister Marjorie, sat round the kitchen table with his folks, laughed at their jokes and shared their food.' And now his first reaction, on finding 'half of poor old Les all over me', was 'Thank God it wasn't me.' That reaction still troubles him today.

The honesty of this book heightens its impact. The description of Buna-Monowitz is stark, and true. By swapping his British army uniform with a Jewish prisoner's striped rags and going into the Jewish section of that vast slave labour camp zone, he became a witness. 'I had to see for myself what was going on,' he writes. Our knowledge of one of the worst corners of the SS kingdom is enhanced because he did so. This book is a tribute both to Denis Avey, and to those whose story he was determined to tell – at the risk of his life.

Sir Martin Gilbert
8 February 2011

Prologue

22 January 2010

A microphone was thrust in front of me as I climbed out of the taxi by the fortified gates of Downing Street. What could I tell them? I was there because of something I did in the war – not my fighting in the Western Desert, not my being captured by the Germans, but because of what happened in Auschwitz.

Back in 1945 no one had wanted to listen, so I stopped talking about it for the best part of sixty years. My first wife saw the worst of it. I would wake up covered in sweat with the sheets soaked, haunted by the same dream. I can still see that poor lad now, standing to attention, drenched in blood and being beaten around the head. I relive it every day, even now, nearly seventy years later. When I met my second wife Audrey she knew something was wrong and she knew it was to do with Auschwitz, but still I couldn't speak to her about it for decades. These days I can't stop going over it and she thinks I'm trapped in the past, that I should move on, look forward. That's not easy at my age.

The polished door of 10 Downing Street that I had seen so often on the news framing the country's leaders opened and I stepped inside. In the hallway they took my coat and ushered me up the stairs, past the framed portraits of former prime ministers. At one point I faced a photograph of Churchill himself, and thought to myself that it was a surprisingly small picture for such a giant of a leader. I paused for breath, leaning on my metal walking stick, before going on past the post-war premiers with Thatcher, Major and Blair towards the top.

I flopped into a chair – I was ninety-one and I needed time to recover from the climb. I looked around in awe at the grandeur of the Terracotta Room with its high ceilings and chandeliers. I knew that prime minister Gordon Brown had announced that morning that he would give evidence before the Chilcot inquiry into the Iraq war and with the general election coming I wondered whether he would have time to meet me.

The mood changed in a flash. The prime minister came into the room, headed straight for me and took my hand. He spoke very softly, almost in a whisper. The room was now full of people but it still felt like an intensely private moment. 'We're very, very proud of you. It's a privilege for us to have you here,' he said. I was touched.

His wife Sarah introduced herself to me. I didn't know what to do so I kissed her hand and said she was more beautiful than on the television. She was, but I still shouldn't have said so. It was the kind of indiscretion that, luckily, a ninety-one-year-old can get away with. I quickly moved to safer ground by adding, 'I liked the speech you made the other day.' She smiled and thanked me.

The press photographers and TV crews wanted their shots of the two of us together. I thought the prime minister was having a rough time politically and I told him I didn't like the way his colleagues were stabbing him in the back, and that if he needed a minder I was ready. He smiled and said he'd bear it in mind. 'I wouldn't do your job for a gold clock,' I said. I may not have voted for him, but he was a decent man and I was impressed by his sincerity.

Gordon Brown's attention was intense and undivided and for a while it felt as if it excluded all the other people in the room. I have a glass eye – another legacy of Auschwitz – and I struggled to focus on him with my good one. Mr Brown is also partially sighted and we sat so close together as we talked, our foreheads were almost touching.

He spoke of 'courage' and 'bravery' and I started to tell him about Auschwitz, IG Farben, the SS, all of it, the details tumbling out in no particular order. At one point I struggled to find a word and '*Häftling*' – the German for prisoner was what came out. 'That happens to me when I remember those days,' a concentration camp survivor in the party said.

To be honoured as one of twenty-seven British 'Heroes of the Holocaust' soon after that was humbling. Most were honoured posthumously. Only two of us were still alive; the other was Sir Nicholas Winton, who had saved more than six hundred children from Czechoslovakia. I emerged with a solid silver medal bearing the words 'In Service of Humanity.' On my way out, I told a journalist that I could now die a happy man. It's taken me almost seventy years to be able to say that.

Now that I can talk about those terrible times, I feel as if a load is slowly lifting. I can think back clearly to the heart of it, the moment of the exchange.

Mid-1944

I knew we had to be quick. I waited, hidden in the little hut. I couldn't even be sure that he would come, but he did and as he ducked inside I pulled off my tunic. He closed the door on the turmoil of that hideous construction site and shuffled out of his grimy striped uniform. He threw the thin garments to me and I pulled them on without hesitation. Then I watched as he dragged on my British army battledress, casting looks over his shoulder at the door as he did it.

He was a Dutch Jew and I knew him as Hans. With that simple exchange between the two of us I had given away the protection of the Geneva Convention: I'd given my uniform, my lifeline, my best chance of surviving that dreadful place, to another man. From now on, wearing his clothes, I would be treated the way he had been treated. If I was caught, the guards would have shot me out of hand as an imposter. No question at all.

It was the middle of 1944 when I entered Auschwitz III of my own free will.

Chapter 1

I never joined up to fight for King and Country, though I was patriotic enough. No, I enlisted for the sheer hell of it, for the adventure. I had no idea how much hell there would be.

There was no sense of heroic departure when I went off to war. We left Liverpool on the troopship *Otranto* on a bright August morning in 1940 with no idea where we were headed.

I looked at the Royal Liver Building, across the broadening strip of brown Mersey water and wondered whether I would ever see the green Liver birds crowning it again. Liverpool had not seen much bombing then. It would get its share a month after I left, but for now it was largely a peaceful city. I was twenty-one years old and I felt indestructible. If I lose a limb, I promised myself, I am not coming home. I was a red-headed soldier with a temperament to match and it would get me into lots of trouble but that is just how I was.

I joined the army because I was in too much of a rush to join the RAF. The paperwork took longer. That was my first lucky escape. Watching the Spitfires plying the clouds overhead I still wanted to fly but joining the RAF then would have meant near certain death. The RAF pilots were the knights of air, but when the Battle of Britain started, the poor buggers didn't live long and I was lucky to be out of it.

I enlisted on 16 October 1939 and I was a crack shot so Rifleman Denis George Avey No. 6914761 was selected to join the 2nd Battalion, The Rifle Brigade, and was packed off for training at a barracks in Winchester.

Rain or shine, it was pretty rigorous. As a 'regular' mob they gave us new recruits a particularly hard time. There was an awful lot of drill, plus physical training and endless obstacle courses so we collapsed exhausted into our bunks each night and were pretty fit by the end of it. We were taught to use every weapon available to the British Army but I had grown up with guns. My father bought me my first shotgun, a 'four-ten', when I was eight years old. It had a specially shortened stock so I could get my arms around it and I have still got it on my wall.

My father insisted on strict discipline with guns. In the country you didn't get the 'yes possiblys' – things were black and white. I grew up in a world of moral certainties and I was expected to stand up for what was right. He taught me to respect humans and animals. Birds were shot for the larder, not for sport. I learnt to shoot on clay pigeons and pretty soon I could throw them in the air myself, pick up the gun and knock them out of the sky before they fell to the ground.

Army rifle shooting was a different ball game but I quickly got the hang of it and I was soon hitting bulls on every range up to 600 yards.

At the end of one particularly long day of physical training, we were on the Winchester rifle range. I squeezed the trigger of the Lee-Enfield .303, felt the kick and hit the bull's eye, no trouble.

The chaps operating the targets were hidden behind an earth mound. They pointed out the hits using a long pole with a twelve-inch white disc on the end. As the chap lifted the pointer hesitantly towards the bull to mark my hit, I pulled back the bolt and shot the white disk clear out of his hand.

The target man wasn't in any danger, but I am ashamed to admit I was showing off. It got me a severe reprimand but it made me popular with the regular soldiers. I was made a 'star' man on account of my marksmanship and wore a badge on my uniform to prove it.

The bayonet training had been pretty grisly. Bayonets are always known as 'swords' in the Rifles. We were being prepared to kill people up close where you could smell a man's breath and see if he had shaved that morning. You were ordered to run at human effigies thirty yards away, screaming and hollering as you charged. You jabbed the blade into the guts, pulled it out and swung the rifle butt around so you could knock his head off as you passed.

Looking on disapprovingly was Sergeant Bendle. He was a thickset man, short and tough. 'Louder, louder' he bellowed at us until he was red in the face. And he wasn't happy until we were screaming as much as he was.

It was psychological warfare and shouting helped you get through it but we still had to do it again and again until we were proficient. I knew if it was a question of me or the other feller, it wasn't going to be me writhing in agony.

Man-to-man bayonet fencing was better because at least it felt like a sport. We had spring-loaded swords fixed to rifles with a protective bauble on the sharp end. If we got a thrust in without it being blocked, the blade was supposed to retract. But of course the Regulars would give it an extra push beyond the stop, giving you an agonising pain in the guts. It was a reminder of what was at stake if you let your guard down.

After Winchester we went to Tidworth on Salisbury Plain. There was one officer there who was especially popular with the lads. He was a dapper-looking gent, well turned-out with a dark pencil moustache and tidy hair. He was a 2nd Lieutenant at the time, I believe, and a cracking officer but he was better known to the rest of us as the gentleman thief, Raffles. The film had come out just before the war and posters were still around. The officer was the suave and sophisticated film star, David Niven.

After one exercise we gathered around him for a debriefing session but we all wanted the gossip from tinsel town. He was comfortable with fans but he had trained at Sandhurst before the war and he was now adjusting back to military life again. He had just appeared opposite Olivia de Havilland in *Raffles* but it was 'Ginger', his co-star in *Bachelor Mother,* he talked about most and we all knew who he meant. There was a good deal of joking around before one of the lads chirped up with, 'I bet you wish you were anywhere else but here, sir?' There was a momentary pause then he said, 'Let's just say I'd sooner be tickling Ginger Rogers' tits.'

Reality hit in the fourth week of May, 1940 when a hundred of us were specially selected and marched down to Tidworth railway station without being told why. We knew things were going badly in France. I was put in charge of about twenty men and told to allocate the mortars, the Bren guns and the rifles.

After an hour, the train came in, billowing clouds of steam and smoke. We climbed in amongst the civvies and began the haul towards the coast.

The British Expeditionary Force was in serious trouble, Calais was besieged and the German noose was tightening. The 1st Battalion, The Rifle Brigade was pinned down there and our unit from the 2nd Battalion had been put on standby to go in to help.

We sat there on the wrong side of the Channel. Staring into the intense coastal light from the safety of England, it was hard to imagine the disaster unfolding across that narrow strip of water but we could hear the concussion of the big guns – an eerie, melancholy sound.

The 1st Battalion had only been in France for two or three days, rushed over to try to keep Calais harbour open and help our army escape. They put up a tough resistance, fighting until there were no more bullets left. A handful of survivors were brought back by the Royal Navy but the rest were killed or captured. Winston Churchill thanked them later. He said their action tied up at least two German armoured divisions while the 'little ships' picked up so many men from Dunkirk.

For us, going in would have been suicide. We would have been wiped out in the water. Happily, the big noises realised that and the plan was abandoned. If I had a guardian angel, she had just appeared again. It would count as my second lucky escape after failing to get into the RAF.

I would finally get to mainland Europe but it would be as a prisoner.

Next, we moved north to Liverpool to camp on Aintree Racecourse, home to the Grand National, though now it was a sea of soldiers waiting to be despatched to who knows where.

We slept al fresco and even in early summer you'd wake with aching limbs and a bedroll damp with dew. Kipping at the Canal Turn with its famous ninety-degree bend was a treat for a lad who had lived and breathed horses on the farm. After three weeks of that we moved to a large civic building and at last we were out of the damp.

It was here I met Eddie Richardson for the first time. He was a fine fellow from an established military family so we called him Regimental Eddie, 'Reggie' for short. He was very well spoken, a little posh perhaps compared to the rest of us, and we shared a room. Months later he was to get into trouble in the desert on the same day as my fortunes turned south.

Training in Liverpool took on a different dimension. We were being prepared for house-to-house fighting in streets set aside for demolition. We learnt the delicate art of making and throwing Molotov cocktails, glass bottles filled with petrol. We mastered the Mills bomb, a hand grenade with a segmented steel shell and the appearance of a mini pineapple. I would become pretty familiar with them in the months ahead. They were mean and simple. You could alter the length of fuse, to give you three, seven or nine seconds before detonation but you had to time it right. The last thing you wanted was the other feller hurling it back at you. You'd pull out the pin, run forward and throw with a straight-armed bowling action as you dived on your stomach. If you didn't blow yourself to kingdom come, the grenade was supposed to end up in a huge pit where the explosion was relatively contained. I had been able to throw a cricket ball a hundred yards when I was sixteen. It was still a game.

We knew as we set off from Liverpool in the *Otranto* that we were leaving Britain in a sorry old state. France had fallen to the Germans in June, Italy had declared war on the Allies, there were regular dogfights between the Luftwaffe and RAF fighters over southern England and the Battle of Britain itself was just starting.

As I boarded the ship, above me the twin dark-rimmed funnels were belching smoke into the air and all around me in the breeze were the chaotic sounds of men searching for a berth. Some were carrying kitbags, hunting for cabins, others were calling out to their chums and finding their way around the ship. Down below us were the vehicles and heavy equipment.

Les Jackson was there from the beginning. He was a corporal then, a regular soldier – a first-class chap with a twinkle in his eye and a wicked sense of humour. He was older than most of us, over thirty, but we had a bond from the start and we would be together at the end, too. Eighteen months later I would be side-by-side with him when we drove head-on into a wall of machine gun fire.

Les had introduced me to his family in Liverpool and I had taken quite a shine to his sister, Marjorie. She was a very attractive fair-haired girl with a gentle Liverpudlian accent, a kind girl and an excellent dancer. I had taken her out a couple of times but we were innocence personified. In those days you could walk a girl home for miles at the end of an evening and the most you expected was a kiss on the cheek. It was still special. His family had shown me such hospitality. He liked his sherbet, Les's old man, but it would be five years before I would cross that threshold again to take him out for a beer and it wouldn't be a happy occasion.

I had Marjorie's picture stuck on the wall of the tiny airless cabin a few decks down that I shared with four other soldiers, but hers wasn't the only one. I had always had lots of girlfriends so I had quite a collection by then.

I was on the top bunk, with Bill Chipperfield below. He was a down-to-earth sort of chap from a very poor family in the south, as honest as they come and always good company. There were two other lads but the poor devils had to sleep on the floor. We were crammed in like sardines and it was impossible to move in the dark without treading on someone.

We had been allowed twenty-four hours' home leave before embarkation, though I'd spent most of that travelling just to get there and back. My family lived far to the south, in the village of North Weald in Essex. They were successful farmers so we never went short and I had enjoyed a comfortable rural childhood.

My mother cried a lot as she kissed me goodbye. I had posed for photographs with my sister Winifred. I've still got that picture, her dark, wavy hair wafting in the breeze. She wore a knitted dress and a string of beads around her neck. I was in uniform, trousers hitched up high, my short tunic pulled in tight at the waist and a forage cap perched on my head at a jaunty angle. It never occurred to me on saying farewell that I might not make it. I felt I could look after myself. Such is youth. Winifred kept her feelings deeply buried. We didn't know what the war would bring, so why worry?

The one who knew but said nothing was my father George. He had fought in the First World War and he knew what was in store: muck, blood, and hardship. He simply shook my hand and wished me luck. He was a fine, proud man with a head of thick, dark hair – a Christian with high standards and the bulging muscles to back them up. He had never been able to show me much warmth but some of what happened later was due to him because he made sure I grew up with the idea that principles had to be put into practice. He was clerk to the council at a time when that post brought respect and local omnipotence but he was popular in the village because he would help anyone in a jam. I learnt later he paid the rates for some of the poor residents out of his own pocket.

He found it hard to show affection at home and praise was dished out sparingly. When I won a coveted sports prize as a child, all he said was, 'Well done, lad', and he never mentioned it again. I only realised how much he thought of me after the war. Shortly after I sailed, he joined up to fight too, lying about his age. I was told later he was always asking after me wherever he was stationed, trying to find out where I might be. I think he fancied he might be able to look after me but of course we never met up. He was captured in Crete and forced to do hard labour in Germany building a mountain railway, despite going down with pneumonia. He spent much of the time hurling nuts and bolts down the hillside to prove he wasn't beaten. He could be stroppy, all right. That's probably where I got it from.

Back on deck, I watched the crew preparing for the threats ahead, the submarines and the mines lurking below the waves, waiting to blast a hole in our side and send us to the bottom. The only real protection against mines was a paravane, a torpedo-shaped device with sharp fins. Hanging over the railings I watched it being lowered over the side and into the waves.

The shark-like object came to life on contact with the water and the fins pulled it down and away from the ship. The heavy cable was reeled out until it was a good distance from the vessel and parallel to it. The cable was meant to wrench the mine from its moorings, to be machine-gunned when it bobbed to the surface, or send it sliding down the wire to hit the paravane, blowing up in a tower of white water but sparing the ship. It gave us some comfort.

I was fascinated by contraptions like that. I had always tinkered with cars and motorbikes but I'd had my heart set on a proper engineering education while I was at still at school. I was uncontainable even then; I had to be the one giving the orders. It had always been like that. As a boy I had my own kid's army and we paraded around shouldering real guns though without ammunition. I was made Head Boy at school and I had the muscle to control the bullying, which I did. Later in life my wife Audrey would tease me that I had become the bully. She was only half joking I suspect. I was certainly fearless.

I went on to Leyton Technical College in East London and did all right. In 1933, as Hitler was becoming the Chancellor of Germany, I walked up on to a stage in Leyton Town Hall and collected a prize for my studies from a man standing behind a desk. I was just fourteen but he should have impressed me more than he did. He was the First World War soldier and poet, Siegfried Sassoon, then in his mid-forties, his hair still dark, swept across a high forehead. He spoke a few words of congratulation and handed me two wine-coloured volumes embossed in gold with a shield and a sword. I had chosen books by Robert Louis Stevenson and Edgar Allan Poe.

That seemed a long time ago. On board ship the mainland was slipping into the smoky haze. The civilised world I had known with its rules and customs, its sense of decency, was also slowly sliding away.

Chapter 2

Les Jackson always knew the shortest distance between two points, he was that kind of chap. He walked into our cabin soon after the *Otranto* had put to sea, stepping over the sleeping bodies on the floor and managing to wake them up anyway. He looked at the row of girls I had stuck to the wall, including his sister Marjorie. I was expecting a sarcastic comment at least but none came. He knew I had a soft spot for Marjorie but he had something else on his mind.

'Avey, I've got a job for you. You're on lavatory-cleaning duty.'

'What? You can't be serious, old boy.'

'It will be worth it.'

He roped in Eddie Richardson as well. Now Eddie was a public school type who could hardly bear to utter the word lavatory never mind clean one. When he found out the weapon of choice was to be the toilet brush he wasn't best pleased but Les was right. Half an hour of toilet cleaning every day and we were rewarded with a feast fit for a king. Egg and bacon sandwiches – as much as we could eat. Splendid. More to the point we were excused all other work for the entire voyage. Les was an operator all right. He was always sailing close to the wind.

Seventeen ships had sailed that day, 5 August 1940. One turned back with engine trouble. The rest of us steamed out into the Irish Sea with our naval escort. We still had no idea where we were going; that information was restricted, even to us. We were barely out of sight of land when the jarring sound of a warning siren, a U-boat alarm, pierced the air above the steady throb of the engines. The ship erupted into action, men running in every direction. I fought my way through the stream of bodies heading for my lifeboat muster station. Men with ashen faces combed the waves with their eyes looking for a periscope or, worse still, a torpedo. I could see signals flashing from *Otranto*'s bridge to faint grey shapes on the horizon. As time passed so too did the sense of alarm as nothing was sighted. They still left us standing around for hours. Life on board ship soon settled down into a monotonous routine.

I was woken from a deep sleep by a violent yank on my arm. The cabin was full of noisy squaddies and I was being pulled from my bunk. 'Wake up, Avey, we've got one for you. It's time to earn your money,' someone said.

Before I could properly focus I was being carried along in the throng of uniforms. Men were chanting and shouting in high spirits all around me. 'This should be one to see,' someone said. 'Wait till he gets a look at this feller. '

I knew I was being delivered somewhere and probably for sacrifice. We went along narrow corridors past countless cabin doors and up steep stairs onto the deck. The sea breeze caught my cheeks and I woke up properly. I was taken along the boat deck past lifeboats hanging in their slings and rows of giant, white tubular air vents like mouthpieces of old telephones. We dropped down towards the stern. To my right a spotty-faced lad was making animated punching gestures with his fists. I was beginning to get the picture.

I saw an open-air boxing ring on the rear deck, complete with ropes. An enormous mast towered over it. Word had got around that I was a boxer and in those days I would have fought anyone at the drop of a hat in or out of the ring. I'd usually come out on top but normally I knew who I was fighting.

My gloves were on before I spotted him and I guessed instantly I'd been set up. He strode into the ring. He wasn't all that tall, maybe five feet nine, but he was well built and definitely strong. He was a Jock from the Black Watch, a hard Highland regiment, and it was clear I was expected to get a pasting.

He was obviously a street fighter, possibly even a professional boxer, but as I limbered up, I got a closer look at him and my nerves settled. His eyebrows were scarred, he had cauliflower ears and a flattened nose. Anyone who had been clobbered like that was either not very good or not very fast. Someone had misjudged but it wasn't me.

I'd been in boxing clubs since I was a boy and I was fast. Where I was agile, he was lumbering around. He almost landed a few punches but I was strong on the left with a quick jab followed by a sharp left hook. I never went for his face but halfway through the second round I struck him hard in the solar plexus and he went down, gasping for breath. It was over.

After that I stayed on deck to watch the action but it wasn't pretty. A Black Watch officer was soon inveigled into taking on one of his own men. He was clearly an unpopular chap and he was pretty hesitant – with good reason. When he finally stepped into the ring he got hammered to blazes, poor man.

Apart from that, most boxing on board ship was fair and pretty good-natured. I'd often do a few rounds with Charles Calistan, dear old Charles. He had trained with me and we had hit it off straight away. He was a handsome chap with a full head of wavy black hair, an Anglo-Indian who spoke Urdu and proved to be a true hero later. He should have got the Victoria Cross. He was also a talented boxer and I used to spar with him regularly on board.

After eleven days we dropped anchor off Freetown, Sierra Leone, the first land we had sighted since leaving the British Isles. It was clear we were going right round the Cape then heading north for Egypt. Two days later, and without setting foot on land, we steamed south again to Cape Town where I looked up at the flat-topped Table Mountain, so familiar from school geography lessons, and dared to believe briefly that paradise was possible.

It was good to be on dry land again and it was the first time I had set foot on foreign soil, unless you count a cricket trip to Sheffield. Cape Town was quite cool at that time of year but it was a tremendous place. On the quayside we were split into groups. Eddie, myself and two others were handed over to a well-to-do middle-aged white South African chap with a light suit and a dark car. He had volunteered to show the lads around the city.

It was all new to me. I had only ever seen one black man before that and he was a chap selling something on Epping market. He certainly gave it some verbiage. He claimed he could stare at the sun without damaging his eyes.

As a first taste of abroad, Cape Town did the trick and we were in clover after being cooped-up four to a cabin designed for two. The man in the cool suit took us back to a colonial-style house with huge grounds and suggested we use the outdoor showers connected to the swimming pool. It made Eddie wonder how bad we smelt. After weeks of occasionally hosing ourselves down in seawater on board ship, I stood beneath a cascade of clean fresh water and felt the weeks of salt and sweat drain away. I could hardly bring myself to get out from under the shower.

Later the same day we stepped, courtesy of our guide, into one of the finest restaurants I had ever seen, right in the heart of the city. There, projected on the ceiling above us, was a pseudo-sky complete with moving clouds. We were awestruck, and there was decent grub to complete the day.

After four days we bade Cape Town farewell. Table Mountain slipped into silhouette and the convoy split once more leaving the *Otranto* as one of ten heading round the cape and up the east coast of Africa. We reached the volcanic island of Perim at the entrance to the Red Sea on 14 September. From there, we set out on the last leg under cover of darkness still guarded by four warships. We would soon be within range of Italian planes and naval forces operating out of Massawa in Eritrea. All lights on the *Otranto* were extinguished, leaving the crew fumbling their way around the ship. The blackout was complete but the night sky was alive with stars and in the phosphorescent waters of the Gulf of Aden I picked out the menacing outline of a giant manta ray.

We were much-needed reinforcements. Anchoring off Port Taufiq at the entrance to the Suez Canal, surrounded by naval vessels, cargo ships, rusty tugs belching black smoke alongside tiny Arab dhows and fishing boats, we were taken to Genefa, a sprawling, tented camp near the Great Bitter Lakes. The battle with thirst had begun but there were huge earthenware jars placed all around the camp, large enough to drown a sergeant and brimming with cool water. That was the good news. The bad news was we were ordered off on a route march the day after we arrived, twenty-five miles out into the desert and round a barren rocky outcrop, nick-named 'The Flea'. Someone felt we needed entertainment.

While I was still in England, attacking straw dummies with a sword, 2RB, as we called the 2nd Battalion, had been sent into the desert.

The Italian dictator Benito Mussolini hadn't yet declared war but it was coming. For six weeks Mussolini made bombastic speeches and the battalion kicked its heels. I remember seeing a magazine photograph showing some of his elite soldiers leaping over a row of razor-sharp bayonets and thinking to myself, many a slip between cup and lip.

The day after war was declared, 7th Armoured Division, which included 2RB, went right up to the Libyan frontier. It wasn't the most modern force in the world. Some of the armoured cars were still the old Rolls-Royce Silver Ghosts that Lawrence of Arabia had been using back in the First World War but they quickly captured frontier posts along the border.

Mussolini made his first real move as our convoy was preparing for the dash though the Red Sea. Il Duce, as they called him, could see what Germany had achieved in Europe and he wanted a bit of the action for himself. He had his eye on the Nile, the Suez Canal and British supply routes to India and beyond. He ordered Marshal Graziani, named 'The Butcher of the Desert' for his savagery in slaughtering an Arab rebellion, to attack Egypt and the British. On 13 September 1940, 85,000 Italian soldiers poured into Egypt from Libya and the much smaller British force was obliged to withdraw. His troops didn't stop until they got to Sidi Barrani, a settlement on the coast, sixty-five miles into Egypt. Il Duce soon claimed in Italian propaganda broadcasts that they had got trams running again in the town. Trams? They didn't know how to spell the word. It was just a handful of buildings and a collection of mud shacks. There had barely been a proper road, let alone a tramway.

The Italians built a chain of elaborate fortified positions starting on the coast and sweeping south-west deep into the desert. Their camps had romantic, aromatic names – Tummar, Rabia and Sofafi – as if they lay on some desert spice trail. Now there were 250,000 on the Italian side and we arrived to join Allied forces which were vastly outnumbered in the air and on the ground, just 100,000 of us in total.

Cairo was our last interlude before the war became real, the last chance to relax before the true toughening-up began, the process that was to prepare me well for captivity and all that followed. Three of us, Charles Calistan, Cecil Plumber and I, set off to discover the dubious delights of the city with a couple of older soldiers who knew their way around. Cecil was a thoughtful bloke, with a high forehead and a keen eye. I knew him as a brilliant wicketkeeper from my local cricket team, back in Essex. Now those breezy days on the village green were a distant memory. Instead of the thrushes and larks, black kites sailed across a city as exotic as it was mysterious, heaving with allied soldiers: New Zealanders, Indians and Australians as well as the British.

A horse-drawn gharrie overtook us crammed with lads dressed in khaki, all in high spirits and heading off for a wild night. I was pained to see the distress of the beast trapped between the shafts. They clambered out in front of us, shouted, 'Three cheers for the gharrie driver', then bolted without paying.

There were camels bearing improbable loads, donkeys being beaten with sticks by riders whose feet scraped the ground and all around us were street urchins calling for 'Baksheesh, baksheesh.' Small boys hawked trinkets of dubious value. Others pressed us to buy suspicious-looking fruit juices and second-rate figs. A dusty tram rattled by at speed, with sparks flying from its wheels. There was a yellow haze in the air, a mixture of fumes and airborne sand particles, all set off with the smell of open sewers.

Stepping off a noisy street, where the horse-drawn vehicles battled for space with trucks, we ducked into the Melody Club. They called it the Sweet Melody. Somebody had a sense of humour. The entrance was veiled by two musty blackout curtains, though outside there were blue streetlamps and lights shining from windows and doorways everywhere. Brushing through the first of them, I tripped on something sack-like on the floor. In the gloom, I picked out the body of an Australian soldier comatose at my feet.

We pushed through the second curtain into the dim light and smoke of a dingy bar. A band was playing on a tiny stage behind a barrier of barbed wire. They needed it. They were struggling to be heard in the raucous atmosphere. The place was crammed, with lads on leave from the desert looking for some kind of release. There were bullet holes in the ceiling and heaven knows what else on the floor. The Australians were usually blamed for it. They were first-class men out on the desert but back in Cairo, drunk, they could be the worst.

There was a destructive excitement in the air. It was no place to relax. We had just got our drinks when there was shouting from a corner table. The lad in the middle of the rumpus picked up a chair and threw it backwards over his head to crash into another table of revellers. One of his own mates then knocked him out cold with a right hook. He might have been finishing the original scrap or maybe pre-empting a major brawl. It calmed things down and the unconscious chair-thrower was carried outside to join the chap blocking the doorway. The rest of them straightened the chairs and their uniforms and the buzz returned to its earlier, rowdy level.

Officers would automatically head for the bars of the famous Shepheard's Hotel where Cairo's high society congregated. Mere soldiers like us had to be well turned out to get in. The cool of the terrace bar was a different world. A suited man played an upright piano; wickerwork armchairs were arranged around the tiled floors; Egyptian waiters wearing long white galabeyas served drinks on shiny trays they balanced on one hand. This was more like it. I was a corporal then and a far better leader than a follower. I was determined to get a field commission and Shepheard's looked more like the life for me.

Later in the cool bustle of the evening, we crossed the English Bridge over the Nile, guarded by four enormous bronze lions. 'See those?' shouted one of the lads. 'Every time a virgin crosses the bridge they roar, so watch it.' There was uncomfortable laughter. With the desert approaching, there was endless talk about girls. Gnawing away at us was the knowledge that we would be facing bullets soon enough. Not surprisingly, sex came up quite often. It turned out that most of us were still virgins and prepared to admit it. I was twenty-one and sex before marriage wasn't on back then.

People wouldn't believe it now. Many of the lads were in the same boat. We were old enough to die and yet sexually we were still innocents. I was super-fit and of course exhausted at the end of a day of training so maybe I didn't think of it. For some it became an obsession.

One street name was often on soldiers' lips. The Berka was the centre of Cairo's oldest profession. It was out of bounds to all ranks, ringed by large, white signs and black crosses and often raided by the military police. That didn't stop the lads but the whole thing offended me somehow. I could understand that young men going into action might want to go there first, but it appalled me and I never followed them. Now, on the eve of heading off into the desert, I knew deep inside I was starting to close down. Distraction could mean the bullet and I was determined to survive whatever they would throw at me. That meant staying focused.

'Pick up your parrots and monkeys, you're off.'

The order sounded comical but we knew what it meant. We were leaving for the desert. They called it going 'on the blue' because it was an exotic, dry sea, a place of wonder to a boy from a green, rainy country. We were joining the 7th Armoured Division, resilient and nomadic, the Desert Rats.

The slow train trundled through stations with improbably playful names like Zagazig. Then it was west along dazzling white sand dunes bordered by a sharp, blue sea, past a stagingpost with a name that meant nothing to us then, El Alamein, and a station named Fuka, which attracted much more comment.

We arrived at Mersa Matruh where the British had dug in, creating a fortress, and were living a troglodyte existence in anticipation of a further Italian advance. We were there to upset the Italians so we headed deeper into the desert. The rutted track south soon widened as convoys of trucks jinked around the trickier patches.

My fantasy of undulating sand dunes sculpted by the wind was replaced by a stony reality: arid and inhospitable with occasional scrub and patches of dull coloured sift-sand. They called it 'porridge country' and this was to be the scene for our struggle.

A tremendous escarpment of great strategic importance dominated the landscape. The 600-foot high Haggag el-Aqaba runs parallel to the sea and eastwards towards Sollum, where its rocky cliffs jut out over the Mediterranean with the hairpin bends of the Halfaya Pass. The British had already seen action there as the Italians advanced. We rechristened it Hellfire Pass.

The battalion was testing Italian positions with night patrols. I was in 'B' Company and at the end of October we began cutting telegraph wires and mining roads to stop Italian reinforcements coming to assist the remote desert fortresses.

I was learning to understand the desert better, feeling the immensity of Africa with its 180 degrees of sky and roasting daytime temperatures that could plunge to near freezing as you lay out below the star-spangled night. There was no escaping the desert dust storms when they arrived. The billowing wall of sand of a *khamsin* would climb high into the air like a moving mountain and sweep across to hide the sun, stripping loose paint from vehicles like a blast of heated iron-filings. The driving grains of sand stung you right through your clothes. During the dust storms you just had to take cover. The only water was to be found in the 'birs', ancient wells and cisterns, some Roman, whose contents were brackish at best and on one occasion contained a floating dead donkey. That quenched our thirst, though not for long.

As night fell we would leaguer up, parking the vehicles, mainly trucks and Bren gun carriers, in a huge defensive square. Guards would be posted on the outside and changed every two hours whilst the rest of us would try to sleep as cooler evenings gave way to chilly nights. There were no campfires in the darkness, just greatcoats, if you had them, for warmth.

I would get to know the Bren gun carrier pretty well over the months to come. It was a nippy, tracked armoured vehicle, completely open, with a powerful Ford V-8 engine in the middle. There was space for one and sometimes two Bren gunners in the back and it had a Boys anti-tank rifle fired by the commander from the front seat right next to the driver.

I got to know the oily underside of the beast as well because at night I would dig a depression in the sand, then run the carrier over it and wriggle down between the heavy tracks for some protection from shrapnel, bombs or bullets. I would spread out my bedroll, which was little more than a thick blanket rolled into a plastic sheet, check my .38 revolver was handy and the grenades were in reach, then get my head down.

We would be woken by the guard well before first light, so a crack on the head from an oily sump offered the usual start to the day. The camp spluttered slowly into life as engines started, not always the first time. We would break up the leaguer, still cold and sleepy, and deploy out into the desert, at least a hundred yards apart, to await a dawn attack. No one wanted to give low-flying Italian Savoia bombers an easy target. Then the chilly wait began as we scanned the horizon. Only when the sky brightened and the contours of the desert gradually emerged could we relax and think about breakfast.

I'd set about making the first brew of the day as if life depended upon it. I'd be cold and hungry and I needed it straight away so I'd do it the desert way. I'd cut an old petrol can in half, fill it with sand, pour high-octane fuel into it and balance the billy-can of water on top. Then, standing well back, I'd throw a match at the lot. 'Whaff!', a cloud of black smoke would rise into the air. The spectacular blast would offer the first warmth of the day and brought the billy to the boil in no time.

We had welcomed the cooler weather at first but it was beginning to get much colder at night now and that wasn't a lot of fun. Then we started to get rain overnight as well, as if our spirits needed further dampening. Ours was still mostly a phoney war then and we were plunged back into more training: PT, map reading, arms drill and the skills of night patrolling. All of which were about to come in handy.

Chapter 3

We went into action. One night we were sent to blow-up an Italian fuel dump, twelve of us under Platoon Sergeant-Major Endean, with three explosive experts to do the damage. The desert belonged to us at night as the Italians didn't move around much. Good navigation made all the difference, knowing how far back to stop the trucks so they wouldn't hear us, but not so far that we couldn't get there on foot in the time available. Before kick-off, we lined up face to face to do a basic visibility check. Anything light on the uniform might be spotted and bring the bullets raining on us. Next, working in twos, we shook each other down. Jangling keys or the rattle of coins could give the game away and sound travelled at night.

With the final weapons checks completed it was evening before the three trucks set off across the rocky landscape. We de-trucked ten miles from the target and, guided by Endean and his trusty compass, we trekked the last section on foot in silence. We were whacked when we arrived but surprise was everything.

As the outline of the dump became visible Endean gave the signal and we crawled forward to take up positions in the gravel. More hand signals and we were fanning out into a semicircle. It was safer that way. The last thing we wanted to do was to knock out our own chaps if a shooting match began.

I lay prostrate in the darkness with the Lee-Enfield trained on the dump. I tried to get comfortable. It might be a long wait.

To my right I saw the outline of the explosives lads going in heads down and crouching low as they went, shadows instantly lost in the darkness. The minutes passed. Silence was always good. More waiting. Suddenly there they were, all three of them, heads down and running like the clappers. We took aim at the camp and waited for the shooting to begin. The first two blasts seemed small and sent rocket-like flashes into the night sky. There was an unnatural pause, probably only seconds, before an enormous explosion and a ball of fire turned the night orange. I pressed deeper into the sand, as the faces around me were suddenly illuminated.

That was when you expected it to come to the boil. The Italians would usually begin firing wildly into the night. This time it was a doddle and we slipped back into the desert. If anyone survived they never bothered to chase us.

We gathered at a rendezvous point a safe distance away, checked everyone was OK and began the long slog back to the trucks. Before the first signs of dawn, we were back safe and hoping to sleep.

When I look back, I can identify the experiences that changed me and prepared me mentally for the deprivation of Auschwitz. Life in the desert often meant being cold and hungry with nothing better to look forward to than bully-beef, and hard tack – dog biscuits to anyone else. Then there was Maconochie's meat stew. They'd had that in the First World War trenches too. Very occasionally, we might shoot a gazelle and we would have a feast that we could make last for days. Some of the lads would try and fire at them from moving vehicles but the desert just wasn't flat enough. Bouncing over the mounds we called camel humps ruined their aim. As a farm boy I knew the best way to do it was on foot so I went stalking.

Sometimes we could barter with the Bedouin but that was rare and fraught with misunderstanding. They waved to greet you with the palms of their hands facing backwards, waggling their fingers as if to beckon you over. When you obliged they would be confused, wondering what it was you wanted. The misunderstanding was worth it if the prize was an egg or two but fruit and vegetables, which was what we really needed, were unheard of. Sometimes we would capture Italian food supplies, tinned tunny fish or rice, but usually just tomato purée. They seemed to eat little else.

Our diet was dreadful and we were all woefully undernourished so we got used to illness. A scratch would soon turn into a suppurating wound that would refuse to heal and could lead to blood poisoning. These desert sores plagued us throughout the campaign. Medics were rare and the only treatment they offered was to lift the scab and hope for the best. I still have the scars along my forearms seventy years later.

Hygiene was poor, as you can imagine with all the flies. We were regularly struck down with 'gyppie-tummy', and diarrhoea in the desert is no fun. Doing the necessary was tricky enough anyway. You would dig a hole and crouch down. Within seconds, flying dung beetles would begin thumping into your backside. They were more accurate than the average Stuka but whereas the Stukas released their bombs and left, these creatures would fly straight into your swaying rear. It was their preferred landing method. They would then flop down into the sand and start rolling up the meagre content of your bowels before retreating backwards with it, God knows where.

When we were in one spot for longer we would carve a desert toilet seat by cutting a hole in the top of one of the wooden cases that the fuel cans came in. They were about three feet tall and you could sit like a king as you surveyed the shifting sands.

Water was handed out at the rate of a gallon per man but we had to top up radiators and do everything with that so there wasn't much to drink. The water came in flimsy metal containers coated with wax, which invariably cracked as the tins had been tossed around. It tasted either of rust or candles. Washing was a luxury we couldn't afford in combat. When the pressure was off we would wash our hands and face as best we could, then use a shaving brush to apply minimal amounts of water to the rest of the body. It usually ran out before the job was done.

All too often we were dependent on the bowser man. I never knew his name. To everyone he was just the bowser man, plain and simple. He roamed the desert with a captured Italian tanker truck almost at will, touring the birs in search of water. He could be gone for days, always alone. He was a small, mysterious man who could read the desert and converse comfortably in Arabic with the Bedouin. Being on the blue had got to him. If he returned and caught you sitting on one of our improvised fuel-case toilets he would go wild, pull out his .38 revolver and drive the bowser round and round, shooting at the box between your legs. Nobody knew why. Despite the indignity of having a wooden lavatory shot from underneath you, he never hurt anyone and, mad though he was, everyone just accepted him.

Then came the biggest show so far. General Wavell decided on a surprise attack on the Italian desert fortresses. The details were kept very quiet of course. Everything was on a 'need to know' basis and the lads didn't need to know. That's how it was. Our part was to go out and chart the Italian minefields and the other defences round their camps so that the tanks leading the assault could charge straight in through the gaps.

On 7 December, vast columns of men and machinery moved into position under cover of darkness as the desert winter began to bite, leaving soldiers shivering and nervous ahead of the battle. Two days later, in the very early morning, tanks, guns and infantry were led to the start line for the attack. The route for the vehicles marked with hurricane lamps which were shielded from the enemy by petrol cans, cut open and tilted over. The soldiers were near enough to smell coffee and the other aromas of breakfast wafting from the Italian camps. At 0700 hours our guns let rip with a massive barrage and then the attack on their positions began. The Italian tanks were useless with very thin armour. We knocked out twenty-three of theirs in the first fifteen minutes then captured thirty-five more and took 2,000 prisoners for the loss of fifty-six men. In the grim arithmetic of war, that was a good start.

The information put together by our night patrols had helped make it a big success. Some of our officers began to measure the number of prisoners by the acre, rather than the thousand. Judging by the documents I have seen since, the congratulatory messages were soon flying back and forth between the top brass. I don't recall a single 'thank you' being passed on to the boys in the desert in all my time in action. I don't think the top brass felt the need.

2RB found a very good cook amongst the Italian prisoners. He was spirited away by our officers and put to work in their mess kitchen as 'Rifleman Antonio'. He lasted four weeks before anyone senior found out, even though he had to share a cave with a colonel during an air raid.

We captured Sidi Barrani, that windblown fort with a battered wall and a few hutments, where Il Duce had boasted that he had got the trams running. That was 10 December and within twenty-four hours the desert greeted the news with a monumental sandstorm.

We didn't have it all our own way. The Italian air force had a habit of spoiling the party, so when there was a whiff of a spotter plane around we were ordered out to churn up the desert. We would head safely away from our main force and skid around frantically with tracks leading all over the place. Our dust cloud, climbing into the air, created the impression of a far bigger force. Then we would retreat with dust coating our faces and lining our mouths and wait for the flying circus to come over and bomb the open desert. They usually obliged.

It didn't always work. We were back in reserve when an Italian fighter screamed overhead, then another. There was no time to run. I hit the deck getting a mouthful of desert and hoping the pilot had had too much coffee. I counted about a dozen CR42s in all, ugly biplanes with a squashed body, but it was the big Savoia bombers I was worried about. They were over us soon enough, a trio of them, lumbering beasts with an extravagant three engines. The first blasts shook the earth but the bombs fell short of the target. Before they could have another go, help arrived. They had far more planes than we did but a few Hurricanes had been sent out to take over from our old Gladiator biplanes and these now showed up. The chase was on high above us and pretty soon we were alone again in the desert.

Three days later they came back in strength at 1100 hours. There were ten Savoias this time and not a Hurricane in the sky. We all hit the deck and one of the bombs fell within thirty yards of me in a small depression in the undulating desert. When the sky cleared and we could stand again I saw from the commotion below me that someone had copped it, a lovely chap called Jumbo Meads. He was a popular sergeant, very tall, blond and handsome and not the average, nasty NCO. We felt his loss all right but you couldn't afford to get bogged down in sorrow. There was never any time.

The Savoia bombers were a nuisance, particularly at night when relays of them would fly around dropping one bomb at a time, to spoil our sleep. That was why I took to kipping under the carrier.

Soon after that I spent a day driving 3rd Lieut. Merlin Montagu Douglas Scott. He was a grandson of the Duke of Buccleuch, related to the royal family, and a first-class officer, both precise and pedantic. We headed for Halfaya Pass and Sollum to see if the enemy was there. Montagu Douglas Scott had a habit of getting a bit too close to the opposition. A few days earlier, he had taken the same route in the middle of a *khamsin* dust storm with hardly any visibility at all to see if the Italians were still holding a large camp at Halfway House, on top of the escarpment. He found it, hidden in the swirling sand. There was a low stone wall right round it and the whole place seemed deserted, shallow trenches everywhere with canvas covers and rocks piled round for protection. They must have left in a hurry. These little dugouts had bottles, camp beds, letters, photos – all kinds of stuff in them. There were two lookout towers swaying in the wind. All he could hear was creaking and the flapping of canvas in the driving sandstorm.

Then he got new orders over the radio. The Italians from the camp were retreating a few miles ahead. He chased after them with his four carriers, capturing stragglers in increasing numbers until all he could do was disarm them and leave them by the road. Soon he started coming across abandoned lorries, out of petrol or with punctured tyres. The *khamsin* was still building and the air was filled with reddish sand. Ten miles on, something dark appeared through the haze, a pair of big Italian trucks towing guns, surrounded by around thirty men. He captured the lot of them but right then the *khamsin* finally lifted and showed him the last thing he wanted to see. He had stumbled into the whole Italian garrison, hundreds of them stretching ahead in a long, long column. Everybody started shooting at point-blank range and he had to beat a hasty retreat.

On this occasion, we got a bit too close again, seeing enemy trucks and motorcycles ahead, appearing and reappearing through the alleys of the little port of Sollum. We could see Italian artillery high above on top of the escarpment but when we had a go at the trucks, the guns started on us so we had to get away pretty sharply.

Montagu Douglas Scott was a strange chap. He never missed a thing. In the middle of all this, he told us how impressed he was with the way Italians built their desert roads. He pulled us through that one and we were mightily relieved when darkness fell and we slipped back into the desert to leaguer up for the night.

I wasn't impressed with the trappings of military rank but I knew I could do the job better than some of the regulars. I had already seen one chap I didn't really rate make it to captain. It was dead men's shoes in those days but the ordinary lads didn't get a look in. It wasn't right. I had been made an acting corporal on merit on account of my shooting, and that was how it should be.

By then Platoon Sergeant-Major Endean was proving to be the bane of my life. He didn't have much time for recruits like us. He was a regular and he treated us as if we'd walked straight off civvy street. Some of us had, but there was a lot of prejudice in those days. People like the PSM didn't see people's strengths.

We got the order to move forward under cover of darkness one night and as I was in charge I sat alongside the driver in the truck with six lads in the back as we picked our way through the rough desert. He was steering around a field of rocks, peering into the night to avoid the worst, and following the vehicle in front when there was an unforgiving thud below and we stopped. I climbed out and looked underneath to find we'd hammered the sump. We weren't going anywhere for a while.

We were pretty vulnerable out there without any cover but the company left us to defend ourselves and carried on.

I arranged a guard so we could rest. In the morning I ordered the lads to break open the emergency tea rations so they could have a brew and thaw out. With the benefit of daylight and a bit of warmth we got the vehicle running again but before we got very far I heard the menacing sound of planes overhead. A handful of Savoias swooped low. There was no anti-aircraft cover, so we were on our own. I managed to get hold of a tommy gun that I had been entrusted with and I let loose most of a magazine. Even at that range it had no effect. It was a clumsy thing. We hit the deck but the bombs exploded well away from us. After one pass the sky was clear and I breathed a little easier. They had better targets that day.

We got moving again and eventually reached the company and safety in numbers. I tracked down PSM Endean immediately and asked permission to replace the emergency tea ration from the stores. It should have been a formality. The lads had been cold and stuck out in the desert and they had needed warmth. It was my decision and it was the right one. Endean refused.

He took it as a breach of regulations and he was aggressive from the start. I was hot-headed at the best of times but I wouldn't stand for pettiness. I wasn't having any of it. He was keeping his distance and had placed himself behind some camouflage netting. He knew I might take a swing at him, officer or not. I was furious but I told him his parents should have married and left it at that. I had given an order in the interest of the men. For God's sake it was a mug of tea, not a feast.

I knew he would get back at me and it didn't take him long. We were always anticipating a dawn attack so we deployed early. I had been suffering from dysentery for days but I struggled to get up and arranged the guard as usual. I was in a terrible state so I collapsed back on my bedroll in pain. I was sitting down when Endean showed up. He accused me of slacking and I was put on a charge straight away. I had obeyed orders and the guard was in place but it made no difference. Ill or not, he had got me.

The disciplinary hearing followed soon after but I was so angry that I refused to ask for mitigation. I couldn't deny it; I knew what was really going on and it had nothing to do with that trumped-up charge. I was sitting on my bedroll because I was ill; it was as simple as that. I wouldn't plead or squirm for them but I knew I was busted. They removed my stripe and messed up my chances. I accepted it but it still smarts after all these years. Fairness matters to me and I wouldn't compromise on that, not even for an officer. I also knew there was no room for bad blood in the desert. I had to be able to rely on the lads at my shoulder and they on me. I got on with it but it still rankles, even now.

In the next few days, we chased the Italians out of Egypt. They retreated west, deeper into Libya, to two seaports with strong defences. The first was Bardia just up the coast from Halfaya Pass. The other, seventy-five miles further west, had a name we had hardly heard of then, a place called Tobruk.

Mussolini gave the job of defending Bardia to the colourful General Bergonzoli, known to the Italians as 'Barba Elletrica' because of his remarkable forked red beard. We were a bit less respectful. We called him 'Electric Whiskers'. Mussolini told him to defend it to the last man.

He didn't.

Bardia was in a little bay with steep cliffs. The Italian garrison was spread out in an eighteen-mile arc around it. The navy shelled them and the RAF bombed them for two days, then on 3 January 1941, the attack started. Our job was to swing round behind, make it look like we were the main attack coming from the far side and stop anyone escaping.

We were mopping up after an attack on an Italian artillery position when I saw odd claw-like marks in the sand next to the body of a dead Italian soldier, lying face down. With the life draining from his body he had made sweeping movements in the sand as if to hide or bury some object. I saw something shiny but was it a weapon or a booby trap? Scanning around for clues, I stepped forward warily. It wasn't metal. The sun was glinting on highly polished leather so I scooped the sand away to reveal a narrow case perhaps five feet long. Inside was a beautiful gold silk flag, broken down to stow away for safety. It had gold pins through the staff and it was crowned with a decorative eagle. In his final moments on earth, the Italian artilleryman had been determined to prevent it falling into the hands of his enemies. I left it with him, buried somewhere in the sands of the desert.

Months later I spotted an old picture of the Pope in Rome done up in all his finery. He was blessing something. It was that same gold-coloured standard with its eagle headpiece.

Bardia fell. They surrendered almost to the last man. They say we took 100,000 prisoners. 'Electric Whiskers' was that last man and he slipped away.

Next it was on to Tobruk to do the same thing all over again. Our task now was to get a full picture of the Italian defences outside the port and that meant constant patrols, which often ended up with gunfights in the dark.

This was when I first experienced going deep into the heart of the enemy. It was the dead of night when we approached one Italian position. We suspected it contained big guns but we had no idea how well defended the camp was. The last thing the lads wanted was to run into something nasty when the attack started. The recce began as usual with the shakedown and noise check.

Crouching in the dark, the boss decided just he and I would go in, leaving the rest on guard outside to offer what cover they could if we had to beat a hasty retreat. The risk of falling on one of your own lads was great in an operation like this. The clicker was all we had to help identification. It was a tiny piece of metal that clicked when you pressed it and identified you as friendly.

The Italian outer defences were made up of two or three machine-gun posts on each side behind simple walls of rocks. They were right out in the desert alone and vulnerable but they were within shouting distance of their comrades. A yelp would have brought the whole shooting match down on our heads and we'd certainly miss breakfast.

The boss gestured silently and we went down on our bellies to begin crawling slowly forward, listening to Italian whispers in the night. It wasn't unusual to find these outer sentries asleep but tonight they were talking and paying little attention. Cough or dislodge a loose rock and they would soon sit up and take notice. Music from a gramophone drifted across the desert from the main camp beyond. After another fifty yards I began to make out more sangars, rings of rock protecting heavier machine-gun nests designed to cut advancing infantrymen to shreds.

There was a sudden movement from the nearest sangar. Had they heard something? We froze, head down in the dirt. My chest was constricted, I hardly dared breathe. The moment passed and we moved slowly onwards, memorising the layout of the base as we went. We were still crawling when we approached the main inner camp. Looking for a place to scramble over the low wall, we settled on a spot midway between the nearest machine guns and slithered across on our bellies.

A big gun loomed dark ahead, one of their direction-finding artillery pieces that could lock on to the source of a radio signal and send over a large shell to spoil the bully-beef. That sounds lethal but it was before the days of computers. This was crude technology.

There were two more machine-gun posts in the central camp, which worried me less now we were inside. I was good at this. All the senses in my body were alert; my pulse was racing but I was in control. This was the education of the desert. I refused to let in fear that might cloud my judgement but I knew that if they raised the alarm we would have to shoot our way out.

Men were moving around between tents. They felt safe. There was the odour of cigar smoke from the officers' tents, garlic from the cooking areas and I fancied you could smell cologne. The voices were louder now, soaring above the camp. There was always a big difference between the officers and men in the Italian military. These were officers and they were clearly living it up. But there was also a noise I hadn't heard for sometime now. Above the deeper voices I caught the sound of women laughing. I don't know if they were prostitutes or ordinary civilians but there they were, as clear as you like and unmistakeable. They seemed to be enjoying the party.

We should probably have returned the way we had come. There was a bit too much action on the base for my taste and we were getting more committed the deeper into the camp we went. Then, just feet away, a tent flap was thrown open, sending a shaft of light out across the camp. Although we were still in the shadows there was no choice. We both knew instantly the only way out was forwards. In the desert both armies looked shabby and identification wasn't easy in the dark, despite our brown woollen hats. The Italians wore all kinds of things – we had even found hairnets in one of the camps we had taken. It must have been the fashion in Rome but it led to a good deal of sniggering.

There was no choice. We got to our feet and without so much as a glance left or right, we walked slowly, and with as much composure as we could muster, past the tents and through the inner camp until we were back in the shadows and could exit the other side. The entire base held perhaps 200 people and we had passed right through the centre of it unchallenged. It was only then that I noticed that the boss had his torch switched on and shining out of his pocket the whole time.

That was the routine, patrols at night then grab what sleep you could because the chances were you'd be off again as the next night fell. These patrols weren't always plain sailing and soon I had a very close call. I had picked up a small wound on my forearm. It wouldn't heal. It was bandaged up, but the sand got everywhere and it was a mess. The sleeve of my uniform kept the white bandage hidden and providing it stayed covered and out of the moonlight I could go on patrol.

One night, we were sent to capture prisoners in an outlying post. If they could be persuaded to sing, the intelligence could be invaluable when we attacked. We were widely spread out so essentially I was on my own. I heard a single metallic click some distance away so I knew one of the lads was getting nervous.

I dropped down into a *wadi* some five or six feet deep and skirted around hoping to get a better vantage point. Knowledge was power on night patrols and you had to know the full story before you made a move. After a good distance in the gulley I began slowly climbing up, taking great pains not to dislodge any rocks. I heard a noise and stopped, pressed against the side of the shallow ravine. It was the sound of boots on stony ground. Someone was up there. I heard him take another step to the edge of the *wadi*. Then I saw him, an Italian sentry staring down into the darkness, but although he was looking towards me, he was seeing nothing or so I hoped. I was just a few feet below him and I fingered the trigger of my revolver. I was aiming at him and couldn't miss at that distance but I knew that to fire would have woken the entire camp and they'd soon make tomato purée out of us.

The options racing through my mind would all bring catastrophe. I could scramble up and use the knife but he wasn't going to stand there politely whilst I climbed out of the ravine. For all I knew there could be a whole platoon up there enjoying a silent smoke. I stayed put. I would shoot if he made the slightest noise but it could mean fighting a gun battle at close quarters.

Still hidden in the darkness of the *wadi*, I moved my arm a fraction and I saw him stiffen. I knew instantly I had exposed an edge of the white bandage just below my wrist. 'Damn,' I said to myself. Should I shoot, run and take my chances? I couldn't see his face in the darkness but we were both in mortal danger and we knew it. His rifle was by his side. Lifting it to fire would have taken a second at least and I would have pulled the trigger and been running back through the *wadi* before he hit the ground. Instead he froze on the spot, hardly daring to breathe. We were both trapped.

In every dicey situation in the desert to date I'd told myself that too much thought wasted time and that could mean the bullet. You didn't have to think, you had to do. It was my mantra for survival. Instinct told me the right option was to stay frozen to the spot. I waited. The seconds ticked by but he didn't raise the alarm. Instead, he looked left and then right and stepped slowly backwards away from the edge of the *wadi* then turned and walked away and out of sight. I dropped back into the ravine and hastily retraced my steps back to the rest of the platoon. I knew he had seen me and might raise the alarm sooner or later. We had been hopelessly compromised and we slipped away into the night.

We captured four prisoners during that patrol. I grabbed one of them and it was child's play. He was walking around quite alone, oblivious to who was out there. He was tall for an Italian and, despite the dark, I could tell he was clean-shaven and wearing a blue-grey forage cap. I had to get him unawares and that meant stalking him until I was in a position to make a move. I swapped my revolver to my left hand and jumped him from behind, pulling his right arm up behind his back and jabbing the gun in his ribs, withdrawing it quickly in case he spun around. The terror in his eyes told me he got the message.

There was no struggle and I didn't have to say a word. He knew the game was up and he came quietly. But that's when it can get tricky. Once a captive is over the initial shock and knows he is not about to die, if he is any kind of soldier at all he will start looking to turn the tables. I was lucky. My prisoner was petrified and stayed that way until we handed him over later that night and we could finally hit the sack.

Each patrol was becoming a battle for survival. The Italians weren't all Jessies, despite what people made out, and every exchange with the enemy often came down to kill or be killed. I concentrated on staying focused. Occasionally we would get mail from home, passed down the line to us, dog-eared and dusty. Most of the boys scrambled to get hold of the letters before running off to plonk themselves down against the wheel of a truck to read them with smiles of recognition fluttering across their faces at remembrances of home.

I couldn't do that. Home was warmth and civilisation and where I was now just wasn't civilised. I glanced at the letters from my mother and put them away unread. When you speak a language, you think that language. My mother, bless her soul, spoke the language of home. That didn't belong in the desert so, purely for self-preservation, I refused to read her letters. They would have blunted my purpose and made my survival less likely. It might just mean milliseconds but in that time you can get killed. I was closing down still further. In different ways, we all were. I carried a great wodge of those letters with me and didn't read them until I was back in Cairo.

The events of one patrol were to stay with me. The worst of it is, seventy years on, I can barely recall where we were or what we were doing but I can feel it all right. I can still feel everything about it, even now. Patrols were becoming routine, and each one began like the last and ended with us collapsing onto our bedrolls just before the dawn light drove back the stars. I know we were doing a reconnaissance of an Italian position somewhere on the fringes of Tobruk. It was a sizeable camp with strong defences and I feared there'd be some surprises.

I had taken to carrying a knife on patrol. It wasn't a standard issue weapon but it was handy. I had picked it up early on, along with a 9mm Beretta automatic which I had stripped from a surrendering Italian officer. I carried that in a tiny holster under my arm whilst the knife was in a sheath that I had made myself. It was just six inches long, but it was sharpened on both edges and came to a needle-sharp point. I had removed the hilt for a better grip and I knew how to use it. You never grasped a knife in the fist, stabbing downwards like a Hollywood killer. Do that and you're dead: by the time you had raised the blade you'd probably received one in the guts yourself. A fighting blade was always held upwards with the pommel pressed into the palm of the hand and the thumb flat on the steel.

The platoon was spread out around the camp and we had all been given different tasks. I hated patrols where we were so far apart. You were really alone. I knew if I got into a jam it was down to me to fix it quickly and quietly. Shooting would wake the whole camp. I had no intention of ending up in a shallow hole with sand shovelled on my face.

I was somewhere in the outer defences crouching down when I saw him, standing in the shadows just a couple of yards away. I had no real cover other than the night but he hadn't seen me yet. I knew this was bad, very bad. Any moment now he would spot me and the shooting match would start. The wrong decision and I was done for. I took the knife in my hand. There was a sound. He moved; he'd seen me. I sprang on him from the darkness, thrusting the blade up and in below his ribcage. He went down silently and I felt his weight momentarily on my arm as he sagged to the earth and stayed down.

My first response was relief. He could have killed me, but I'd survived. All that bayonet training back home hadn't helped prepare me for this. The screaming, shouting and aggression was designed to make you do it without thinking. This was different – silent, done in the shadows, and I had felt his body weight on me in the darkness. It was him or me. That is how it is in bloody war. You make excuses to yourself all the time.

Back then, I simply thought *I've got away with it; I'm alive*. I just wanted to get back to the desert and the rest of the patrol quickly. I had prevented the operation being compromised and I reported what had happened. There wasn't so much as a thank you.

He was the only man I killed with my bare hands, but it affected me all right, that one. You never forget it, never. A memory is lodged in the mind but a feeling inhabits the whole body. And I have carried the feeling of that night with me for the last seven decades.

Chapter 4

We were getting ready to attack Tobruk, harassing the enemy in the night using the Bren guns and a navy bombardment was coming to soften up the Italian defences. There was still some light when we parked up in the carriers. To one side of the track was a cliff, perhaps fifty feet high. Looking the other way, we could see the Mediterranean.

Instinct is a fine thing in war and it is usually wise to heed it. I had a strange feeling and suggested that we should move the carriers further along the road. Minutes later there was a deafening blast, sending shock waves through the carriers and everyone in them. The sound rumbled around, reverberating off the rocks and our ears were left squealing with that high-pitched sound you get after an explosion. Our language was unrepeatable. The Royal Navy could deliver a devastating punch and you were better out of the way when it did. Their opening shot had fallen close to where we had been just minutes before.

Normally I'd have said to myself, 'A miss is as good as a mile', but that was just the first shell and a naval bombardment is not something to witness at close quarters. Before the dust settled I slammed the carrier into gear and we were on the move. It was just as well because another friendly shell thumped into the rock face close behind us. We didn't stop.

The attack began early in the morning with the Australians hitting the defences from the south. We could see thick black smoke coming from the docks where the Italians had set fire to oil tanks. Their cruiser, the *San Giorgio*, was in the harbour after being badly damaged by the RAF. They beached her and set her on fire as well.

One of our officers, Tom Bird, broke through the defences with the 'S' Company carriers, capturing scores of guns, 2,000 prisoners and, best of all, the contents of an Italian officers' mess. The tanks came in behind him and white flags started appearing everywhere. They took more than 25,000 prisoners in Tobruk, but 'Electric Whiskers' wasn't one of them. He'd slipped away again.

The Italians had done a lot of damage to the harbour but the best news was there was lots of water in the reservoirs to quench our thirst.

Now Tobruk had fallen we could return to our nomadic ways and around then I got to know one of our best officers, 2nd Lieutenant Mike Mosley. It didn't start well. I was driving a truck with him in the passenger seat when we hit soft sand and the wheels started spinning hopelessly. We were soon up to the axles and going nowhere fast. He wasn't exactly pleased.

'Didn't you see it?' he asked. 'What kind of a driver are you, Avey? You're supposed to look where you're going.'

I was stung. I didn't take comments like that from anyone, officer or not. I fancied I was a good driver and the snipe was worse coming from an officer I really respected. I bit my lip and that was rare in those days. With Mosley looking on, we began digging the truck out, laying out the perforated metal sand-trays to give the tyres something to bite on and we were soon back on the road.

I usually drove a Bren gun carrier. Someone had spotted I was a handy mechanic. The carriers were nippy enough, you could get nearly 40 mph out of them and despite their clunky tracks and their armour plate, they were manoeuvrable. You steered with fine movements of the wheel. Turn left to brake the left track and you pivoted round it, turn the wheel right and you did the opposite.

A bit later we were on a dusty hillside. A lengthy column of trucks had parked up along an escarpment track, pressed tightly against the uphill side of the road. The other edge was marked by a drop sheer enough to make you queasy.

Mike Mosley spotted me in my carrier. 'Take me along the column and back,' he said, climbing in and standing bolt upright in the commander's seat. He obviously wanted to be seen by the troops as if he was expecting to take a drive-by salute. My chance had come. I turned the switch to bring on the ignition light and pressed the starter button. The V-8 engine spluttered into life. I slammed it into gear and slithered off. I was soon accelerating without mercy as Mosley hung on to the armour plating trying to keep his breakfast down and staring into the void. With just twelve inches to spare on each side I reached full speed with my eyes fixed on the narrow track and Mosley looking increasingly green around the gills. A minor flick of the wheel would have locked one of the tracks and we'd have been airborne. It put the wind up him all right. I turned at the end of the column and repeated the trick before the clouds of dust from the first pass had settled. He climbed out, just managing a stifled thank you. 'Touché,' I said to myself. I'd made my point. He was pretty civil after that.

'B' Company was under the command of Major Viscount Hugo Garmoyle and we were sent ahead of the rest of the battalion. We were behind the tanks, heading across the desert on the way to Benghazi, the next big target. The landscape became increasingly barren the further we got from the sea. Fifty miles inland, vegetation was sparse, the landscape was dry and stony with patches of reddish sift-sand, occasional hills and deep depressions or *nullahs* that had been scoured into the landscape.

It was good to be alongside Les again for the first time since getting out on the blue. As a Lance-Sergeant he was the carrier commander. He got things done and he trusted me. Not even the desert sores, terrible grub and lack of proper sleep dented his humour. He was still sharp.

On the evening of 23 January the armour ahead of us got into a major duffy with the Italians on the track to Mechili. They were up against seventy tanks, who put up quite a fight. Our lot knocked out nine of theirs but we paid a hefty price. It was all over when we caught up. The Italian tanks were smashed and left littered across the desert. *Heaven help anyone in there*, I thought to myself looking at a burnt-out Italian M13. Their armour was like cheese. Those inside had simply fried.

One of the others had clambered on to an M13 which at first glance didn't look as badly damaged. 'Oh my God, look at this. There's someone alive in this one,' he said. The soldier was standing at the side of the turret and he had one hand on the stubby barrel, staring through the hatch, unable to pull himself away.

I swung up under the gun and looked in. The tank commander was inside and still sitting down. His guts were spread out, dark and crimson all across his lap. He moved just slightly. It would have been ridiculous to try to lift him out. He would have been in agony and he wasn't going to live long anyway.

For a moment I was seventeen years old again and back in Essex. I was on a pheasant shoot with my father and his friends. We were walking with the dogs bounding around us in the deep undergrowth. I was enjoying the warm weather and the adult company. There was a distant flapping as one of the dogs put a cock pheasant to flight a hundred yards away. I raised the shotgun and fired the barrel with the chokebore to get the range, feeling the recoil in my shoulder. I watched the bird come down and knew I'd killed it. The dogs retrieved it and I tramped back through the long grass to the party, holding it aloft by the tail feathers, beaming proudly. But when I saw my father's face I knew instantly something was wrong.

'I suppose you think that was a good shot,' he said.

'Yes, I do,' I replied.

'Well it wasn't, I can tell you. At that distance it was purely accidental.'

I knew better than to protest.

'You could have wounded that bird at that range and it would have been in pain for days. Now get off the shoot.'

My father had always taught me to respect people and animals but I was humiliated in front of all those men. He was right, of course, but I hated it at the time. I turned and left in shame.

Now, not many years later, I was standing on an Italian tank looking down on a man who had been an enemy but was now a suffering human being with no prospect of life.

I never saw his face, thankfully, but I raised my weapon and did what I thought was right. I was reported for that and I had to go and speak to a senior officer later that day. He was sitting on a pile of wooden boxes. He wanted to hear the whole story and, as a seasoned soldier, I think he understood. No more was said about it.

I decided not to sleep below the carrier that night and dug my usual grave-shaped sand bed away from the vehicles but still safely within the leaguer. I checked my weapons and turned in along with the rest – no hearty campfires of brothers in arms below a desert sky, just dog-tired men sleeping in the sand.

In the desert I always slept with my ears cocked. The slightest unfamiliar noise and I was there, alert and ready. It got worse the more patrols I did. I knew how easy it was to slip into a camp undetected at night; to move around in the shadows, smelling the domestic smells, even hearing 'O Sole Mio' sung by men who felt completely safe. I also knew that a soldier entering an enemy camp at night would be fired up, ready to kill to escape. He'd do what I had done.

It was the miserable sound of rain that woke me. I fumbled around in the wet, dark sand until my hands settled on the cold, knobbly metal of the Mills bombs and breathed a little easier. The Beretta was still under my arm and the .38 was in reach. Prepared, I drifted back into a sort of sleep listening to the patter of rain and the distant sound of snoring. Later I woke shivering, with an unexpected weight pressing down on me. The bedroll was stiff and I could barely move. It was covered in ice.

Next, it was on to Fort Mechili. We meant to cut off the Italians but we just missed them. Our maps weren't up to much and they found a way out on a track we didn't know about. They had abandoned the whole position overnight leaving vehicles and stores behind. Once again they were retreating.

These long journeys in a carrier were not pleasant. It was open to the elements. The driver's seat could be dropped in combat so you were below the armour plating but you were fully exposed when driving and the drag created a vacuum, pulling airborne sand in around you and coating everything. We were close to Fort Mechili when a violent *khamsin* whipped up from nowhere. It would be bully-beef and gravel for dinner as usual.

The convoy pulled up for a break and before I could get out Eddie Richardson was alongside.

'You won't get into Shepheard's looking like that, old chap,' he said.

The sand glued to my cheeks cracked as I smiled. I climbed out, flicked the dust from my stiff hair using both hands, took a swig of waxy water and went to work. The tracks on a Bren carrier needed a lot of attention, especially on stony ground. I began by checking the pivot pins that linked each segment of the tracks together. A carrier without its tracks was a sitting target, so any doubts and I would swap them. I'd knock out the old pin using a heavy hammer and bash in the replacement, chasing the old one out. It would be good for a few more miles.

On 28 January we settled down to hold the fort and maintain the carriers, and the rest of 2RB caught up with us a few days later. They'd had a bit of a time with the Italian air force, with fighters strafing them and a few very near misses from bombers. They were told they could have a breather, and that we wouldn't have to move again for the best part of two weeks.

That was a good joke as it turned out. Two weeks turned out to be more like two hours.

The trucks had their bonnets up, the lads were washing and shaving. Some of the officers had gone on leave or were getting ready to go. That was when the big cheese, General 'Jumbo' Wilson, arrived. The buzz soon spread. Something big was happening. The RAF had spotted long columns of enemy leaving Benghazi and the top brass guessed rightly the Italians were quitting the whole area, leaving Cyrenaica. We were well inland, in the middle of a bulge of Africa sticking up north into the Mediterranean. The Italians were departing down the left-hand coast of that bulge. A hundred and fifty miles of desert lay between them and us. A bold strike could deliver a decisive blow but it was a journey, we were told later, that not even camel trains would attempt. We grabbed what sleep we could.

It was a race. At first light, engines spluttered and the column began to roll, tanks, armoured cars, trucks and the carriers in a long line, spread out against air attack. If the whole Italian army was really on the move, we would still be heavily outnumbered even if we got there in time to block their way. That first eighty miles was purgatory. It was a forbidding landscape scattered with slab-rocks and scoured with *wadis* and hidden patches of sift-sand. If you drifted into one of those you'd be there until next Christmas. Tracked vehicles like the one I was driving were bucking and rearing over the boulders, ditches and camels humps, constantly at risk of shedding a track. I replaced at least twelve pins to keep the carrier rolling on that journey alone. It was imperative to look after it. No feet, no horse, as simple as that. All our vehicles were long overdue for proper repair. The light tanks kept breaking down and had to be left behind with their crews, hoping for recovery.

The weather was making it hard too. Visibility was terrible in the endless blast of sand and dust, then we would run into an icy rain storm. The commanders got the worst of it, standing in the backs of trucks like desert mariners, frozen stiff. We were soon running dangerously short of fuel. At the best of times the carriers did five miles to a gallon. On this bad ground it was more like one or two and the crashing around was springing leaks in our spare cans. If the fuel tanks got close to empty, the dregs of sand in the bottom would be sucked into the carburettor and we would shudder to a halt. We were running short of water too, getting by on just a glass per man per day.

Near Msus, sixty or seventy miles from the coast, the column closed up. Our aircraft had run out of spare engines, but one single working Hurricane reported a long column of Italian vehicles heading south from Benghazi.

We were given new orders. The tanks and carriers couldn't travel fast enough. They quickly put together a special force in the faster vehicles to race south-west and block the Italians' way. Two thousand of us were chosen for this 'Combeforce', commanded by Lieutenant-Colonel John Combe of the 11th Hussars. We left the carriers behind to follow up later.

I picked up belts of ammunition and my bedroll and I climbed into the back of the nearest truck, leaving everything else behind in the carrier. By 1300 hours we were rolling again, this time more quickly.

We had to stop at nightfall because the Italians had spread thermos bombs across our path. They were nasty little cylinders shaped like a vacuum flask but they were no picnic. We were moving again by sunrise, tearing along on a compass course to cut the road at Sidi Saleh, engines boiling. The desert was giving way to a more forgiving landscape, with a little more greenery and signs of cultivation. We were emerging from the wilderness into what had once been the granary of the Roman Empire.

Three Italian fighters dropped out of the sky at a brief rest halt, machine guns blazing. We hit the ground but the scream of propeller engines soon became a distant drone. They had achieved nothing but someone knew we were here. Given that the dash had been designed to take the Italians by surprise, it was worrying.

In the early afternoon, about 1400 hours, we reached the road near the derelict village of Beda Fomm. In almost a day and a half we had covered around 160 miles over some of the roughest ground the desert could throw at us. Not only that, we could see nothing coming from the north. We had got there before the Italians but, as it turned out, only just.

The road ran through sandy ground with low ridges running north–south. The sea and the coastal dunes were two miles to our west. We were working hard to get the guns deployed across both sides of the road. Captain Tom Pearson was in charge and he began to lay a minefield. We barely had time to dig in before the enemy showed up in force.

The first Italians came into view and imagine how they felt. They thought the nearest enemy was at least a hundred miles away so they were convinced the vehicles ahead of them must be friendly until our artillery opened up. It was a complete shock. They careered off the road, trying to get out of harm's way, and then the fighting really began. They outnumbered us by a huge margin but luckily they didn't know that. They launched some wild attacks and we threw them back each time but more and more of them were coming down the road.

Late in the afternoon, our armour caught up, peeling off to attack to the north of us, halfway down the long Italian column. There were burning Italian vehicles everywhere by the time dusk fell and we had already taken a thousand prisoners but there were more Italians arriving all the time. What we didn't know then was that 'Electric Whiskers' was in the column and he'd been given orders to break out of the trap. He should have been able to, because it wasn't great territory for such an unbalanced battle, with flat terrain spreading out both sides of our roadblock. Our orders were clear: the Italians must not be allowed to break through between the road and the sea.

Tom Pearson was one our best officers and he knew we had to convince the Italians there were far more of us out there in the darkness or they would drive straight round us. In the evening, he decided to send out a harassing force right along the Italian column.

Mike Mosley took two platoons including mine, and a small section of artillery to do the job. I was relieved to be going into battle with Mosley. He was a bit of an enigma, a bishop's only son who had himself been heading for the church until the war came along. A naturally curious man and a brilliant soldier, he didn't have a fear in his body in battle. Since I had given him a fright in the carrier, I felt the slate had been wiped clean. I trusted him as much as any officer. That night he was to win the Military Cross.

I locked the side handle on the Bren, checked the curved magazine and climbed into the back of the nearest truck. Mosley clambered up after me, pulled out his revolver, gave a bang on the roof of the cab and we lurched off in the dark.

It must have been about midnight when the drone of engine exhausts told us another column was approaching from the north. My night vision was starting to kick in and we could make out the outline of trucks, tanks and big guns about 250 yards away in the night. There were 200 vehicles or more, stretching way back along the track. There weren't nearly enough of us to stop them breaking out, so we began to create an illusion.

I aimed my Bren low to allow for the recoil which always lifted it up and over the target. You had to force it down with pressure on the side handle. Mosley pointed at the target with his revolver and gave the order, 'Bursts of five, when you're ready.'

It was pretty accurate at that range. The flames engulfed the first trucks quickly and those behind were caught in the orange light making them easier targets. In seconds, shadowy figures were running into the sand beyond.

Our bigger guns began barking explosive shells towards the enemy and we moved off down the column; sometimes stopping to aim, often just firing on the move. Some gunners liked to spray bullets wildly. I never fired more than five in a batch; I didn't need to. We'd put the occasional tracer bullet in to see how we were doing and we would see them arcing over in the darkness.

That column was the best part of three miles long and we brought it to a halt. When we got to the end, we spun around and prepared to cause more trouble on the return journey. They were firing back, of course, but not having much joy. We kept it up for three hours but a couple of our trucks were in trouble, so we had to head back for repairs. We were getting short of food and ammunition. There was a squally wind with bursts of heavy rain so you often couldn't see much. The artillery couldn't move because the armour needed all the petrol and some of the guns only had thirty rounds left each.

The Italians weren't giving up. It went on all that day, with sporadic attacks, gunfights and blown-up vehicles everywhere with soldiers crouched behind them. The CO of our headquarters company arrived during an uncharacteristic lull and decided what we most needed was a mess tent, so he put up a big white marquee right by us. What a silly arse. It made a beautiful target and Italian shells started arriving immediately. The main battle was now three miles north where our tanks were attacking the Italians on the road round the hill we called 'the Pimple'. We were the 'longstop', the cork in the bottle, and they kept trying to break through.

We were getting more and more stretched. A group of Italian tanks was heading straight for battalion headquarters and we only stopped them a hundred yards short. White flags began appearing and by the end of the day about 10,000 prisoners had been taken but the rest still kept attacking.

Somewhere out in the dunes towards the sea, one of our NCOs, Platoon Sergeant-Major Jarvis, was guarding 500 prisoners with the help of Rifleman Gillan. They saw two big Italian tanks coming so they decided to rush them, two men on foot against tanks. The Italian prisoners, seeing a chance to escape, joined the rush and the puzzled Italian officer in the leading tank opened his turret hatch to see what was going on. Jarvis clubbed him on the head with his rifle then fired in through the slits and the crew surrendered. Gillan did much the same with the other tank and they captured both of them. They both got the DCM for that but when an officer congratulated them, Jarvis just replied, 'Yes, it was all right, sir, because the rifleman and me had a nice, warm place to spend the night.'

In the darkness, we could hear the rumble of heavy vehicle engines. It was clear they were planning something. Just before dawn we spotted them. A large force headed by thirty tanks was approaching the roadblock where it dispersed quickly as if to surround the barrier. It was their last all-out throw of the dice and when they broke through our forward positions, it looked like it might work. The lads had no choice but to drop back. We had eleven anti-tank guns left at the start and as we knocked out the tanks, they were knocking out our guns. The story goes that in the end we had just one gun working and the crew of that gun accounted for five tanks with their last five rounds. I'm not sure it was quite that close but that last Italian tank got to within twenty yards of our HQ tent before we stopped it.

We dealt with the infantry following the armour and by that time, everyone could hear our tanks coming from the north to join in. White flags began appearing along the road and Italian soldiers started to emerge, many no doubt glad it was all over. I kept some pressure on the trigger. It could still turn nasty. Later we heard of an officer who had been attacked with an axe by a prisoner who had already surrendered. It paid to be cautious.

The man was walking alongside the column when I saw him, past burnt-out trucks and hideously distorted tanks. More Italian soldiers with white flags appeared as he passed by. There are different accounts but I can still see him wearing a long cape open at the front. There were the occasional flashes of his uniform underneath and you could see he had more gold braid on him than Soft Mick. General Annibale Bergonzoli, 'Electric Whiskers' himself, was surrendering. He had escaped Bardia and Tobruk but he was now in our hands along with a clutch of other generals.

As his dusty cape parted I noticed that he still had what looked like a small ivory-handled automatic pistol on him. I stepped forward and gestured towards the gun at his side. He stared at me defiantly, he knew what I wanted. Hardly pausing, he patted the tiny weapon with his right hand and then wagged his finger. I understood straight away. He was not giving up his pistol and surrendering formally to anyone less than an officer. I stood aside and waved him on in their direction. I believe it was Captain Tom Pearson who finally got it off him.

And that was the battle of Beda Fomm. In just a couple of months we had taken a 130,000 prisoners. Our breathless race across the desert had allowed us to finish off the Italian 10th Army entirely, but there was no jubilation in our camp, only relief.

Two days after the shooting stopped I picked my way through the tangled metal and twisted carcasses of vehicles. The danger that had kept me alert and focused during battle was gone. Mangled bodies were scattered around in the dust already attracting flies. There were severed arms and legs spread out over a wide area, cut off by explosives or even concentrated machine gun fire. Wounded Italians were propped up against odd-looking rocks like gateposts. There was a solitary tree. Most of the injured had been taken away but some were still lying in the dirt, too weak to groan. It was a ghastly situation.

Everyone copes in his own way, I suppose. I ran into Mike Mosley again. The great war hero was mooching around amongst the sand dunes staring at the ground. He straightened his back and came across to me.

'Do you know, Avey,' he said, 'I've found no less that twelve species of wildflower in this little patch of sand alone. Amazing.'

Chapter 5

Despite the pasting the Italians had received during the battle, we had captured quite a few weapons and vehicles intact. I was told to list all the useful Italian clobber we could salvage. There were private cars in that last desperate column. Their polished fenders were now coated in thick dust. There were coaches too, which had carried prostitutes from the Italian bordellos of Benghazi. The women were packed off with the rest of the civilians back the way they had come, to the annoyance of some of the lads.

Later, Bergonzoli claimed he lost partly because all those civilians, over 1,000 of them, got in his way. Ridiculous. He had the grace to admit that what he called 'the excellent marksmanship of The Rifle Brigade' had something to do with it as well.

It is surprising what you find after a defeat. I came across a splendid collection of cockade hats all with their own flourish of feathers. The generals wouldn't be needing those any more. I kept one. Then there was a beautifully crafted set of surgeon's tools in a hand-sewn leather case with dried blood still on the scalpels. I was more interested in water. Rations hadn't improved much and I was desperately thirsty.

My eye was soon drawn to a largely intact group of trucks. They carried hundreds of wooden crates, each two feet square and about eight inches deep. I was suddenly energised by the thought that the crates might contain food or drink. There was another chap with me. We hopped up onto the first truck. 'Come on, look lively,' I said, 'Get your sword on to it.'

He hacked a hole in the plywood. I was immediately disappointed. There were no bottles or cans, just printed paper. He prised the top off altogether. 'Good heavens above, take a look at that,' I said. The crate was stuffed with thousands and thousands of crisp, newly printed Italian banknotes.

The second crate was the same and the next and so on and so on. The trucks belonged to the Italian army pay corps and there was enough money to pay an entire army but to us, those millions of lira didn't mean a thing. I found out later you could change them in Cairo at 600 to the pound but I would have swapped the whole lot for a few bottles of clean fresh water and some decent grub.

I reported it and that was that. We threw a couple of crates onto the pick-up and forgot about them. Some of the lads used Italian money to light their fags, even taking handfuls off into the desert to wipe their backsides, enjoying the joke as they crouched. The Cairo exchange rate on those might have been a bit worse. We were more impressed with the rice and tomato purée we salvaged later. You could eat that.

We waited for days to be relieved by another column coming down from the north. Eventually the order came to head up towards Benghazi to try and make contact with them en route. The crates of cash were still in the pick-up when we set off.

It was a journey of seventy miles with glimpses of the sea from time to time to remind us the whole world wasn't dusty. We came to a halt in a traffic jam in the outskirts of Benghazi. Then above the sound of exhausts and honking horns a shot rang out followed rapidly by another and the zinging sound of a bullet deflecting off something hard. There was a sniper on the loose. I spun the pick-up around and retreated rapidly back down the road. I drove until the streets felt calmer and stopped outside a smart-looking bar.

I wasn't keen on the sherbet then, alcohol didn't impress me much at all, but with throats like cardboard, it was an easy choice. The five of us went in and we took a crate of lira with us.

We walked into the most beautiful place I had seen since leaving Cairo, a cool and airy room at least a hundred feet long and thirty feet wide. The walls and ceiling were covered with elaborately etched glass mirrors. There was a long marble bar down one side and it was crowded.

There was a muffled scream from one of the few women and a sharp intake of breath from the rest of the clientele. Everyone was watching us, and they were terrified. One glance at the wall of mirrors and I could see why. We were desert desperados, battle-stained and grimy, and we looked ready to shoot the place up.

We didn't hang about. Two of the lads went straight through to check out the kitchens and backrooms for anything suspicious. Someone had been taking shots at us just ten minutes before and the last thing we needed was any more surprises. When we were satisfied, we headed for a table and the occupants quickly made space for us. We sat down on the polished metal armchairs, keeping an eye on the doors.

A small chap approached cautiously and said something I didn't understand in Italian. He was aged about forty with a carefully trimmed black moustache and a white jacket. We guessed he was the owner.

'Drinks all round,' I said pointing to a glass and signalling around the room with my hand. He got the message, there was a snap of his fingers and a few words of Italian. Drinks started to appear, including beers for the lads, and the atmosphere eased a notch. The customers were never going to relax fully with a gang of enemy soldiers, fresh from battle, making jokes in the middle of the joint.

The bar was filled mostly with Italian civilians and they had every right to be jumpy. They had been in the evacuation of Benghazi. Many of them had witnessed the battle before we sent them packing back here again.

'You know,' I said to the lads, rocking backwards on my chair, 'we could probably buy this place outright, what do you reckon?'

A smile spread across their faces. We were getting back our sense of fun after some pretty rotten months. We lifted the crate onto the marble bar and called the owner across.

'How much for the whole place?' I asked with a smile, gesturing around. He looked blankly back at me. I tried again a little more slowly, exaggerating the hand gestures.

'We want to buy the bar – all of it: tables, chairs, the lot. We have lira, how much?' Still no understanding.

I pulled out my sword, which made him flinch. Prising open the top of the crate, I gestured with the point to the contents. 'Look, money, your money. Lira, lira, lots of lira.'

His eyes widened, he was certainly interested. It was just wads of paper to us but the man with the moustache was beginning to see the possibilities.

We stayed for half an hour and that was long enough for word to spread. We had no idea if the area was safe and it was time to make our excuses and leave. The owner and his family scarpered before we did and he took the crate of lira with him. I'm sure it was more than a fair price and I still like to say I own property in Libya.

We returned to the ordered chaos of the battalion. The lads felt we should have pushed on to Tripoli whilst we had the momentum, but the big noises thought otherwise. They were starting to plan our withdrawal. They had a point because most of our vehicles were long overdue for some proper care. The whole of 7th Armoured Division was mechanically clapped-out.

We were still basking in the glow of overwhelming victory when an omen appeared in the sky. At 0630 hours on 12 February a bomber was spotted by the patrol flying at just fifty feet along the road. It dropped several heavy bombs and disappeared into the distant haze. It wasn't a clumsy three-engined Savoia. It was a Junkers Ju 88 with black crosses on the wings. The Luftwaffe had arrived. That same day, Rommel flew to Tripoli to take over the desert war and the Germans began to put together a new fighting force, the Afrika Korps. We would not have it so easy again.

Early in the morning of 21 February, and with less than twenty-four hours' notice, we set off back to Cairo via Tobruk. I was with Charles Calistan. It seemed like an eternity since we had explored Cairo together. We had all been bloodied since then. Progress was slow. We were supposed to drive in formation with a hundred yards between vehicles and crawling at fifteen miles an hour even when the going was good and no more than eight on the worst sections of desert. Tom 'Dicky' Bird was the trusty battalion navigator. We had rations and water on board for two days but it was a long, dry haul. No crocked vehicles were to be left behind. Nothing could be spared. If possible we had to tow everything home.

On the second day there was an almighty blast. One of the carriers had hit something. Approaching the wreckage, it looked like one chap was already dead. We spotted another fellow writhing in agony on the ground and screaming loudly. It was George Sherlock, an older soldier and another keen battalion boxer. The natural reaction was to run to help but that could be deadly if they had strayed into a minefield. Gathering in one spot also offered a better target if you came under attack so after a blast you needed to work out what had happened before you did anything stupid. We approached carefully, shouting out for him to hold on, but his calls grew more frantic. It might have been a mine or a booby trap but it turned out to be a thermos bomb dropped a fortnight earlier. George was bleeding badly but he had energy enough to shout, which was a good sign. His leg looked badly mangled and his arm wasn't much better. He wouldn't be landing any punches for a while and he became still more agitated as I approached him.

'No! No! Don't let Avey near me,' he screamed, stopping me in my tracks. I was stunned. He needed help quickly.

'Don't let him near me, he'll shoot, I know he will, he'll shoot!'

Now I knew he had heard about the Italian tank commander.

He was panicking and losing a lot of blood but I was taken aback by his fear of me. I didn't want to make it worse, so I let the others patch him up.

His words preyed on my mind. We got him to hospital in Tobruk where we handed over our captured Italian lorries. We swapped our other vehicles for ten trucks for the final leg back to Cairo. That evening, Tobruk was heavily bombed; the Germans were making their presence felt all right. They were kind enough to include us in the itinerary too and lobbed some bombs our way on their way home.

As a man who liked speed, I was pleased to find the trucks could hit a headlong twenty miles an hour but I was beginning to feel rough. With the months of stress, toil and combat behind me, my defences were down. I started to feel very ill indeed.

By the afternoon of 28 February we were safely back at Mena on the edge of Cairo where our advance party had got the camp well under construction. The tents and wooden huts were luxury to behold but I was already in hospital with a mystery illness. The refit began but the desert didn't want to leave us alone. As I lay sweating and confused, the others were having their new uniforms christened by a violent sandstorm.

German aircraft were dropping mines in the Suez Canal nearby. 2RB had to line the banks and spot where the mines fell. At night they decided to spread a net over the water, so that in the morning you could see the holes where the mines had gone through. To demonstrate the principle in daylight, two aircraft turned up to drop dummies. They were only expecting one. It took a while to realise the second aircraft was German and the mine was real.

I didn't see any of that. The luxurious camp proved to be a double-edged sword. Unknown to us, the mud-brick walls put up to protect the tents from bomb blast were a perfect breeding ground for sandflies. They came out at night to bite us. My resistance was low. I got sandfly fever: a soaring temperature, headache, aching limbs, burning eyes, the works. The doctor said my liver and spleen had swollen up. It would be a while before I'd be back in working order. There was an epidemic that summer and it didn't end until they learnt to spray with DDT.

I was ill for a long time. The battalion stayed around Cairo until the end of April but the desert war began to take a different turn. The Australians and the New Zealanders were taken off to fight in Greece and so the remaining forces with their battered equipment had to pull back. Soon Rommel's Afrika Korps was all over the desert and we were back where we started. In April, Rommel laid siege to Tobruk. Then he crossed the Egyptian border at Halfaya Pass and 2RB was sent out into the desert again to take on the Panzers.

It started badly. Rommel pushed them back to Buq Buq. That's where I caught up with them to learn that Montagu Douglas Scott, an officer I had respected, had been killed at Halfaya, the very place where I had driven him just months before. Once again a *khamsin* had lifted leaving him far too close to the enemy and this time he didn't make it. He was the first officer of my battalion to die in the desert.

Buq Buq was by the sea and when four or five of us were given permission to get cleaned up, we didn't need to be told twice. It was a beautiful beach: shell-white sand, bleached and fine, as far as you could see around the bay. The sea was a deep azure blue and there were prodigious waves, curling and foaming with brutal power.

We were drying off and larking about a bit when we heard a shout for help. It took a while to identify the source then we saw a man, obviously in trouble and thrashing about helplessly, at least a hundred yards out to sea. There must have been an undertow.

I had started to get dressed after my welcome but salty wash. I ripped off my clothes again and I sprinted down the beach to get a better look. I screwed up my eyes looking into the glare of surf and sky. The violent noise of the breaking waves blocked out any other sound.

He wasn't the only one out there. A more distant shape was appearing and disappearing in the peaks and troughs, at least thirty yards beyond him, seemingly going under. I ran in to the water, leaping the remnants of waves in the shallows, then forcing my legs forward. When I could wade no further I began to swim against the waves.

I reached him and managed to tow him through the water. By the time we reached wading depth again, some of the lads had caught up and they helped me drag him ashore.

I wasn't sure he was even alive, he was just a body flopped on the beach. I wanted to collapse but I quickly realised no one else knew what to do. It just so happened I had gone to life-saving classes to fill the time on the long voyage out from Liverpool. I picked myself up and started to do artificial respiration, lungs straining with the exertion. Liquid was soon erupting from his mouth.

I turned my attention to the second man out at sea but he was gone. The man I'd saved was a Royal Artillery officer. He was now conscious and breathing. It was Eddie Richardson who reported it. I think he just wanted the old man to know what I'd done. He was like that, Eddie.

The NCO found me as a *khamsin* hit the battalion. The billowing wall of hot sand whipped through the unit, penetrating everything. You could hardly see a hand before your face and many of us had blankets over our heads for protection. Mine was supplemented by a bandage that I wrapped across my nose and mouth to filter the hot air. I was so well hidden that someone had to point me out to him when he arrived, shielded by a scarf across his own face. With all that it was a muffled conversation.

'I understand you have been making yourself useful on the beach, Avey. Is that right?'

'Yes,' I said pulling the bandage away from my face to speak.

'Saving an officer, no less.'

'That's right.'

'You understand, of course,' he went on almost shouting now, 'I can't give you anything for it.'

'Yes.'

'What I'll do is this. We need someone extra to escort prisoners to South Africa, so pick up your parrots and monkeys, you're off.'

'What, now?'

'Yes, now. Keep your nose clean and you could make it until the end of the war. Is that clear?'

I can't remember what I said to him but he was soon gone, another covered shadow in the sandstorm. I had fond memories of South Africa but fate was cruel. I was beginning to feel ill all over again. My head was throbbing, my muscles were starting to ache.

I left for Cairo on the next convoy of supply trucks with the *khamsin* still blowing, my head pounding and my face covered to keep the flying grit out of my nose and eyes. There were a couple of chaps with me, and I was soon lying on the truck floor being thrown around with a tempest raging outside and another raging in my head. I was becoming delirious; this time it was malaria.

Thank God it weakened me. I don't know why I did it but one of the chaps told me about it afterwards. The fighting had already taken me to many terrible places. I don't know which one it was that I revisited on the hard floor of that truck but in my delirium I suffered a sudden paroxysm of panic and fear. They told me I lunged forward trying to wrestle a revolver off one of the lads, convinced that the survival of us all depended upon it. Luckily I was overpowered.

They whipped me into a hospital tent. I lost track of the days but I was there at least a fortnight though it could have been much longer. The nursing staff were splendid; the quinine treatment was bitter and ghastly. That's about all I remember, and the heavy bombing, of course. There was plenty of that during my recovery and when you're under canvas, it's alarming.

I pulled through and was soon with the boys again. Not long after I was back on my feet again I was sitting in the breakfast tent when an orderly officer spotted me. 'What the hell are you doing here, Avey? You're supposed to be in South Africa.'

I had assumed the malaria episode had ended that little escapade. He disappeared before hearing an explanation. A couple of hours later he turned up again. 'Right, that's sorted. I have got a ship for you, so pick up your kit and get off to the harbour on the double. They need two men. You can pick someone to go with you, but make it quick.'

I scanned the wooden tables and settled on Bill Chipperfield. Bill had been in my cabin on the *Otranto*. He was as honest as the day is long and it just felt right.

They dropped us down to the harbour in a pick-up. I needed a shave, my uniform was filthy and oil-stained and when I saw the ship we were sailing in, I felt very unsuitably dressed. She was the famous *Île de France*, a crack French liner, requisitioned by the British Admiralty when Paris fell. She had three tall funnels surrounded by broad promenade decks but the black and white livery which had accented her sleek lines was lost beneath a coat of battleship grey.

She had been noted for her art deco interior with its paintings and sculptures plus a Parisian street café, swimming pools, and gyms. Now she was a troop carrier but you could still detect the elegance and grandeur.

'You have been given one of the state rooms,' the guide leading the way announced. It wasn't a mistake; this was a floating luxury apartment.

You could almost smell the perfume of elegant Parisian women; imagine them dressing for dinner in one of the luxury dining rooms on board before stepping out, immaculately presented, for a promenade around the deck.

Instead, I felt the scratch of the desert sand in my stiff and dirty uniform more then ever. Once in my cabin I ran my calloused hands across the soft bed sheets and dreamt. The desert sores on my arms now seemed more of a social embarrassment than a badge of service.

There was a cough. I looked up and now standing before me were not one but two Indian stewards.

'Is everything to your liking, sir?'

'Eh, first class,' I mumbled hesitantly. For months now I had had many orders, few choices and no comforts. Now the choices and comforts were making up for lost time.

'Do you have everything you need?

'Everything I need? Yes, everything.'

'Jolly good.' He was still not satisfied. 'What temperature do you like your bath, sir?'

I felt a wry smile spread across my lips.

There were hundreds of Italian prisoners on board ship. Our job was to guard the gangways leading to their quarters and prevent them breaking out or, worse still, taking over the vessel. I was appalled to be handed an Italian rifle to do the job. *They must be able to do better than that*, I thought, *our Lee-Enfield was the best rifle in service*. But most of the Italians were relieved to be out of the war so the risk wasn't that great.

After the desert it was all a breeze. I sometimes ate at the captain's table. It was the first time I had seen white bread in an age. There hadn't been any bread at all in the desert.

On arrival in Durban, we left the prisoners to someone else to unload and reported to Clarewood Camp nearby. The first part of the job was done.

There was an air of unreality about South Africa this time around. But I was determined to explore and I was pointed to the Navy League Club, a fine colonial-style place with a long, cool bar. There was music and human beings as I used to know them, people whose daily concerns weren't just about staying alive. A stream of folk wanted to hear about the desert. We were minor celebrities. That became a bit too much for me but at least you could drink tea and they had decent bread too.

I met a lovely girl there by the name of Joyce, a manageress with the Stinkwood Furniture Company which made tables and chairs out of an expensive hardwood and got its name from the odour the timber gave off when it was worked. I was soon invited back to meet her parents and after a couple of social visits they suggested I should stay with them rather than at the barracks. That was not unusual, other lads at the camp had managed to move in with South African families and most, Bill included, had a wonderful time. The Merrit family lived in a comfortable apartment on a broad road with palm trees that led down towards the Esplanade.

Life was good and the war was a million miles away. I was fond of Joyce and I guess now you'd say she was a girlfriend, we certainly spent a lot of time together. She was a good yachtswoman who would take me sailing off the coast and a strong swimmer who would not so much as flinch when the klaxons sounded, warning of sharks. She was quite a girl.

My job took all of half an hour per day. I was handed a list of prisoner numbers at Clarewood Camp and had to pass them to HQ in Durban. I enjoyed life with Joyce's family. There were the chauffeur-driven trips to the bioscope, where we'd watch a movie with a drink in hand, sitting in Lloyd Loom-style armchairs with waitresses serving us hand and foot.

Joyce was able to get some time off work and she suggested we made a tour together, knowing I was unhappy with always being asked questions about the war. The battalion had obviously sent me for a break and, to my surprise, my request for time off was approved, so we set off to travel the length and breadth of South Africa. In the north we crossed into Rhodesia, as it was then. The landscape was heaven-sent and there were servants running after us constantly. You hardly dared do anything for yourself. It was the summer of 1941, the middle of the war, and I was enjoying Africa.

Perhaps I had cracked it. Perhaps this could be somewhere to settle in the future, but back in Durban something was stirring inside me. I was constantly seeing the men coming in on the ships and preparing to go up onto the blue. It began to prick my conscience. And then I came across George Sherlock in the street and I think that did it. I was with Joyce when I met him. He shouted and was hobbling across the road on crutches before I realised where the voice had come from. It was wonderful to see a man I had last encountered writhing in agony and crying out in panic, looking so well despite losing his foot to a thermos bomb. We were delighted to see each other.

That made up my mind; I needed to get back to the battalion. I found out that the *Mauretania* was leaving for Suez and got on board in a crowd of other lads. I planned to report myself as soon as we set sail.

I told Joyce's family vaguely that I would be going away for a while. I didn't make a big song and dance about it. To be honest I never really spelt out to Joyce what I was doing; that I was going on the blue and that I might not be coming back. You never really allowed anyone to get close to you in wartime; maybe I had crossed a line. I was about to exchange one world for another. It had to be like flipping a switch. It was the only way I could do it. I wrote to her once afterwards from Egypt and tried to explain but what was done was done. Joyce visited England five years after the war and wrote to see how I was. How I was, was married. I never saw her again.

I had been given a ticket to safety in South Africa and I had ripped it up; I was heading back to the fight. I felt I had to, but I was leaving Joyce behind and who knows what might have become of us, had I stayed. Such are the bloody stupid things we do.

The ship was full of South Africans in a valiant mood and there was a lot of singing on board, much of it in Afrikaans. I never mastered the language but the tunes that drifted across the darkened decks at night stay with me still.

It was hard to share their high spirits. I knew what was in store for them but I was reluctant to spoil the party. They would have a rough time on the blue, the South Africans, and I was to witness some of it. It wasn't going to be easy for any of us.

When we were out of reach of the coast, I reported myself to a British officer on board. The response was predictable and direct. 'Well that was a bloody silly trick' was all he said. He was clearly perplexed. They soon found a berth for me but with the heat as it was, we mostly slept on deck.

There was more trouble when I got back on the blue. I had disobeyed orders in coming back, but being *present* without leave was an unusual charge to make stick. I got a standard 'fizza' but they needed men urgently. The Germans were hammering at the door. Our past victories were dead and buried. They belonged to a different war. Erwin Rommel, the Desert Fox, was the name on everybody's lips. The Germans had stormed all the way to the Egyptian frontier and the garrison at Tobruk was under siege.

Chapter 6

We picked up the Bren gun carriers at Mersa Matruh and headed off to join the battalion. Now I was with some of the old crew again and when Les Jackson turned up we were complete. We were delighted to see each other but not much was said. I'm glad he didn't ask me about where I'd been. While I'd been learning to tack with a beautiful young yachtswoman during the day, and waited on hand and foot in the evenings, Les and the lads had been forcing down bully-beef or greasy Maconochie's stew in Wavell's sandpit. That was now Auchinleck's sandpit anyway because Wavell had been replaced as Commander in Chief, Middle East, after the failure of an operation or two, much to my horror.

Les was all right. He didn't like to crack the whip, but he always got things done and, if he was commanding the carrier, then I was going to drive it. There was no argument. He had confidence in me and he left me to instruct our new gunner. We loaded the back of the carrier with ammunition and prepared to leave, heading for our final act together.

The offensive to relieve Tobruk would become notorious as Operation Crusader. As ever, we were kept in the dark but by now we could make pretty good guesses. The aim was to rescue the port city and push Rommel all the way back, recapturing lost territory. The main assault would be on the Trigh Capuzzo, a long desert track past Sidi Rezegh, south of Tobruk. It was meant to force the enemy to fight a huge tank battle on terrain of our own choosing. The besieged Tobruk garrison was supposed to break out and join us.

That name, Sidi Rezegh, meant nothing to me when I first heard it.

I was still in 'B' Company commanded by Tony Franklyn and we were part of Hugo Column, named after the major who lead us, Viscount Hugo Garmoyle. Our job was to engage the enemy to the west of the main advance.

That part of the desert was pitted with deep depressions, so many in fact that the maps list ten alternative names for their subtle variations. A dip in the ground could be described as an *agheiret*, or an *agheret*, unless it was a *ghot*, a *giof*, a *gof* or a *got*. Alternatively it could be termed a *hatiet*, a *rugbet* or even a *sghifet* and it was not to be confused with a *deir* which was the kind of depression you could camp in. Big ones could be useful to hide in. Small ones could break your tracks.

We gathered close to the Libyan frontier, forty miles south of the sea, in a forbidding but now familiar landscape of sand and gravel with lots of tiny saltpans which had once been lakes. At 0600 hours the next morning, 18 November, we cut through the wire and set off. As the sun rose, it was bright but not hot. There was no mirage and all around, we could see tanks and other vehicles streaming across the desert towards Tobruk.

Many had passed here before us. The arid landscape was dotted with Muslim graves, large and small and usually marked by cairns of stones; there were Roman water cisterns and even cave dwellings in the outcrops of rock. Many might have passed but few had stayed and you could see why.

Even at the best of times the carriers were as thirsty as an Aussie rifleman in the Sweet Melody, but we were struggling along in low gear, negotiating patches of soft sand, so we were knocking back fuel like nobody's business. As ever, I was focused on keeping the tracks on, the engine running and the sand out of my eyes.

Battalion HQ was coming along three hours behind us. Later,

they described the 'subdued atmosphere of excitement' that pervaded the column. I don't recall feeling especially jolly. Les and I were a unit and we just got on with it. HQ even found time to stop for a wash, a shave and breakfast.

The RAF were doing a good job. There was no sign of enemy aircraft all day although we passed the remnants of two crashed and burned Stukas, which gave us some comfort. Our first real contact with the enemy came in the late afternoon, when we got into a brief duffy with five Italian tanks. Back at HQ, spirits were high. They were joking about 'beer in Tripoli'. As it turned out they'd be lucky to survive for a beer in Cairo. I don't remember the same feeling where we were leaguered. We spent the night in a series of small hills surrounded by vast depressions, sleeping on gravelly earth in a landscape peppered with tombs.

We got going early to make sure nobody caught us napping. It was a clear cold morning and it began with the sort of action we were used to, a dust-up with another bunch of Italian tanks. We chased them north towards the well at Bir Gubi, with 22nd Armoured Brigade's new Crusader tanks joining in. Gubi was surrounded by enemy trucks, a tempting target, but what happened next was thrilling and horrible in equal parts.

We had grandstand seats for what they say was the nearest thing to a cavalry charge by tanks seen in the whole war but those enemy trucks were not what they seemed. They were a disguise for well-dug-in anti-tank guns. Soon all you could see was dust and smoke. Our tanks ran right through the middle of the enemy positions, running over them in their trenches but they were no match for the guns and they were decimated in the process.

Orders came through on the wireless for us to go in and collect prisoners. They claimed Gubi had been captured but the smoke cleared enough for us to see that it was still very lively indeed and spitting both artillery and anti-tank fire, so Captain Franklyn countermanded the orders, luckily for us. By late afternoon, 22nd

Armoured had knocked out sixty Italian tanks but they had lost twenty-five new Crusaders. It didn't bode well for when they would come up against the Panzers.

As it got dark, we went in to see if any of our disabled tanks could be recovered. Some of them were still smoking and there were dead and wounded from both sides spread all around the battlefield. At least two of our tanks had simply shed their tracks. There was a lot of engine noise and shouting coming from Gubi and, hearing people approaching, we managed to catch a prisoner.

The next day, 20 November, we buried my friend Bill Manley. Dear old Bill. It must have been a clean shot because he was dead when I got to him and I don't recall seeing much damage to his body. The rest of us just had to deal with it. It was towards first light when we buried him. There was no ceremony, no ritual about it. I got on my knees, pulled as much sift-sand away as I could, trying to prevent it trickling back into the shallow grave. We removed one half of the dog tag from around his neck and dropped him into a shallow dent in the desert. I tried not to look at his face as I pushed the sand back over him. Bill was one of those prepared to talk about home, his family – the things that mattered – and generally you didn't do that. None of us wanted to get too close and at moments like this, knees in the dirt, pushing sand over a human face, we knew why. We piled what stones we could find on top to stop the wild dogs getting at him and stood up without so much as a prayer. I pulled the bolt out of his rifle, attached the sword to the end and rammed it barrel first into the sand at his feet. I turned away and left him alone in the desert.

Long after it was over, they came and cleaned up the site of those battles. They moved buried bodies to the military cemeteries but there were a lot they couldn't find, so they listed them on the Alamein memorial. Bill's name is there, so he still lies where I left him somewhere in the shifting sands south of Sidi Rezegh.

We were ordered forward again to see if Gubi was still occupied. We found out when all sorts of heavy artillery and anti-tank fire opened up. The South African Brigade arrived soon after that and we tried to warn them but their leading armed company sailed straight into the danger area and got badly smashed up, poor devils. Some of them were without doubt the boys whose hearty songs had raised our spirits on the *Mauretania* as we sailed up the coast of Africa.

Thankfully, one of our officers managed to get to the main body of their troop-carrying lorries before they came in range and they dug themselves in. Twenty-seven Stuka dive-bombers, complete with fighter escort, appeared overhead. Usually they were flown by crack pilots but this lot delivered their bombs into an empty patch of desert. Only one managed the usual steep dive, though he spoilt it by failing to pull out in time and followed his bomb into the ground. It prompted quips that the pilots must have been Italian but I found it hard to believe the Germans would allow Italian pilots to fly their planes. Perhaps they were novices.

We were getting near our objective. Fifteen miles to the north was the ridge, overlooking the Trigh Capuzzo track. On that ridge was the mosque tomb of Sidi Rezegh, a white building with a dome, and a big airfield. 7th Armoured Brigade had already rampaged across it, destroying Messerschmitts and Stukas, crushing their fuselages with the tanks. It came at a high price in casualties. My friends in Major Sinclair's 'A' company had suffered, losing two carriers to anti-tank guns. Looking back, I find it was described later as 'one of the outstanding exploits of the desert war'.

Seizing the ridge allowed our forces to overlook the so-called Axis road towards Tobruk but the assault was making slow progress, not enough for the besieged garrison to break out to meet us.

I've read the military histories so now I know what went wrong.

The Germans didn't share our appetite for a set-piece tank battle. They chose their moments and used their superior weapons to take us on in separate, unconnected fights that cost us dear. They were good at it. That morning, 21 November, I drove the carrier up out of a *nullah* and as I crested the brow I saw a German tank a thousand yards away. The gun swivelled and he was firing on us in a flash. I only just had time to do a skid turn and drop back down into the dip.

Major Sinclair's 'A' Company met the Germans in the early afternoon when seventy-five panzers came straight at them in a confusion of dust, shell bursts and burning vehicles. Our men were hopelessly outnumbered and their anti-tank guns had been knocked out. The survivors took to the *wadi*s for protection and were soon trapped between tanks to the south and infantry to the north as the light faded. Soon he and his men were in the bag.

Les and I had been buzzing around in the carrier for most of the night with the rest of Hugo Garmoyle's column. In the morning we were sheltering in the valley south of the airfield when we heard despairing messages from Battalion HQ, which was pinned down. It was no more than three small pick-ups with wireless masts, completely exposed on bare ground, the HQ staff crouching down for shelter behind the trucks. We heard them on the radio.

Five Crusader tanks were sent to their rescue but they were set on fire straight away. With two of the pick-ups burning, HQ radioed that they were taking to slit trenches. Among the few guns left working was a Bofors anti-aircraft gun but its unsuitable shells just bounced off the German tanks. The crew of an anti-tank gun, mounted on a truck, were knocked out. One of our officers, Lieutenant Ward Gunn, ran 150 yards under heavy fire to take it over. He got two enemy tanks before he was killed and won a posthumous VC for that. Some of the HQ staff crawled to safety as German infantry bore down on them.

Just as Major Sinclair and his men were being brought in, a

salvo of shells landed in the middle of the group of prisoners and in the dust and confusion, he ran for it. He found a sangar and hid under a groundsheet until dark while Germans looted a truck ten yards away. He spent a chilly night under the stars before he made it back. At the end of it all, two officers from 'A' Company and forty men were missing. Only twenty made it out safely. 'A' Company was no more.

Operation Crusader was in disarray. We were running out of tanks and ammunition. The Sidi Rezegh aerodrome had been recaptured by the enemy, which would have devastating consequences for the men immediately around me. We had watched at a distance, seeing the shell bursts on the aerodrome where 'A' company had been pinned down, but now we were at the centre of the battle.

The 4th Armoured Brigade began withdrawing through our position, and carriers on the aerodrome were also being forced slowly backwards.

At that point a bunch of enemy tanks appeared on the ridge to the south of the airfield and not more than half a mile away. The panzers passed thirty yards from one of our platoons but even at that range none of our weapons, the Brens and the useless Boys anti-tank rifle, made any impression on them. The battle between our twenty-five-pounder field guns and their heavily armoured tanks was hopelessly uneven but Garmoyle kept them at it, going from one gun to the next, encouraging the gunners and giving orders. I didn't see it but there's a story that a shell fell right by him as he walked calmly around. A rifleman said to his mate, 'Hey, look, a shell fell right on the Major.'

'What did he do?' asked the other.

'Took a longer stride.'

Those gunners, and Garmoyle's encouragement, held up the German advance until nightfall but many of our vehicles were captured before they could get back out of range.

That last night of freedom was relatively quiet considering the chaos all around it. We withdrew well away from the ridge. Other units were leaguered up with us by now. Right through the night, small groups of tanks from the 22nd Armoured Brigade kept turning up. I swapped my desert boots for heavy leather ones and put on my leather jerkin. I expected something bad to happen.

At first light on the morning of 22 November we were right back in it again. Fifty of our surviving tanks held an enemy panzer attack at bay. Then came a false dawn as the light tanks of 4th Armoured Brigade raced up having fought their way north-west. Brigadier Jock Campbell led them into battle, racing along in front in a pick-up, flying his blue scarf as a flag. They rushed straight into combat but the attack was more gallant than effective. They arrived in small groups and were destroyed in small groups.

We were now in a precarious position on the edge of the Sidi Rezegh aerodrome. There was a lot of confused discussion on the wireless because we were using a different set of place names to those issued to the 11th Hussars. It didn't bode well. We were ordered to follow a bearing of 22 degrees as the most suitable line of attack across a featureless expanse. They told us to beware of enemy tanks, which were prowling around looking for prey.

With two blue flags held stretched out at arm's length the platoon commander ordered us to advance line abreast. I adjusted my leather jerkin as the carrier engines growled around me. It was hot and sweaty and I had a white handkerchief tied to the steering wheel to wipe my brow. I crunched the carrier into gear and we lurched forward, rocking on the tracks as we picked up speed until we were just a neck ahead of the other four. We had no idea what they had ordered us into.

The ground suddenly dropped away ahead of us and I had to swerve eastward along the edge of an escarpment. Then from nowhere machine guns opened up and the armour plating was soon ringing like hammer blows on an anvil. We were for it now all right.

Les said nothing. 'Fire, for God's sake,' I shouted at the gunner behind me. I heard the metallic bursts of the Bren firing above me. The sound was deafening. I could feel the heat from the Bren's muzzle. Used cartridges showered down on to my neck and into the driver's foot-well.

There was a pause behind and a clash of metal as the gunner changed magazines. The bullets were still smacking into us, sending vibrations through the carrier as if a pneumatic drill was at work on the armour plating.

Les was focused on firing the Boys anti-tank rifle alongside me. I had my seat dropped down in its action position and, instead of looking over the top of the armour, I was peering through the glass in the tiny windscreen slit. I was leaning to my right, away from Les, looking through the screen at an angle in case a bullet came through it.

The recoil of each shot kicked him backwards, its echoing blast lost behind the clatter of incoming machine gun fire. Another pause and I could hear the frantic sound of the gunner changing magazines again. The armour plating was zinging with incoming fire. I was struggling to control the carrier and empty cartridges started spitting down on me again, then suddenly that stopped. All around the din continued but the Bren was still. My ears were ringing but the silence from our gunner was awful. I knew instantly he'd copped it. Then they opened up on us from both sides.

We were driving into a narrowing funnel of German gunners. On our left, they were hidden below the lip of the escarpment. On the right, they were level with us. Les, who had been firing and reloading without pause, wanted to take aim at a gun position.

'Stop!' he screamed.

'Not bloody likely! We'll be a sitting target.'

They were already firing at the tracks and the wheel assemblies. If they knocked those out, they could pick us off at will.

We were bearing down on one of the machine-gun posts in a blizzard of crossfire. With the gunner out of action and Les struggling with the anti-tank rifle, the only really useful weapons I had to hand were a pile of hand grenades next to the seat, and the carrier itself, which could still do some damage.

'I'll get the buggers,' I shouted to Les, more in defiance than hope, as we ploughed into the machine-gun post. The carrier lurched again on its tracks as we mounted their position to the sound of metal being crushed and twisted below the tracks. I was sure the machine gunners were killed instantly but we were surrounded. It hardly made a difference now.

I grabbed a grenade, pulled the pin with my teeth and lobbed it with my arm arcing above the armour plating. It was impossible to know if the blast had any effect. I couldn't see. The air was full of flying metal. I threw another grenade and another, hoping desperately that each blast would bring silence. It never came.

It didn't feel like a bullet that hit me. It was just a smashing blow to my upper body as I stretched up to hurl my last grenade. I had been shot.

I was barely aware of the spud-masher grenade bouncing into the carrier.

I had been knocked down, stunned, into the driver's well. Then there was an almighty blast. It was like having two heavy steel spikes hammered into my ears. Slowed down, it seemed as if my head was expanding and contracting with the force of accelerating air.

If the grenade had bounced down my side of the carrier, I would have been finished but the transmission casing between me and Les saved me by deflecting the hot metal up and away. I must have been knocked out by the blast and the carrier had plunged thirty feet off the edge of the escarpment.

When I came around the inside of the carrier was red and I was covered in gore, warm and sticky. I had half of poor old Les all over me; blood and God knows what else.

It wasn't over. A German soldier towered over me silhouetted against the glare. If he chose to shoot me, that would be it. He was dragging me out of the carrier. He was angry and I didn't expect special treatment, not here, not after what I'd done. I had just crushed his comrades. It was all the same to me now what happened. And there was dear old Les. A human shape was recognisable but little else. The grenade had exploded right in his lap.

The soldier didn't shoot. I saw his lips move. He was rifling through the carrier hunting for the ammunition. Through the high-pitched squealing in my ears I could still hear gunfire in the distance. The other carriers were in trouble. Then I saw the gunner, crumpled on the ground. He wasn't moving and his arm was badly mangled. Another young German came up. He looked at all the bright dents in the sides of the carrier where hundreds of bullets had hit. He ran his fingertips over them, smiling as if pleased with the accuracy of his aim.

Looking down at my leather jerkin with remnants of Les all over it, I knew straight away why I had been spared in those first few seconds of capture. It looked like I'd been blown apart too. They had taken me for dead.

My first reaction on seeing that Les had been blasted to kingdom come was, 'Thank God it wasn't me'. Later, much later, people would tell me that everyone wants to survive and that it was a normal response, but was it? I don't know. I still don't know. Like I said, in war you make excuses to yourself all the time.

Les was the chap with the twinkling eyes. I had come all the way from Liverpool with him, I'd danced with his sister Marjorie, sat around the kitchen table with his folks, laughed at their jokes and shared their food. It didn't seem right. It troubles me as much now as it did seventy years ago. But you do what you have to do, to get through. The mind is a powerful thing. It can take you through walls.

Sidi Rezegh would become known to us as the forgotten battle, and to be a footnote within a forgotten battle is something indeed.

Chapter 7

The gunner was in a terrible state. His arm was all but severed by bullets and he was losing a lot of blood. I didn't expect him to live. A German soldier applied a tourniquet. He made twisting gestures towards me with his hands and I caught the words, '*Jede fünfzehn Minuten.*' He wanted me to release it regularly but I never had the chance. I was lifted onto a stretcher and taken away, leaving the shot-up carrier and Les behind.

I never found out what they did with his body. His remains were still there, slumped forward in his seat when they took me. His name is on the Alamein memorial. I hope someone gave him a proper burial.

Forgotten battle? It was a bloody disaster. Four of the carriers were lost in that action alone. I had minor wounds to my leg and my head and a more serious one to my upper arm. It would be some time before I learnt that Eddie Richardson, Regimental Eddie, had survived it. His carrier had launched off the escarpment at speed and made a lucky soft landing on a giant pile of jerry cans. He survived both the ambush and the flight and was taken prisoner. I think I saw him in the distance in a transit camp months later but I couldn't get to him.

Bill Chipperfield, who had shared my cabin on the *Otranto* and had come to South Africa with me, was dead together with twenty lads from 2RB killed in the first two days of the Sidi Rezegh battle. Many more from other units perished; I'd seen their corpses all over the battlefield. 2nd Lieut. Jimmy McGrigor was killed when a shell hit Hugo Column HQ. He was all right, Jimmy. He talked to us like people, not layabouts.

The siege of Tobruk was lifted but that didn't stop Rommel. He attacked again, advanced deep into Egypt and wasn't stopped until the following summer when he reached El Alamein just a day or two's march from Alexandria. There, the 8th Army, by then under Montgomery, turned the tables for the last time, pushing Rommel out of Egypt once and for all, pressing on through Libya and into Tunisia. Charles Calistan played a heroic part at El Alamein, destroying a score of German tanks almost single-handedly, but by then I was in another world entirely.

The German stretcher-bearers brought me to an advanced dressing station where I was placed on a metal table. They removed my bloodstained jerkin. A *Stabsarzt* came, a surgeon with the rank of major. I felt his hands all over my body as he checked for further injuries. I lay staring at the heavy canvas roof of the bell tent. There was an interruption as they brought in an Italian officer with his foot blown off. To my astonishment, the *Stabsarzt* ordered them sharply out of the tent so he could concentrate on me. It was a strange feeling, given that I was now a helpless prisoner dependent on an enemy doctor. He dug at my wounds to get the filth and shrapnel out of them and I was bandaged up. Thankfully, the bullet had missed the bone. I was mightily relieved.

I wasn't scared. I remember thinking how the hell had I allowed myself to be caught and that now I would never get to be an officer. I was moved to a bigger tent with boxes of supplies piled in the corner. It was strange being undercover again. You didn't see many tents in the desert; we always slept al fresco.

'Would you like to eat something?' The words took me by surprise. The speaker was a young lad with sun-bleached hair. The Afrika Korps had many educated people in its ranks and quite a lot spoke English. I hadn't eaten properly for days. The answer was obvious. He came back carrying some bread and jam or 'Marmelade' as he called it. I was astounded. I hadn't seen bread since South Africa.

It was then I realised I was going to survive this. I was well looked after in a silent and dispassionate sort of way. I assumed good treatment was the order of the day. Later, when I encountered a different sort of German soldier, I realised the Afrika Korps were in a league of their own.

They told me my war was over but I knew it wasn't. I was still on duty and I would stay on duty until the end. It was a promise I made to myself then and it was to my own detriment later. Still, they had patched me up and probably saved my life so it was an oddly calm interlude. There was no guard inside the tent at night; the medical staff had no fear of me at all, they knew I wasn't capable of escape. I don't know how long it was before I was moved but eventually I was loaded, still lying down, into the back of a small vehicle. There was another wounded soldier in there with me but he barely spoke.

It was a long and painful journey. The roads were rough and I was struggling to breathe in the back. I tried to remember the odd bits of German I had learnt at school. After a while I managed to raise myself up and bash on the back of the cab. There was no response. We needed air. '*Luft*, *Luft*,' I called out, thumping the metalwork again.

The truck stopped. I heard the driver coming round to the back. The doors opened and he shouted something I didn't understand. The engine fired and we set off again with the door pinned back. It was very dusty but it was better than suffocating. That journey must have been more than 300 miles. We stopped several times, maybe even overnight, I don't remember. At Benghazi I was taken to a large hospital building and put in an iron bed at the end of a long, clean ward with tall windows. I was the only allied soldier in my section, kept away from the Italian and German wounded at the other end.

The female nurses were German and Italian and they only

spoke to me when they had to. They'd arrive with a clean dressing on a tray, instruct me to move this way and that, do the job and then leave. I slept a lot. Slowly I was getting stronger and the first cooked food in ages was welcome.

I still had my leather jerkin. It was badly cut up by the blast but I managed to get the worst of the gore off it and the rest dried into a permanent stain. I couldn't wear it without being reminded of Les.

Then I was moved quickly and without much explanation. The British were advancing on Benghazi and the Germans didn't want to give back any prisoners, wounded or not. I was driven to the harbour in the back of a truck. Scores of other allied prisoners, perhaps a hundred or more, were waiting to be loaded on board a battered cargo boat. I couldn't say how many were already down below. Wooden packing cases were piled on the decks. We were bound for Italy and there was no chance to escape. We were led up a gangway at the stern and down into a hold. I hadn't had contact with any allied prisoners since my capture but I folded up my jerkin as a pillow, collapsed against the bulkhead and kept myself to myself. It was pretty cramped and the air was hot and foul with human filth. Soon after setting sail we were given our rations, an enormous dog biscuit perhaps eight inches square, so hard you couldn't break it with your teeth. It was the only food we would get.

After some time, the steady throb of the engines and a swaying sensation told me we were moving and by now the fetid air was barely breathable. We began to holler, '*Luft*, *Luft*, *Luft*', our hands cupping our mouths megaphone-style. It became a raucous, desperate game and everyone joined in. We were hoarse with shouting when part of the hatch was opened. We gulped in fresh sea air, filling our lungs as if oxygen had been rationed and then settled down to endure the rest of the voyage, sitting and sleeping on the same patch of hard steel as the hours passed.

We were there through one whole night and most of the next day. The dog biscuit didn't get any more appetising. I looked up through the gap in the hatch covering and saw we were heading towards evening. The light above was sharper and more intense as the sun dropped in the sky.

I don't remember any warning. There was a crushing blast from the forward section of the vessel. It lurched violently in the water as if buffeted by a huge wave. Another explosion followed. I knew it was serious.

The panic began almost immediately. Men turned and headed for the narrow metal stairways up to the deck. I saw guards with guns blocking their way as they fought to get up. It was a dreadful scene. There was no order or discipline; people didn't help each other. They fought to save themselves alone. It was ugly but I would have to do the same.

I could still see the sky. A thin rope that had secured one corner of the tarpaulin over the hatch was now hanging down into the hold. I grabbed it and found it was firmly attached to something above. Despite the wound in my arm I began pulling myself up, hand over hand, with the rope twisted between my feet to ease the pressure. It was something I had done countless times as a child. I reached the end of the rope and gripped the hanging corner of the tarpaulin itself, shinning up that until I reached the rim and swung my legs over the edge of the hatch. The ship was in trouble and down at the bow. I never thought about it for a second. The sea was not too rough so I tore my boots off and dived straight in. With the muffled sound of water fizzing and popping in my ears, time slowed for an instant. I knew there were many men still trapped in that hold; I knew they might never get out and those closer to the blast would be dead already.

I surfaced though a layer of thick oil that stuck to my face and hair as I came up. I didn't want that filth in my lungs. It was dark, heavy stuff and it felt like it would drag me to the bottom. It could only be a matter of time before the ship went down with all those still trapped inside. I knew I had to swim away from it to avoid being sucked under so I kicked hard and managed a crawl through the oil.

More danger. There were other men in the water now, some flailing helplessly. A fast boat, like a small destroyer, was in amongst us almost immediately. It was an Italian subchaser and it hadn't come to help. I knew then that the explosions were tin fish, not mines; we'd been torpedoed by an allied submarine, which was still down there below my legs. The subchaser was scything through the survivors in huge arcs, whipping back and forth trying to find the sub below. It towered above us like a cliff of grey steel. There was panic in the water.

I heard Italian and German voices calling out but anyone caught in the path of the subchaser was mangled in its props or overwhelmed by the wash. Then it began to drop its depth charges. First there was a silence then from far below, a muffled thud, which felt like a hammer blow to the chest. It burst to the surface in a blast that sent a column of water high into the air and turned the sea around it white. I was a hundred yards away and it slammed my whole body. There was another blast, then several more until after a final pass the subchaser was receding on the skyline.

We were alone. The light was fading fast. From water level, the stricken vessel was nowhere to be seen. She had been perilously low in the water and some of the deck cargo had been blown off into the sea. I always assumed she went down.

I saw a large wooden packing case floating in the water and swam for it, churning through the oil. It seemed to take for ever and when I got there, there were several Italians already clinging to it. Through a hole in one corner I could see the case was empty. I got my breath back. This creaking box would be the only life raft we had. I knew something had to be done or I would die in the Mediterranean winter water. I struggled to get a grip on the slippery timbers and after falling back several times I heaved myself up on top, fully out of the water. I didn't fight anyone to do it but had anyone tried to pull me off I would have fought them. If you are really resolved you can do these things but it took an enormous effort and I was clapped out when I got there. I collapsed and lay on my stomach.

I saw then that the case was fragile and might not hold together long in the waves which were now beginning to whip up. The others were just too weak to pull themselves out. I didn't think of helping any of them. To offer a hand would have risked being pulled in. I had to think of number one. Without number one there was nothing. The sea remained choppy. They slipped off silently one by one. They were there and then they were gone. That's how it was.

As the sun dipped below the sea, the waves settled. There was no land in sight and the warmth in my body was draining away. It was soon dark and I was under the sky once again with the light of the stars amidst a lonely soundscape of waves, wind, and creaking timbers.

I held on through that long cold night in the hope of rescue but the sea was empty. I slid in and out of consciousness as I lay on my belly. As the sun came up I fancied I saw land, a golden city on a hill. It could have been the sun on stone buildings; it could have been an hallucination. Time passed and I drifted briefly into consciousness again and this time there really was land in sight, startlingly close. Waves were rolling onto the rocks at the base of a light coloured headland. It brought little comfort. Even that distance was too much to swim.

When I became fully conscious again I was trapped between two pillars of rock and just clear of the water. I was alive and the embrace of the solid rock was welcome after the swaying and groaning of the timbers in the waves. I was still covered in oil.

I could hear the gentle rhythm of the waves and I was convinced the earth below me was rising and settling with the swell. My throat was parched, my lips had the scratch and taste of salt, oil and filth. It was some time before any strength returned and I tried to move.

I was on the edge of a rock-strewn cove. I got to my knees and tried to stand but my legs gave way the second I put any weight on them so I lay a while longer summoning the energy to try again. I must have been on that wooden container for about twenty hours. There had been just one night that I could remember, but with bouts of unconsciousness even that was vague.

When I was able to walk again, I found a landscape of scrub-land and poor soil behind the cove, with hills beyond. The scattered trees would give me some cover but I had no strength in my limbs and my spirits were low. I started to think I would have to give myself up or starve. My bare feet had become soft with immersion in water. The stones hurt them.

I stumbled along until I came upon an old man working outside a small, wooden peasant hut. I didn't stop to wonder whether he was friendly or not but went straight up to him and signalled for water. I had no choice. He hadn't heard me approaching and he recoiled instantly when he saw me. I was soaking wet and had oil deep in the pores of my skin.

His face was lined and weathered but his tousled hair was dark and strong. He didn't run but he kept his distance and looked behind me to see if I was alone. When he spoke it didn't sound like Italian and that made me wonder. Perhaps this wasn't Italy at all.

'English, English,' I said and crossed my wrists to suggest that I had been shackled. His expression eased but he kept his eyes on me and he never came closer. I pointed back along the track towards the sea, making wave-like gestures and an explosive sound mimicking a sinking ship. He stared back, silent and expressionless, then seemed to come to a decision. He mumbled something and gestured me towards the hut's door. It was dark inside and he relaxed just a little when we were out of sight.

I sat down and he handed me water in a battered tin cup. It was my first drink in at least twenty-four hours and I gulped it down in seconds. He brought me more. Now I became aware of its earthy taste but I gulped just as fast. He stood there with his eyes fixed on me. 'Food?' I said gesturing to my mouth. 'Eat?' He cast around in the dark then gave me a handful of raisins. The strong taste stung my palate. After bread and more water, I flopped in the corner and slept.

I awoke feeling groggy. The old man was still there. He brought me eggs and a pastry with dried fruit in it. I nodded gratefully as he withdrew and watched me eat. After the dog biscuit on the boat it was a feast. I asked where I was and got a blank stare and more words I couldn't understand. An idea dawned on me so I took a stick and drew a vague map of Greece in the dirt floor, struggling to give it recognisable shape. He stared at the squiggles more baffled than ever until I added the unmistakable boot shape of Italy to the left and he came to life with an explosion of repetitive language. He took the stick and pointed with conviction to the three fingers I had drawn to represent southern Greece. So that was where I was. I could tell from his vehemence that he hated the Italians who had occupied his country.

I revived a lot with food and rest and I don't know now how long he sheltered me for but I couldn't stay there for ever. If I was caught with him he would get a bullet, it was as simple as that. I wasn't really sure how far I could trust him, though, looking back, that assessment now seems harsh. I wanted to get away.

He gave me some old canvas sandals, which I tied to my bare feet with a bit of cord and he produced a coarse shirt that I put on under my tunic. I was reluctant to dump my military clothing. I knew the risk. Disguised as a civilian I could be shot as a spy. I am sure he was relieved to see me go.

It was a solitary journey and I had to stay out of sight: the oil stains would attract attention. Added to this, my geography of the region was poor and I couldn't visualise what lay ahead. My watch had survived the water and I used it to find north. I avoided roads, trekking over hills and through olive groves. I kept away from settlements and drank water from tiny streams when I could find them. I was weak and lethargic but forced myself to keep going. I was beyond the stage of having hunger pains and I knew from now on I would have to steal to eat. Every contact risked betrayal. If anyone helped me they might be shot. Theft was the better option for everyone.

During the day people were usually working outdoors, often some distance away from their huts. It was easy to break in and a bit like being on patrol in the desert again: find a good vantage point, hunker down and observe. When I knew it was safe I'd go in but there were only slim pickings to be had. The people were poor and suffering from the Italian occupation. I never left with a full stomach but on one occasion I found the same sort of dried fruit pastry the old boy had given me.

When I realised I was in Greece I had dared to think I might stay out of the bag a little longer but it was hard to imagine getting right across occupied Europe and home. As the days passed, I grew weaker. Still smeared with oil and now caked in earth, I stumbled into a small band of men and women working in a field. I scared them more than they scared me. I asked for water. They understood and handed me a long, skin flask. I drank what I could and headed off quickly.

Soon after that I saw there were armed men on my tail. I suspected they were Italians. Someone had reported me. I ran into a large olive grove and crouched down to hide but it was hopeless. They began shooting, there was nowhere to run and they would have killed me. Surrounded, I emerged with my arms up. They tied my hands and walked me to a truck. I was in the bag again.

It was a long journey. I was taken to a crowded camp full of allied prisoners, British and South Africans alongside Greek partisans. It was a dreadful place made up of bivouac tents in a field. There was a lot of rain and even snow. Many of the prisoners were severely ill with dysentery and other diseases. There were no latrines when I arrived so the prisoners had to go where they could and they were so ill that meant anywhere. It was a dreadful place, that field, and the prisoners quickly named it 'Dysentery Acre'. Eventually the Italians relented and a trench was dug about four feet by ten and four feet deep. It was soon full: 160 cubic feet of human excrement. It stank.

There was no room for embarrassment. I'd had dysentery on the blue and I knew what it was like, the sickness, the stomach pains and the urgency. You lined up cheek by jowl, a row of backsides sticking out over the edge of the banking. I remember one thin-faced chap crouching next to me in a sorry old state. Somehow he lost his balance and slipped down the banking into the hole. He was waist-deep in it, poor feller.

'That's the second time I've been in here today' he said.

After that I was moved north and held in a large warehouse near Patras. We had bread and water and nothing more but at least we were led out by a guard when we needed the latrine. He stood and watched as we crouched over a shallow stream. The conditions were a little better but that didn't last.

Chapter 8

We were loaded on board another ship. It was warm down below, a pleasant change from the chilly camp and this time, we didn't have to travel in a cargo hold. There were Italian soldiers on board, going home on leave. One tried to talk to me as we filed past, asking in Italian, then in French who we were and where we had come from. He didn't get very far.

One torpedoing had been quite enough for me but looking at the maps now, I think we took the safe route, hugging the Greek coast inside the islands of Cephalonia and Lefkas before entering the Strait of Corfu to make a rapid dash across the Strait of Otranto to the heel of Italy.

We spent the journey sitting on the floor. At night an Irishman with a tender voice sang a sad song and two South Africans talked about their home. We arrived at a harbour full of guards, maybe Bari or Brindisi, and were marched off to a tree-lined field with a little grass. There were hundreds of us by now and there was no barbed-wire fence so they needed more soldiers to watch us. Some of the lads there were in a terrible state, with swollen faces and limbs from lack of vitamins.

They gave us little to eat and those who had any strength left soon kicked up a rumpus about it. We shouted and jostled the guards until it all got out of hand. We were lucky no one was shot. In the end they regained control and five of us were isolated from the rest. They chained us to trees, shackling our arms and legs and we cursed our way through a miserable day. I'd usually been the one in charge. Now I was tethered like an animal. It seemed an age since I'd set off from Liverpool in the *Otranto*, expecting adventure. We stayed in that field for three or four days and then we were moved to a proper camp.

It had long low barracks of stone and concrete, divided into five bays with timber bunks for around fifty people in each. We were given a couple of warm blankets and a thin palliasse stuffed with straw for a mattress. This was Campo Concentramento Prigioniero di Guerra, Sessantacinque. That's Prisoner of War Camp PG 65 to you and me. It was close to Altamura in southern Italy.

One of the Italian officers was a major who looked like Jimmy Cagney. He was a reasonable feller and he was as pleased as punch when we told him. There was no forced labour and no brutality but the extreme lack of food made it a shocking place.

We had an outdoor cookhouse and the Italians dumped trees in the camp to fuel the fire. One of the lads who still had some strength chopped them up. He probably got extra rations. A huge cooking pot was placed on the flames and in it went whatever they had, which was usually not much more than macaroni. When the soup was done it was carried around the camp in ten-gallon aluminium containers and dished out, just one ladle of thin liquid per man, per day. To start with we got a small piece of bread on top but that was soon halved in size. There was a slurp of ersatz coffee for breakfast and that was it. I started to feel my body deteriorating and none of us were well to start with.

The lice in our clothes had a better diet. I could take my shirt off and squash a hundred between my fingers. Within half an hour there would be a hundred more. They drove you scatty.

Soon after arriving we were lined up and asked what we did in civvy-street. The interpreter's English wasn't great and I remained suspicious, so said I was a cat burglar. He looked up from his list, clearly baffled.

'What?'

'Cat burglar,' I repeated.

'Gat bugglar?' he said looking towards his superior for a reaction. There wasn't one. He wrote something down and moved on to the next man.

When the first Red Cross parcels arrived we thought we were in heaven, though we had to share each parcel between many people. There would be a tin of powdered Klim – milk spelt backwards – a little coffee or tea, a tin of vegetables or some processed cheese, sometimes dried eggs, plus a small bar of chocolate, sugar or raisins.

The boredom was crushing. There was no military discipline in the camp. We had to look after ourselves. We had nothing to cut the bread with but we did have tiny metal mirrors and I found a way of splitting them to create blades. I added wooden handles to make pretty good bread knives and traded them for extra food. The camps worked on barter. You had to have something to swap. As the months passed, I set about making a sort of small suitcase out of flattened Klim containers. God knows why. I had hardly anything to put in it and it was not part of any daring escape plan. I flattened the cans then folded over the edges to link them together in larger sheets that I could bend into shape. It helped me get through the long days and a tin box of sorts emerged at the end of it.

Although we had Red Cross tea and coffee, we had no easy way to boil water. I decided to improvise so I made an enclosed drum with revolving fan blades inside like a sealed hamster wheel. I connected it by a pipe to a tiny metal box filled with cinders, lit a fire around them and when I cranked the fan, it created a mini blast-furnace. The cinders glowed red-hot and you could boil a tin of water on top. I was terribly proud of it and it meant we could drink tea for the first time. Others went on to adapt and perfect the blowers and they were a great success.

I suspect now that the Italians simply didn't have the food to give us. Some of the ordinary guards had little more than we did. We even dried out our used tea leaves to trade with them.

I was still suffering from the ignominy of capture. I barely trusted anybody and I kept largely to myself. I do remember a couple of prisoners. There was a cockney called Partridge who would do favours without wanting anything in return. Then there was another chap called Bouchard who was desperately thin and dying on his feet. He spent his days scavenging for food around the camp. We talked sometimes but never about home. Why torture ourselves?

I heard later that some of those from other camps were taken outside to be disinfected, only to be spat on and abused by the public. We stayed where we were. Occasionally a Catholic priest would turn up and conduct a service for some of the more religious lads. Even that was done through the barbed-wire fence. He never came in.

There were other attempts to ease the monotony. If you knew anything about anything, you could hold a talk about it. The subjects ranged from history and geography to engineering. One chap talked for hours about his lathe and the principles of turning wood and metal and how to cut threads.

After a while they began building extra huts; we were already overcrowded and the camp was to expand. We didn't usually do forced labour in Italy but when we were offered 150 grams of extra bread a day to help with construction we took it. The food situation was dire.

The huts we were to build were sited outside the perimeter. The plan was to complete them first and then extend the fence around them. Going outside the wire was a thrill in itself. There could be food to filch or a chance to get away.

I was one of six lads sent onto the roof to fasten tiles down with cement. It gave me my first real view of the surrounding land. There was just one guard watching over us and he was down below. My belly ached with hunger. It couldn't be any worse on the run. I chose my moment and asked the guard if I could climb down to relieve myself. He reluctantly said yes, although I knew he couldn't keep an eye on all of us.

Once out of sight I didn't waste a second and bolted straight away.

I expected the hullabaloo at any moment but nothing happened and I managed to put some distance between me and the camp before resting. I have no idea when he raised the alarm but I was certainly well away.

I had a piece of bread with me and a tiny chunk of cheese. It was the only preparation I had made. I decided to avoid the coast and head north towards neutral Switzerland. I tried to be optimistic. A home run was more likely from here than Greece but it was still hundreds of miles over enemy territory.

The journey felt familiar. I avoided roads and large settlements and scavenged for food in remote farm outhouses. I didn't get caught at it but I didn't get much food either. The best I managed was the odd dodgy vegetable and something that tasted of aniseed, possibly fennel. I have never been able to eat it since. I covered a lot of distance on foot over the next three or four days but I was getting weak and hungry. I came across a small crop of wheat but it was going grey and rotting in the fields. Italy was not a happy place. It began to rain like the devil.

I took cover in a small deserted building and waited for the rain to stop. It was dark outside when I heard voices calling. My shelter had been surrounded and they were ordering me to come out. I had been spotted.

I stepped into the gloom. I was anxious. I couldn't see how many Italian soldiers were waiting for me but it hardly mattered, they'd got me. I was put on a lorry and taken away. They never bothered to tie my hands and I wasn't knocked about. They got me back to the camp quickly and I spent a day and a night in a punishment cell. Then the dreadful routine resumed. It had been an unplanned effort born out of frustration. I was back in the bag and I'd have to lump it.

Dysentery dominated life in the camp – not just some slightly inconvenient type of stomach upset but a life-threatening, demeaning illness which sapped all our energy leaving us weak, listless and in pain. We were all losing weight and with so many sick people, embarrassing accidents were common. Once you had messed yourself, getting properly clean was almost impossible with just cold water to do it. I saw lads in tears with the humiliation of it, grown men caked in diarrhoea. Many people in that camp died of preventable diseases and neglect. One man's body was kept lying around for days in a shed before he was buried. I remember it because I inherited his trousers. Mine were ripped and filthy and the rest of my uniform was almost as bad.

I was relieved to have them, whether they had been taken from a corpse or not. It was practical. But as the days went by I started to itch badly, and this time it was more than lice. A blotchy, lumpy, red rash appeared on the insides of my thighs. It spread quickly until I had it all around the groin and God knows where else. I had picked up scabies. Tiny mites had burrowed into my flesh, and laid their eggs. As I scratched, the skin broke and bled and I knew it could get infected in all the filth. I'd survive a painful day but at night it seemed my skin was inflamed and crawling.

The bouts of dysentery and constant hunger meant I was horribly lethargic and getting thinner. If I stood up quickly, I would black out and keel over. After a while I began doing it on purpose just to knock myself out behind the barracks. It made the time pass more quickly. When I was out cold there was relief from the hunger, the lice and the torment of the bleeding rash. Most of us did it. The torment of scabies went on for weeks, maybe even months. Not until a bar of carbolic soap appeared in the camp to wash with did I start to bring it under control. My body was in a shocking state, but in my head, I wasn't a prisoner at all. The enemy had done many things to me but they hadn't captured my mind.

That year in Italy was hellish. Many of the lads died of disease and neglect. When news came that some of us were being moved I felt it couldn't get much worse. I was too weak to march out of the camp. There were no officers with us and no military discipline to speak of. The best any of us could muster was a slow listless walk to the lorries. We were loaded into cattle trucks at a railway siding. In better days I would have leapt straight in but it was now a struggle to get up. A sign on the outside said 'Forty men or ten horses'. There was one bucket for everything. I wanted to be as far away from that as possible. Many of the lads still had dysentery. I dropped down in the corner, relieved to have found a place below the only window. It was a twelve-inch square gap with barbed wire stretched across. It provided air, light and a restricted view of the world rolling by. It was also the only place to empty the bucket, which was soon overflowing. Something had to be done.

A couple of the boys lifted it to the window but pouring a bucket of excrement through a wired-up hole above head height was messy. Much of it blew back and ran down the inside of the carriage where I had sat. There was some verbiage about that. All the shit from Shanghai and I was sat underneath it.

We had the same old dog biscuit to eat and a container of water between us all. We didn't know where we were going. As the train wound its way slowly north, we passed miles of deserted beaches and I saw a sign with the name 'Rimini'. I had heard of that before the war. We turned inland and passed through villages where people came out to wave. Maybe they thought we were Italians.

I had no idea then that this was the same route they would use to transport Italy's Jews and other enemies of the Reich northwards to the concentration camps. Our trucks might be stinking and filthy, but at least we had the space to lie down. The Jews were crammed in much tighter, weaving their way across Europe to a fearful destination with no protection at all from the Geneva Convention, not that it had done us much good so far.

After days on the move the track began to twist and climb and trundled through the Brenner Pass. We had reached Austria. I got my first sight of the Alps through the barbed wire. I was awestruck by their magnificence and troubled by a contradiction. I associated myself with the countryside I had grown up with. Its beauty seemed to me to be linked to the beauty in mankind. It had made me the man I was. I wondered how such frightful things could be happening in a place of such natural splendour. I hadn't seen the half of it.

When the train came to a halt, the station signs said 'Innsbruck Hauptbahnhof'. We were shunted into a siding and put into covered lorries. Now the guards were German. After a long journey mostly through open countryside the truck stopped in a small forest clearing where we were allowed to get down to relieve ourselves. Instantly I was on edge. The German guards began setting up a machine gun on a tripod. It was facing our way. I thought they might shoot the lot of us there and then. We were miles from anywhere with no witnesses. If they began shooting should I run or try to attack the gunners? The moment passed. They dismantled the weapon and we got back on the trucks.

Over the next few months I passed through a number of camps. I wasn't always sure where I was and looking back it's hard to be certain in which order I visited them. After a lengthy journey we arrived at one camp where we were put in a compound and there were Russians on the other side of a barbed wire fence.

I tried to speak to them over the days but with no common language we didn't get very far. I could see they were in a terrible state. They were trying to keep their spirits up and they put on a show for us, dancing behind the wire, but they were frail and malnourished and they could barely manage it. It was a sorry sight. There was a terrible stench and it was days before we learnt why. The putrid smell came from decaying corpses. The Russians were being slowly worked and starved to death. Their rations were insufficient to sustain them and we were told that in desperation they kept their dead alongside them in their bunks to claim their food for a few extra days.

The rats were thriving. They were the size of cats and certainly eating human flesh. I could smell it on them. They had no respect for barbed-wire fences. I slept on the floor and woke at night to find them running across my bed. I felt their breath on my face. They stank. One of my ancestors had been a rat catcher centuries ago. If he could have seen us in the middle of the twentieth century, an era of industrial miracles, with rats feasting on people, he'd have thought civilisation had collapsed. He would have been right. I felt the bite of strange creatures larger than cat fleas. We called them bed bugs. I don't know what they were but when I squashed them, the blood they had drunk burst from them.

I was soon in trouble. Crossing the camp one day, I was pulled up short by a German officer who was screaming at me. I had failed to salute him. I tried to explain that in the British Army we didn't salute anyone without a cap. He wasn't having it. One of the lads shouted that I should salute and forget it. Reluctantly I did and the officer let it go.

After a while we were split into groups and I was sent to work with the Russians down a coal mine. I stepped into the lift-cage at the pithead and dropped into the darkness, the fragile frame creaking and bending under the strain, on the verge of falling apart. The armed guards at the bottom of the shaft ordered us to walk until we reached the seam. They barely spoke to the Russians at all, they just clobbered them instead. There was brutality there all right. I was the only Englishmen on that face and they were easier on me. I was set to work shovelling coal into a skip from morning until night. I worked standing in water. It was cold and grim. There were no helmets or protective clothing for anyone, but the Russians had the worst of it. Many were toiling barefoot, hacking at the seam with heavy tools. I was not allowed to talk to them.

I had been down there for three days when I heard screaming from one of the guards. The aggression in his voice drowned out the scraping of shovels and the sound of picks in the darkness.

They were knocking one of the Russians about. He had improvised some protection from the sharp rocks by tying thin strips of rubber to his bare feet. I knew straight away he had cut them from a disused conveyor belt I had seen in an abandoned side tunnel.

The guard was hysterical and shouting about sabotage. More Russians were dragged from the coalface and all ten of us were shoved up against the tunnel wall, faces blackened and smeared. There was no begging or pleading. There wasn't time. I wasn't aware of an order. The shouting stopped. The five soldiers lifted their guns and one fired without hesitation. A deafening shot reverberated around the network of tunnels and poorly lit passages. It was followed by another, the second guard firing as the first pulled back the bolt to reload.

I had only seconds to react. There was nowhere to run. If I was going to die in that godforsaken pit I would take one of them with me. That much I could do. It would have been death whatever happened. There were more shots in rapid succession. Then it stopped. Five bullets and five dead Russians in the coal dust. I had been the eighth in line.

My eyes had been fixed on the firing squad so I never saw the Russian bodies hit the ground. My ears were still ringing as we were bundled away. I had faced death before but with a fighting chance. This time survival had been down to the whims of a brutal enemy. I had come as close to capitulation as I was to get. I had played no part in my own salvation. What happened in that satanic hole shook me more than anything before or possibly since.

I was taken to a sparsely furnished room. The guard gave me a violent shove towards a chair and the questions began. In broken English, the officer asked if I was behind the 'sabotage'. Had I put the Russians up to it? Who had given the order? There was nothing I could say. There had been no plan, just an exhausted wretch trying to protect his cold, injured feet. If I was planning anything, they said I would be shot. I believed them.

The threats unnerved me but I still had a motor inside that

wasn't completely broken. I was marched to a train and thrown in with another group of prisoners. They were normal rail carriages with a corridor down one side and small, basic compartments. We didn't know where we were going. I asked to be allowed to use the toilet and realised it was at the end of the carriage and near the door. The guard was standing far away. I didn't know the other lads at all but I spotted a possibility. As the train came to a stop we got the door open, jumped onto the tracks and ran for the nearby fields. About half a dozen of us got out before the train began to move. There was no coordination and we scattered, running in all directions.

I was mentally exhausted. The shooting in the mine had taken its toll.

I should have learnt the lesson from Italy: you had to plan an escape properly to be successful. We were in uniform and stood out a mile. I don't know how many were caught but I was soon looking down the barrel of a gun again. There was no shooting thankfully but it was over and I was taken to a room questioned and knocked about a bit. After that I was sent to a camp that I believe was Lamsdorf. I never got to find out. My card had been marked. I was a habitual troublemaker.

I was transferred almost immediately to the punishment camp at Graudenz in northern Poland. I was told to strip and a man puffed pungent white powder over me, between my legs and under my arms. My hair was cropped short and I was photographed like a criminal from the front and the side with a number board around my neck. I was Prisoner 220543.

They led me to a spartan barracks with three English fellers and a Scot already inside. They were rough types with shaven heads and they looked like they deserved to be there. We didn't have much in common. We were allowed out briefly for exercise into a small yard surrounded by high walls. There was nothing to do but walk in endless circles. I didn't have much to say. The shooting in the mine still weighed heavily on me.

There were no mattresses just bare timber bunks. To sleep I had to remove the wooden laths in the middle to give my bony hips space, otherwise it was agony. The wood-fibre blanket was so thin I could see through it. I turned too quickly on the first night and my elbow ripped a hole in the middle of it.

In the morning I was taken into another bare room with two officers sitting behind a table. As the questioning began again the guards moved in to stand on each side of me. I saw their heavy polished boots. It felt like I was going to get a pasting but they were going through the motions. I was relieved. They still thought I had been involved in something with the Russians but my uniform gave me some protection unless they could prove something.

I heard of terrible things going on around me in other parts of that huge camp but I was OK. I had been sent there as a punishment but at least I wasn't working in that awful mine any more. After about three weeks I was on the move again, this time by train with a couple of guards.

Chapter 9

We arrived at a small station. The platform was very low and I had to climb down some steps to get off the train. I was marched off straight away down a rough track and after about two miles we came to a camp in quite pleasant countryside. Compared to where I'd been recently I couldn't believe it. There were ten well-built wooden huts, grass in the compound and just a single wire fence at the perimeter. *We'll have some fun here*, I thought. A few hundred allied prisoners were already inside. There were electric lights, running water, lavatories you could sit on and central heating pipes. The twin bunks had straw filled mattresses, even decent blankets. I heard it had been built for the Hitler Youth. It certainly looked like it.

The other prisoners told me where we were, a little south of a Polish town called Oswiecim.

The next morning we were woken at 0630 hours and marched out of the gates, through fields and woods for a mile and a half until the countryside abruptly vanished. Ahead was a vast, sprawling building site, stretching far away. Smoke plumed from chimneys and steam cranes. The dark bones of a satanic factory complex were rising from the mud in concrete and iron. Above them, a screen of barrage balloons bobbed on steel cables. We were marched in.

The whole site was crawling with strange, slow-moving figures – hundreds, no, thousands of them. All were dressed in tattered, ill-fitting striped shirts and trousers that were more like pyjamas than work clothes. Their faces were grey, their heads were roughly shaven and partly covered by tiny caps. They were like moving shadows, shapeless and indistinct, as if they could fade away any moment. I couldn't tell who they were, what they were.

The rest of the lads called them the 'stripeys'. They told me the Germanised name of this Polish town, Oswiecim. It was Auschwitz.

I recognised these poor wraiths as my fellow beings though much that marks humanity had been stripped from them. I could see that already. They wore the Star of David badge. They were Jews.

We were split into work *Kommandos* of twenty to thirty men and sent off to different contractors, all within their own fenced-off areas. The work began immediately, shifting and carrying building materials and heavy pipework around the site and laying cables. Right away, I saw how it was. When something needed to be shifted, they would call for the poor stripeys, who would appear as if from the earth and swarm around the pipe, valve or cable to be lifted. It took so many because they were so weak. There were men hauling huge bags of cement on their backs, others struggling with wheelbarrows.

Brutal foremen, wielding clubs or heavy knotted ropes, stood over them. These were criminals recruited as *Kapos*, prisoners who had the power of life or death over the others and they used it freely. I hated them instantly. I witnessed my first beating straight away and found it hard to believe that life was now so cheap. Even in the desert, we had taken more notice of death. Here they didn't run to the cost of a bullet to end a stripey's life when boots and clubs would do it for them.

At this point, they kept these Jewish prisoners away from us. Talk to us and they risked being shot or beaten to death. At night we returned to our half-decent camp and they were marched off, God knows where.

The massive factory was being built by the chemicals giant, IG Farben, primarily to manufacture 'buna', synthetic rubber for

Hitler's war effort, as well as methanol for fuel. The site was two miles long from east to west and almost a mile deep. Within that wired compound, laid out like a massive grid, there were countless individual '*Baus*' or building sites and the place was dominated by a large industrial plant with four tall chimneys. We called it the *Queen Mary* after the three-funnelled liner. Somebody couldn't count. There were buildings, towers and chimneys going up everywhere, gantries and plumbing on a giant scale, with narrow railway lines along each block, bringing in all that was needed to get this place up and working. Everywhere, in the nooks and crannies of this industrial nightmare, were the poor creatures in their filthy zebra uniforms, many too weak to stand, let alone shift and carry. I knew by now that this was no ordinary labour camp. They were being deliberately worked to death.

It was hell on earth. Hell on earth. There was no grass, no greenery of any sort, just mud in winter, dust in summer. Nature – not to mention the Grand Architect himself – had abandoned that place. I never saw a butterfly, a bird or a bee the whole time I was there.

It was soon clear that the guards could not enforce the rigid separation of groups. It slowed things down and they needed the work done quickly.

We were soon working alongside the Jews. From then on we shared their labours but not the lashes or the random killings. We were not supposed to die here and they were. That was the difference. When the wind came from the west, there was a sickly sweet stench from some distant chimneys.

For a few days I worked alongside one poor chap, I think they called him Franz. I had started to recognise him in the crowd. Then one day he just wasn't there any more. I snatched a moment when the *Kapos* weren't looking to ask one of the men in his *Kommando* what had happened to him. He gestured upwards with both hands and then said, 'He has gone up the chimney.'

The scales were lifted from my eyes. Those too weak to work

were being killed and burnt. The stench was the smell from the distant crematoria chimneys. I knew it now but being told was not enough for me.

On one march back from IG Farben a row broke out between some of the British prisoners and the Wehrmacht guards or *Postens*, as they called them. Our lads were winding them up, booing and jeering and I was caught up in the middle of it. There was a fracas and the *Postens* were quickly in amongst us trying to restore control, jostling and shoving us around. The *Feldwebel* – sergeant – was shouting orders. He was a tall feller and he focused on me the moment I emerged from the melee. He grabbed a rifle from a *Posten*, seized it with both hands and swung it with all his might towards my head. I saw it coming and ducked out of the way. There was a thud; the sound of crushing bone. One of the Germans immediately behind me had taken the full force of the blow to the side of his head. He went down straight away, his face losing shape. The butt of a nine-pound rifle swung with force at the temple didn't leave much doubt. If he wasn't dead already, he didn't live long. We got back into line and prepared for retribution. It didn't come. I never saw that particular *Feldwebel* again.

Our camp was too good to last. One day in early 1944 we were moved to a site only yards outside the southern edge of the IG Farben complex. The stripeys were somewhere to the east of us, close enough that at night we could hear screams and sometimes gunshots coming from their camp.

Our new prison compound was bare and basic and more crowded than the first. Icicles hung from the barracks ceiling in winter and mosquitoes swarmed in the warmer months. There was a crude latrine, just a row of holes in a plank over a pit and even those were few in number for a camp the size of ours.

We heard that E715, as it was named, had housed Russian prisoners. The rumours said the SS cleared them out to make way for us, herded them into the crude tunnel which was later to be our air-raid shelter and killed them there with poisoned gas. It was hard to know whether it was true or not. In a place like that anything was possible.

I now know that Soviet POWs were the victims of the first experiments using poisoned gas. In September 1941 hundreds of them were murdered using Zyklon B gas in a basement at the main Auschwitz camp. It worked but it wasn't efficient enough for the camp commanders so they adapted a crematorium building to allow the gas crystals to be dropped in through holes in the roof. Nine hundred died in that experiment. The wheels of mechanised murder had begun to turn.

Back then the rumours that gassings had taken place in our own camp simply fuelled my frustration and the need for certainty. The Russians were treated nearly as badly as the Jews. We were luckier than either group. Our guards were usually the Wehrmacht, the German Army, less brutal than the SS but here they had none of the humanity of the Afrika Korps.

The German officer we saw most in E715 was an NCO called Mieser. He'd turn up if there was trouble to be sorted and he was there for the morning roll call.

We would be as unruly as we dared, we were not being counted for our benefit.

Mieser's shouts for us to be silent –'*ruhig*' in German – were quickly echoed by the lads. Whenever he appeared we barracked him, repeating it mercilessly in chorus. So *Ruhig*, was the name we gave him. It was schoolboy stuff but good for morale. *Ruhig* could be officious and some hated him but he was not one of the worst.

We rarely saw the commandant or *Hauptman* as we called him. I had reason to face him on one occasion. We were returning from work one night in the rain. I was standing next to a cockney lad called Phil Hagen. We were in a small barbed-wire compound near the entrance to the camp and the guards began to search us. It didn't take them long to find that Phil had a dead fowl stuffed down his trousers, a chicken or maybe a duck, which he'd managed to get hold of somewhere.

They always punished more than one if we got caught. There was a lot of shouting and hollering and the lads soon began to jeer, forcing the guards to take out their weapons and loose a few shots into the air to get control.

I was close to Phil so the two of us were carted off and locked up for the night in a freezing cold punishment cell towards the front of the camp. There was no food or water. When we were brought before the commandant the next morning, Phil claimed the creature had attacked him and he had been forced to kill it in self-defence. There was a pause for the translation, then the commandant burst out laughing and the tension was defused. No more was said about it.

There were two particular atrocities against our men that were widely discussed in the camp. I wasn't on the spot but I heard all about them.

'Jock' Campbell was a sharp-witted lad and despite camp conditions he was usually well turned out, even dapper. The story goes that the column was returning to camp one evening when Jock spotted a female forced-labourer struggling to carry a heavy canister.

When Jock saw what was happening, he broke out of the column and went to help. He was ordered back in line. When he refused he was bayonetted, though not fatally it turned out. Some accounts have pointed the finger at a soldier named Benno Franz. I never saw the incident so I can't say. What I did see was Campbell lying in the dirt being attended to by some of the lads when we were marched past. It was nasty but it can't have been a full thrust and I am now fairly sure he recovered.

On 23 February 1944 a corporal from the Royal Army Service Corps was hard at work on the Buna-Werke site when he was ordered to climb seventy feet up a steel gantry covered in ice. He refused, saying that without the proper footwear it would be lethal. He was shot dead on the spot. His name was Corporal Reynolds. Some accused an officer called Rittler, others said it was the soldier Benno Franz again. I recall hearing a shot that day and never went to look as it was not an unusual sound. Those events doused what good humour there was.

Some in E715 decided the best way to cope was to fill what little spare time they had with creative activity. They tried putting on theatre productions in the barracks to raise morale, to show we weren't beaten. Some bright spark had the idea of dramatising the story of Sweeney Todd, as if we needed the demon barber to add spice to our mundane lives. People were being dispatched all the time.

Perhaps someone was attempting a subversive allegory. If they were I can't remember much of it other than the German guards and censors coming to check what we were up to. There were other dubious productions but it wasn't my way of coping. We were witnessing a never-ending atrocity and I didn't want diversion.

I changed my mind when it came to football and so did many of the lads, we were only human. A few T-shirts and some shorts were brought into the camp and someone dreamt up the idea of an international tournament of sorts. The teams were to be England, Scotland, Wales and South Africa but there weren't enough of each nation. Burt Cook was the only South African to play, as far as I can recall, so they were just team names really. I played two games on the right wing for the South African team, I scored in the final and we won.

The matches took place on a field to the east of the main entrance and I fancy there were machine guns set up to stop us getting too frisky. Doug Bond, who became a friend of mine years later, was goalkeeper for England, though I didn't know him at the time. The chance of a game had been hard to turn down and right or wrong I enjoyed it enormously.

Looking back we were perhaps naive. We were lined up for

team photos afterwards and we can all be seen smiling, fresh-faced, into the lens. Now I think we were part of an elaborate propaganda exercise. The photographer was a civilian, as I recall, and the photos were handed out to us later. Around the same time we received some fresh uniforms, they weren't new but they were smarter than what we had. Many of the lads were lined up and photographed in those too.

It was a gift to the Germans. It helped the Wehrmacht to put some distance between their treatment of us and the methods the SS used on the Jews. Someone was anticipating the questions that would come in the post-war period. I have no doubt it also helped the camp commanders keep the visitors from the Red Cross off their backs. They had proved to be highly gullible anyway. Some of their reports into conditions in our camp I saw later bore little resemblance to the truth.

They suggested we had been able to play football whenever there were enough guards. It was utter balderdash. One Red Cross report claimed that the work was not hard and that there were no complaints about it.

They said we had hot running water, and even more ridiculous that they had seen inmates playing tennis. The Red Cross did report that the pit latrines were insufficient in number and that the drinking water was unfit for consumption, something the Germans had at least confirmed to them.

This was not a cosy environment. I never knew who I could trust. There was constant talk of spies in our ranks, ferrets we called them. I was aware of the story of Miller, I recall seeing him. He was a well-spoken chap. He had arrived alone from Lambsdorf camp and told the lads he had served with the Green Howards, one of the smaller regiments. He had aroused suspicion immediately. Details of his war service and his knowledge of the regiment didn't add up, so the story went. Some of the boys started fishing around. They concluded Miller was a ferret – a spy placed in the camp to get information from us.

What we heard was that they jumped him in the latrines, killed him and threw his body into the pit below. I wasn't in on that one, but I never doubted it at the time. There were plenty of men capable of doing a job like that in the camp. The Germans never responded to the fact that a man had gone missing.

The IG Farben Industrial Complex, Buna-Monowitz in 1944

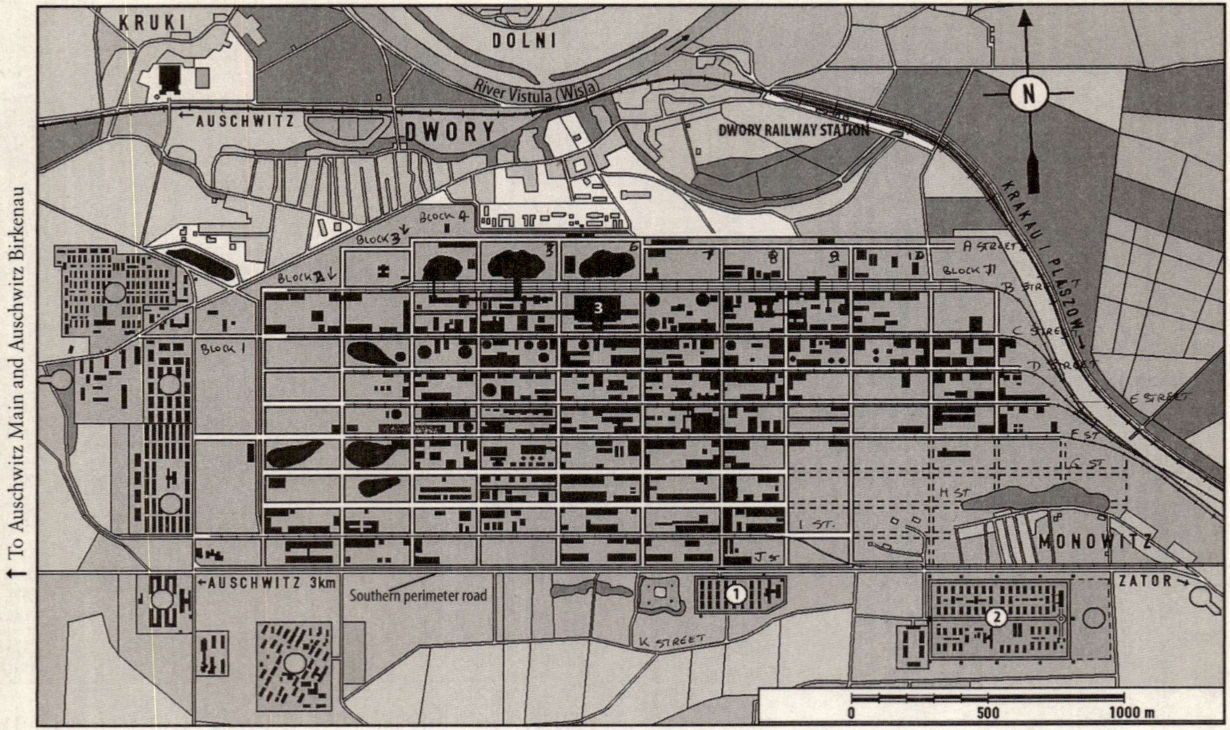

1 E715, the POW Camp
2 Auschwitz III, Monowitz
3 The 'Queen Mary'

Auschwitz III, Buna-Monowitz at the end of 1944

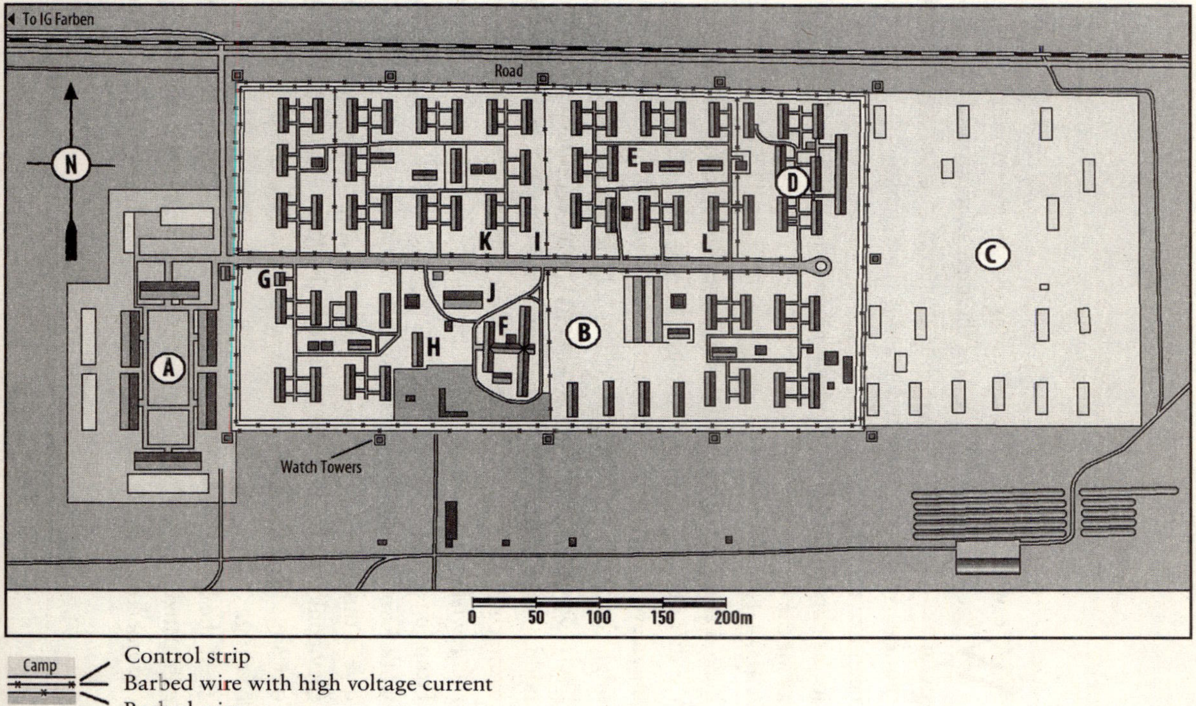

Control strip
Barbed wire with high voltage current
Barbed wire

A SS barracks
B The Appelplatz – The Parade Ground
C Planned Camp expansion never completed
D Barracks for sick prisoners/ mortuary
E Punishment Bunker
F Prisoners Kitchen
G Prisoners Orchestra
H Brothel, Denis calls this the *Frauenhaus*
I Clothing Store
J Forge
K Warehouse
L Camp Canteen/Prisoner Orchestra

Chapter 10

We worked eleven hours a day. Forget everything you have seen in war movies where the men swan around in cricket sweaters, doing a bit of gardening or gym to cover their escape tunnels, smoking pipes and teasing the Germans. It may have been like that in the officers' camps but for us, the 'other ranks', it was hard, physical work, though it was not nearly as hard for us as for the stripeys.

Each day I saw Jews being killed on the factory site. Some were kicked and beaten to death, others simply collapsed and died in the dirt of exhaustion and hunger. I knew the same was happening in every corner of the camp, in every work detail. These Jews might be able to prolong their lives a little but the outcome was likely to be the same. They weren't fed enough to survive. Around midday the dreadful cabbage soup arrived. We could barely stomach it, though ours offered some nutrition while the stuff the Jewish prisoners had was little more than stinking water. From time to time we managed to exaggerate the numbers on our work *Kommando* to get more soup than we needed. We couldn't give it directly to the Jews but we left it standing around where they could get to it. If the guards or the *Kapos* saw them eating our soup they kicked it over to stop them. There was usually a beating.

At the Buna-Werke they sucked the life and labour from each exhausted man and when he was spent, he was sent to be killed. I did not know the names then but they went west, either to the original brick-built camp, Auschwitz One, or the vast new wooden sprawl of Auschwitz-Birkenau. There they would be killed sooner rather than later, many immediately on arrival. Behind it all stood the SS and the executives of IG Farben itself. The *Kapos*, the prisoners put in charge of their fellows, became the focus of my anger. They were evil men and many wore the green triangle of the career criminal. Their survival depended on keeping the rest of the prisoners in line. If they lost their privileged job they were friendless and then they didn't live long.

People talk about man's inhumanity to man, but that wasn't human or inhuman – it was bestial. Love and hate meant nothing there. It was indifference. I felt degraded by each mindless murder I witnessed and could do nothing about. I was living in obscenity.

For the Jewish prisoners anything that could be traded or swallowed had value. It might offer them the chance to live a bit longer. They all had to find a niche, a way of securing a few extra calories a day, or they died. The risks for them were enormous.

We were privileged in comparison, but only in comparison. We argued for the occasional Sunday off and there was a slight easement in our conditions. Not before I got into an unexpected row with one of the senior contractors on the IG Farben site.

A little knowledge can be a dangerous thing. A little knowledge of a language in a place like Auschwitz could be deadly. I had accused one of the managers on site of being a '*Schwindler*' to his face for making us work seven days a week without a break. He went berserk. I knew I had misjudged the word when the guards were called to take me away.

In the end a translator was called in to mediate, a Scottish soldier with better German than mine. He argued that in English to call someone a 'swindler' was a mild criticism, like calling him a rogue. Clearly in German it was much worse. Actually '*Schwindler*' was mild compared to what I really thought but that plea took the heat out of the row and calmed things down. I had been lucky again.

It was generally hard graft and we were angry that our forced labour could help the German war effort. We complained that the work was in breach of the Geneva Convention. To my surprise the complaint was passed on and we were summoned to an office building on the IG Farben site. I was one of five lads chosen to go and make the case. I was amazed they were prepared to listen at all but when we were ushered into the office and saw that a senior officer was going to preside over the meeting I knew that it didn't bode well.

He listened to the complaint then he took his Luger pistol from his holster, slammed it on the table and said. 'That's my Geneva Convention. You will do what I say.' We were sent back to work but we were determined to do whatever we could to hinder what was going on.

I was often ordered to make deliveries to the office of one German engineer. He wore a trilby hat and high boots or gaiters when he was out on the site but he was chatty and seemed to like me. We had some plans to subvert the work the Germans were making us do and that connection made the subterfuge easier. That's where I got to know Paulina, a young Ukrainian who worked there. After Germany attacked the Soviet Union she and many other Ukrainian women had been transported across Europe and press-ganged to work for the Nazis. They had more freedom than the Jewish prisoners. They didn't wear striped uniforms and they were not there to be exterminated but life was still precarious for them. They had to have courage to help us and Paulina helped us a lot. She came from somewhere on the Black Sea, she was young, had a broad face and wavy blond hair. She tipped us off when special shipments of machinery or components were expected to come in so that we could try and arrange some sort of sabotage.

When it was too tricky to meet in the engineer's office we'd tie up in a small boiler house. The boiler man was a forced labourer and I'd warn him in advance. He knew what was going on but he teased us anyway, linking his fingers together whilst whispering the words '*amour, amour*' suggestively.

He had unscrewed a sheet of corrugated iron from the structure behind the boiler so that if the SS came into the shed when we were talking one of us could escape out the back of the building. I never had to.

The information Paulina gave us was vital. We swapped labels on railway trucks hoping they would go to the wrong places. We slipped sand into axle-bearings so they would run hot and wear out. We twisted the blades on cooling fans so that they would vibrate and gradually damage the machinery. We even laid sharp stones under electrical cables in trenches in the hope they would eventually sever the supply. When we were directed to rivet the huge gasometers, we developed a way of peening the rivet head so it looked neatly finished but would work loose in time and cause a leak. I would sneak into the contractors' yards, find the bottles of oxygen for oxyacetylene welding and use a removable key I had made to open the valves and release the gas. Acetylene could be smelt; oxygen couldn't. It was the perfect crime. My engineering expertise came in handy for the first time since the desert. I was glad to be of use.

Paulina did more for me than supply information. She managed to get me cooked food to eat on a couple of occasions, better still, she gave it to me on a plate. I don't know where it came from but I appreciated it. She liked me, that's as far as it went. There was nothing between us but when she gave me her photograph I kept it safe all the same. I carried it in my uniform and I brought it home with me. I still have it today. She also gave me a simple signet ring with the mysterious initials FD inscribed on it and the date 1943. Even casual gifts were rare in that place and had a human value so I carried that all the way home too.

Much of the sabotage we pulled off wouldn't have happened without her. They were all slow-burn projects. They had to be. Anything dramatic would be detected and someone would pay for it. It was too risky.

The ground for the buna rubber plant had been broken in April

1941. Heinrich Himmler, the Reichsführer-SS, had promised IG Farben thousands of slave labourers to build it. Not a single batch of buna rubber was ever produced in that plant and I'd like to think we played our part.

The inhumanity was all around. One day I was looking towards the canteen buildings on the IG Farben site when I saw a Jewish prisoner rummaging in a dustbin for something to eat or trade, some mouldy greens perhaps or a cigarette butt or a piece of wire. He was moving slowly. Hunger and exhaustion had blunted his senses to everything other than the need to eat or die.

There was no time to warn him. He didn't see the female guard in uniform, one of very few on the site, until she was right behind him. She knocked him to the floor with a single blow and stood astride him. It didn't take much. She picked up a large rock in her leather-gloved hands, raised it above her head and smashed his skull with it.

She wasn't the only female guard I saw. Someone pointed out a woman in a well-cut uniform in a party walking through the site. Her hard expression disfigured a youthful face. They told me she was Irma Grese, the notorious guard from the Birkenau extermination camp on the other side of the town. Her sadistic acts led to her execution in December 1945.

Some of the SS guards were old or had been injured in combat but I had no sympathy for any of them. They were not the Afrika Korps. They could see what was happening in Auschwitz. There was no hiding it.

On one occasion an SS man came up to me as I was working outside. He had deeply sunken eyes and a combat injury to his arm. He stood by my shoulder and, staring straight ahead, he began to talk as if to himself. He had been a machine gunner on the eastern front and he described a Russian attack that began with the blow of a whistle. There were thousands of them, he said, and no matter how many he mowed down they kept coming. He was reliving it by my side. The barrel of his machine

Me and my 'Lads Army'. I am the first from the left holding a French bayonet. The villagers gave me the nickname 'Ero'.

Hands in pockets with friends at Butlin's Holiday Camp Skegness, late 1930s.

My father George enjoying a day by the sea.

Sitting on the running board of my Wolsey Hornet Trinity at Butlin's, late 1930s.

My sister Winifred and I during my brief embarkation leave prior to leaving for Egypt in August, 1940.

During training at Winchester, 1939-40. I am on the left.

Myself (right) with Charles Calistan (centre) and Cecil Plummer (left) relaxing in Cairo before going to the desert, 1940. Charles and I had friendly boxing matches. He was an Anglo-Indian who won both the Military Medal and the DCM and I believe should have had the Victoria Cross too for his bravery at El Alamein. He was killed in Italy in 1944.

A British Bren gun carrier in Egypt, 1940. The driver and commander dropped down behind the armour during combat but we were open to the air and vulnerable to grenades. The Bren gunner behind was the most exposed.

A British soldier fixing the tracks on a Bren gun carrier, a job I did many times in the desert.

Italian prisoners resting after a long march are guarded by a Bren gun carrier in the Western Desert, December 1940.

A Bren gunner in action around Tobruk, late 1941.

A Ukrainian woman called Paulina (left) and an unknown friend. She worked in the offices of one of the German engineers at the IG Farben site and tipped off the POWs when shipments of materials were expected so we could plan sabotage. I carried the photo home inside my uniform.

A corner of the sprawling IG Farben site showing the building we POWs called the Queen Mary because of its chimneys. The site contained many separate construction sites and miles of pipework on overhead gantries.

The South Africa football team at E715. I am on the left of the front row. I have always suspected the photographs were a propaganda ploy by the Wehrmacht to distinguish their handling of the POWs from the SS treatment of the Jews.

Prisoners marching from the direction of Buna-Monowitz (Auschwitz III) towards IG Farben, a journey I made twice. The striped uniforms of the concentration camp prisoners can be seen towards the back of the column. The SS barracks are visible in the distance and the legs of a watchtower and a small earth covered bomb shelter for the *Postens* are in the foreground. The entrance to Auschwitz III is hidden behind the watchtower.

Huts believed to be part of Auschwitz III in the snow.

At my desk as Chief Engineer of UMP in the 1960s. I had a successful business career but it was years before my nightmares about Auschwitz III eased.

The receipt for compensation offered by the British Government for my time spent as a POW. I thought it was an insult.

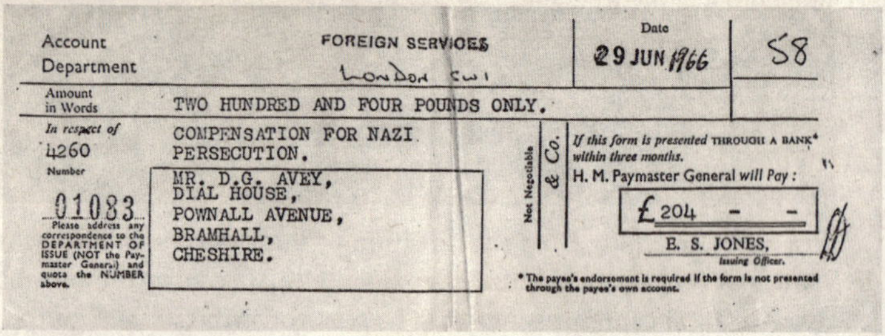

Account Department
FOREIGN SERVICES
LONDON SW1
Date 29 JUN 1966
58

Amount in Words: TWO HUNDRED AND FOUR POUNDS ONLY.

In respect of 4260
COMPENSATION FOR NAZI PERSECUTION.

Number 01083
Please address any correspondence to the DEPARTMENT OF ISSUE (NOT the Paymaster General) and quote the NUMBER above.

MR. D.G. AVEY,
DIAL HOUSE,
POWNALL AVENUE,
BRAMHALL,
CHESHIRE.

Not Negotiable
& Co.

If this form is presented THROUGH A BANK* *within three months.*
H. M. Paymaster General *will Pay* :
£204 - -
B. S. JONES,
Issuing Officer.

* The payee's endorsement is required if the form is not presented through the payee's own account.

Riding Ryedale after a dressage competition, part of a three day event.

Audrey and I enjoying an evening together.

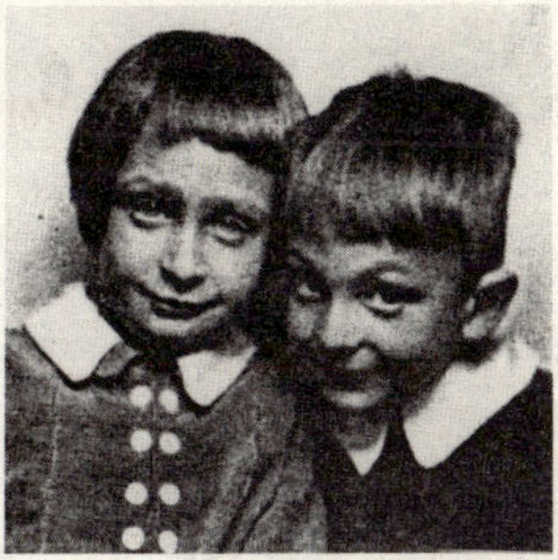

Susanne and Ernst Lobethal as children in pre-war Breslau.

Ernst as a young man. He changed his name to Ernie Lobet on reaching America. I was shocked to learn that, having survived Auschwitz Ernie was drafted to fight in the Korean War.

Meeting Ernie's sister Susanne again after sixty-four years. When we first met in 1945 I was a deeply traumatised soldier unable to bring her any comfort about the fate of her brother.

Ernie (Ernst) Lobet, taken from his remarkable video testimony for the Shoah Foundation. This was how I first heard his story.

Head to head with prime minister Gordon Brown at 10 Downing Street on 22 January 2010. In March 2010 I was presented with a medal as one of twenty-seven British *Heroes of the Holocaust*. All but two of us received the award posthumously.

September 2010: now I can talk about those terrible times, I feel as if a load is slowly lifting.

gun soon warped with the heat of endless firing. It was useless. They were unstoppable. He was wounded and perhaps part of his mind had gone. I said nothing. How could anyone sympathise in that place?

At the end of his monologue, he picked himself up and walked off without as much as a goodbye. I saw him again three days later. He looked right through me.

I remember holding the metal pipes so that a blond, fresh-faced twenty-year-old could weld flanges onto them. He was a German civilian worker. These workers were a mystery to us but he intrigued me. I tried to appeal to him as a young man, quizzed him about music, and why the Nazis hated jazz. I thought if I caught him off guard he might speak about his past, reveal something useful. He was already poisoned by hatred. He said the Jews had destroyed his country. There was no meeting of minds but suddenly he stopped welding and sang.

'Küss mich, bitte bitte küss mich,
Eh' die letzte Bahn kommt,
Küss mich ohne Pause'
('Kiss me, please, please kiss me,
till the last tram comes,
Kiss me without stopping')

If those innocent lyrics were at odds with that monstrous place he didn't notice. He went back to his welding.

Another prisoner stood out for me amongst the wise and the accomplished brought down by the Nazis. His name was Victor Perez, a Sephardic Jew born in French Tunisia. In his day he had been a world champion flyweight boxer but he had been arrested in Paris in 1943. As a boy keen on the sport I knew him as 'Young' Perez who had come and fought in Britain in the early 1930s. I talked to him just once inside IG Farben and then very briefly. When I told him I knew of his big fight against Johnny

King in Manchester he had to stop and think before he could remember. He was a shadow of the handsome young fighter whose photos I had seen. Years later I learnt he had been forced to box on the *Appelplatz* – the Auschwitz III parade ground – whilst the SS laid bets on the outcome. He was shot by the SS in January 1945.

Our little acts of sabotage weren't enough for me. The ground we trod on had absorbed much blood. That terrible stench still hung across the camp and mixed with the filth and fumes in the air. The questions were building up.

I thought I had become inured to the brutality of the place. I had to be just to survive. Everyone caught up in Auschwitz had a story, a history, but the scale of it meant each person's personal tragedy was lost in the mass of it. Then, when I least expected it, two individuals stepped out of the crowd. The collective suffering of thousands became the fate of real people once again. So it was with Hans and Ernst, the two Jewish prisoners who got to me for very different reasons.

I met Hans whilst working on the first floor of a brick building that was slowly taking shape. It was still open to the sky but they had begun installing heavy piping along a corridor. I was out of sight in that passageway but the layout meant I could be easily surprised if a guard came prowling.

What was I doing? I was scribbling a mathematical formula in chalk on one of the large pipes lined-up waiting to be connected. I was oblivious to my surroundings. It was an idle act but I was trying to salvage something of my pre-war self, the certainties I had known. What I was wrestling to remember was a cumbersome method for calculating the area of a triangle: Heron's formula.

$$A=\sqrt{s(s-a)(s-b)(s-c)}$$

There I was chalk in hand in a half-finished passageway close to the epicentre of the Nazi killing machine, staring at the chalky letters and symbols on a pipe.

Hans saw I was alone and took his chance. He came straight up and asked me if I had a cigarette. Then he caught sight of my mathematical scrawl. When he spoke it was in German. All he said was 'I know what that is.' ('*Ich weiss was das ist.*') The daily jostle for food and survival was momentarily forgotten. The two of us stopped and stared at that strange formula and for a few heartbeats it felt like we were communing with the centuries of human wisdom and ingenuity, the world of decency and learning that had been swept away.

Hans was a Dutch Jew with high cheekbones and a thin face. He was an educated chap, I recognised that the moment I met him. I found out later that his family had run a department store, or something like it, in Amsterdam before the war. I never knew much more about him than that. I'm not even sure Hans was his real name but it was what I called him. Knowing names was dangerous. If they interrogated you that was it, they'd get it out of you somehow and someone would be for the bullet. If I identified myself at all I called myself Ginger.

When my focus returned I realised he was in danger and I shooed him away. If he was seen talking to me he would be for it. He was gone in an instant but those brief moments had made a deep impression on me and I looked out for him from then on.

That meeting with Hans was to be the beginning of the most foolhardy venture I have ever been involved in but first I had troubles of my own to resolve because soon after Hans left, a guard stumbled across the chalked letters. He summoned help. A uniformed delegation appeared and stood around in baffled silence contemplating the mysterious symbols on the pipe. Then the inevitable happened. I was taken to a small glass box of an office on the ground floor for questioning.

There were only two SS officers present and they were convinced my scribble was a secret coded message of some sort, but what did it mean and who was it for?

'It's not a code it's a formula,' I said. 'It's a bit like Pythagoras' Theorem ... only different.' I knew this was going to be hard to explain. They looked unconvinced. 'It's to do with triangles,' I said, 'calculating the area of triangles.' There I was, trying to explain Heron and Pythagoras to the SS. With their broken English and my basic German we weren't getting very far. My actions didn't make any sense to them. The truth was it was just one of those weird things I do.

It was a cold day when I met the second of the prisoners who left an indelible mark on my life. My back was aching with the strain of hauling loads of pipes across the site to have flanges welded onto them. The three-storey filtration plant was practically finished. Now the bigger job of installing the equipment inside was underway.

I never really smoked in those days but cigarettes were the only universal currency in Auschwitz. You could almost buy a man's life with them. They had other uses too.

A number of senior German engineers overseeing the project arrived to review progress. They walked about, rolling and unrolling their plans and taking notes then standing around looking important and talking to each other.

I did what I always did when they were around. I got as close as I could and lit a cigarette with the sole purpose of blowing the smoke in their faces. They didn't appreciate it much. The other lads followed suit. We had to do it subtly. Too aggressive or obvious about it and there could be trouble, but they got the message.

Smoking was also a way to get cigarettes to the Jewish prisoners without attracting attention. I hated them having to scramble in the dirt for them when I threw the butts away but it was better than doing nothing. Even a cigarette end could be bartered.

I emerged from the filtration plant, leaving the sound of hammering and bright flashes from the welders' torches behind. I noticed straight away that a young Jewish prisoner had his eye on me. I guessed he was probably waiting to see if I would drop a cigarette. His head was shaved like the others but there was something special about him. He had more expression in his face. He didn't look like a corpse but I knew he soon would. They all did eventually. I remember the transports of Hungarian Jews arriving. They were big strapping fellers some of them. Within four months they were skin and bone and many of them were already dead.

This lad was around nineteen and somehow different. I noticed straight away that his zebra uniform was thicker than most, not quite so worn out, maybe even cleaner than the others. It made me cautious at first. Perhaps he was one of the favoured few, the *Prominente*, who had found questionable ways of rising up the camp hierarchy. It didn't seem likely but I couldn't be sure.

'What's your name?' I asked.

'Ernst,' he replied. 'What is yours?'

Somehow his manner overcame my caution. There was something likeable about him.

'Call me Ginger,' I said. I think I gave him a cigarette and then we parted. That was it.

It was a few days before I saw him again. We didn't look at each other, that was too dangerous in the open, so we talked as we walked. He was struggling with his English but as soon as I understood what he was trying to tell me it changed everything. He said something like, 'Me sister in England . . .'

These simple words stopped me in my tracks. Had I understood him correctly? He had a sister in England? I was astonished. I looked at him. He was tired but he wasn't as drawn-looking as the others. He explained in a mixture of English and German that his sister had managed to escape to Britain in 1939, one of the last to leave Germany. Her name was Susanne, he said and she had made it to Birmingham. Just hearing the name of a familiar British city on the lips of one of those poor devils was unsettling.

A link had been made, I felt closer to him. I was not an emotional man but I realised how much I blotted out just to survive there. His sister was safe in Birmingham and he was stuck in this hateful cauldron.

'Do you have an address?' I asked. He said he did but he needed to remember it. I wondered whether he was checking me out. He probably realised he had one chance and he wanted to get it right. I had to wait.

The next time I met him he had his sister's address clear in his mind. He told me straight away. It was 7 Tixall Road, Birmingham and I memorised it immediately. I said I would try to get a letter to her. That simple promise was the beginning of a mystery that would stretch across almost seven decades.

Ernst had an impish, intelligent face. In the few months I knew him I never saw him get beaten, but it was just a matter of time for most of them. An injury or a beating would hasten his decline.

Back in the camp I thought long and hard before deciding on the best way to make contact with his sister. She might not read English yet. She might not trust me. In the end I decided to do it through my mother who would probably understand how to interpret my obscure messages.

When I put pen to paper I told my mother to write to Susanne and tell her that I was with her brother in the British camp. I gave the impression that he was an English soldier and that he had a wound to his hand and couldn't write but other than that he was OK. It was a load of rubbish, of course. I think I even created a false regiment for him. Through my mother I told Susanne as directly as I dared that the only way to help him was to send cigarettes, as many as she could afford, to me by post. I said I would try and get them to him a little at a time. I knew it was a long shot but if my letter got through, at the very least Susanne would know Ernst was still alive. It was worth a try.

That letter was written in normal English. Usually I wrote to my mother using a childish code my sister and I had developed.

Those letters were full of references to things on our farm. I'd write about our cattle being sent to the abattoir. To get across the numbers of concentration camp prisoners I referred to the herd then say it was to the power of three or whatever it was. I even tried biblical terminology and references to Moses. It was clumsy stuff but it was the best I could do.

To underline that I was talking about the Jews I referred to Queen Victoria's prime minister, but without using Disraeli's name. Alternatively I would mention Epping Town where my mother knew a number of Jews lived. She needed a lot of imagination to get any of it but I learnt later she had grasped what I was trying to do.

I desperately wanted the world to know what was going on. I tried to tell her to pass the information on to the War Office but I couldn't do it openly so I began referring to a man my parents knew about who had worked at the War Office before 1939. He lived in Ongar and I had often been in the same train to London with him when I was studying. I hinted as clearly as I dared that she should try to contact him. In the end she chose a different method and wrote two letters to the War Office. It was very general information and I don't know how she phrased it. She wasn't well but she tried.

I had no idea what the outside world knew about the death camps then. I had been in the army since 1939 and there wasn't much news reaching us in the desert. In captivity there was even less. Now I think the allies knew a lot about the concentration camps by that time.

We did have some information coming in. There was a radio hidden away inside our camp, E715. I never saw it myself but I was told it was a basic crystal set. One of the lads had put it together, bartering and smuggling the parts with anyone who had contact with the outside world. It was kept well hidden. And it was usually assumed that someone had it secreted away somewhere.

Most of us heard the news from the radio second-hand through a fellow prisoner we nicknamed '*Stimmt*', probably from a German phrase he liked to repeat, '*das stimmt*', meaning 'that's true'. I think his real name was George O'Mara, a pleasant feller who would trip around the huts passing on what he knew, a sort of whispering town crier.

We saw German newspapers from time to time, particularly when we were using the latrines inside the Buna-Werke. I found a copy of one publication – probably the *Völkischer Beobachter* – with an edict from the SS printed in it, boasting of their plans for Britain when they were victorious. They said they would govern from Whitehall, execute all prisoners of war and allow their brave soldiers to impregnate English girls with good Aryan blood. Just right for the latrines.

It was chilling propaganda but it only served to enrage me more. Like I said before, I hadn't joined up for King and country but youthful adventure had now become a moral conflict for me at the very time I could do little about it.

I could move around quite easily between bouts of work. If I put a pipe on my shoulder I could cross the entire building site without anyone asking me questions. We all did it. Occasionally I would come across Ernst.

Once I was in a hut in a contractor's yard with a couple of other British chaps when he came in. We had been talking for a few minutes when we heard a noise and realised a guard was mooching around. Ernst couldn't get out in time so he hid at the back behind some upturned tables.

The guard stepped inside, looked around and demanded to know what we were up to. I managed to keep him occupied but I was talking utter rubbish to him in broken German and in the end we went outside leaving Ernst hidden in there. It was a while before he dared to come out. It sounds dramatic now but the British prisoners pulled off tricks like that all the time. He must have been scared but he never mentioned it. The next time we managed to speak, when the *Kapos* were out of range, all he said was that my German was very good. It wasn't, but I appreciated his words.

Ernst never told me about his family in any of our furtive meetings. I knew of his sister in England and that was it. The letter I had written seemed unlikely to get through and the address was probably wrong. I didn't hold out much hope. What with Allied bombing, theft and general wartime disruption I thought it was highly unlikely any cigarettes would arrive.

Chapter 11

The next time I saw Hans we were both struggling to shift pipes around. For eleven hours each day we'd heave and carry the heavy-duty components, piling up the weighty stop-taps on low trolleys that ran on the narrow gauge line between the buildings. Once the bogeys were loaded we'd push them across the site to where the valves and piping were needed. Our conversations had to be snatched between the loading and unloading of those heavy tubes and the valves that went with them. That was what we were doing when we hatched our plan.

We were sometimes shoulder to shoulder, straining together but even close up, speaking German out of the side of my mouth wasn't easy.

This time they were being welded into place behind another dark brick façade, that of a three-storied filtration plant slowly taking shape. Metal staircases wound up through the unfinished building. The prize being wrought here in human lives was buna, artificial rubber to keep the Nazi's war machine rolling. We knew the site as the Buna-Werke.

They say, 'stone walls do not a prison make nor iron bars a cage'. It was a quotation I knew as a boy. I had made it my own back then. I knew they couldn't capture my mind. Whilst I could still think, I was free. I had always been a fighter, I had never knowingly walked away from a challenge but it was different now. I had little knowledge of eastern religions or philosophies then but I knew the mind could take you through brick walls. It was my mind that was supplying the muscle.

We were all forced to work for Hitler's war effort, the slave labourers from the Auschwitz Concentration Camps, the civilian forced workers and the British POWs. We did similar backbreaking work to the Jews with one crucial difference. The programme known as '*Vernichtung durch Arbeit*', extermination through labour, did not apply to us.

When night fell we were marched to our respective camps; the Jews to Auschwitz III, sometimes called Monowitz and about which we knew little, and the British POWs to our camp E715, on the southern margin of the building site.

Every night, I went back to something more or less predictable, a spartan hut and poor food, but at least I could be fairly sure I would still be alive in the morning. For Hans and all the other stripeys there was no certainty of survival at all, not even to the next day.

The Jews had had their human dignity stripped from them but they had a chance if they had something to gamble with. All attempts to gain an extra crust came down to a gamble in the end, the roll of a dice.

There wasn't much I could do but I was tormented by the need to know, to see what I could. As the weeks passed I managed to speak to Hans from time to time and as we spoke the idea of swapping with him took hold of me. That way I could see what was happening. I began to hang out the bait.

If we could organise an '*Umtausch*' – an exchange – he could come into the British camp overnight to rest. He'd get better food and more of it, possibly even eggs. To cement the friendship I gave him part of a German sausage, which I had won. Whenever we received one in the British camp we drew lots for it. If we divided it evenly the wurst was hardly worth having. If one person got it at least he had something to chew on. It was hard to eat for us but when I gave it furtively to Hans it was more nutrition than he'd had in weeks.

I supplied cigarettes for him to trade. They were like gold dust in the camps and I was lucky enough to have an uncle who tried to send a batch of 555s each month.

They didn't all get through, far from it, but my father still paid him back the full amount after the war. It cost him a pretty penny.

There were people to bribe and things to acquire but I had enough cigarettes for what I needed. I had sown the seed carefully with Hans because you trusted no one really. Not even a man who understood Heron's formula. The idea had slowly begun to take hold in his mind, and over the weeks it matured into something approaching a plan.

There were just two lads in our camp that I let in on the plot, Bill Hedges and Jimmy Fleet. They told me I was an idiot but they went along with it. Bill's bunk was above mine in the back corner of the hut and he handled most of the subterfuge. It was his job to secrete Hans away. To the rest, the story was to be that I was ill and had taken to my bed.

Bill had worked in a hardware shop up north before the war; that was all I knew about him. I'm afraid I called the shots even then and most people tended to go along with me. They were both sworn to secrecy about it. Like I said, we didn't trust anyone.

The swap took weeks of meticulous planning and observation. I studied the movements of the Jewish prisoners, I knew where and when they would gather to march back to their camp, learnt to copy their weariness, the stoop, the shambling gait.

I taught myself to walk in the crude wooden clogs they wore. I traded cigarettes for a pair, wrapped rags around my feet to cushion the rough edges and practised shuffling in them. Those clogs could be a thing of torture on the site; they helped finish many men's lives if their feet began to swell or they couldn't move fast enough. I had to get that right.

One of the stripeys pointed me towards an older *Kapo* who I was told was less brutal than the rest. He was thickset with a dark weather-beaten face and from the stubble you could tell he used to have black hair in better times. I managed to get him onside with a bribe of fifty cigarettes – twenty-five now and twenty-five when I had returned successfully from the swap. This was without doubt the riskiest part. In a place like Auschwitz everyone had to fend for themselves. I could easily have been betrayed if he had seen a minor advantage to himself and I had seen *Kapos* kill people.

Through Hans, I got cigarettes to two of his companions in his work *Kommando*. They would have to guide me, show me where to go. When the time was right, I hacked at my hair with a pair of old scissors and then shaved off the rest with a blunt razor.

As the shift neared its end, I smeared dirt on my face especially on my cheeks and under my eyes to gain the grey pallor of exhaustion. I thought of the endless patrols into enemy camps in the desert. I was ready.

But why did I do it? Why did I, voluntarily, give up the status of a protected British POW to enter a place where hope and humanity had been vanquished?

I'll tell you why. I knew that the inmates of Auschwitz were being treated worse than animals. I didn't know then what the various Jewish camps were, that Auschwitz I to our west was the brutal extermination camp until Auschwitz-Birkenau was built further west again and redefined the definitions of industrial slaughter. I didn't know then that Auschwitz III-Monowitz, the camp next door to us, was, relatively speaking, the least lethal of the three. What I did know was that Jews were being killed in front of me and that those too weak to work any more were being sent for extermination. When I looked into the faces of the Jewish prisoners, with their hollowed-out cheeks and dark sunken eyes, it was as if there was nothing there. All feeling and emotion had been cauterised in them. I had to see for myself what was going on. I had to get myself in there.

Again and again, they begged us to tell the world what we had seen if we ever got home. The stripeys understood what was happening. The stench from the crematoria told them all they needed to know. So yes, we had all heard the talk of gas chambers and selections but for me it was no good just hearing about it. The words conjecture and speculation were never in my vocabulary. I might not have known which camp was which but I needed to see what turned ordinary human beings into these shadows.

This, Auschwitz, IG Farben's Buna-Werke with all the slave labourers in it, this was the inferno itself no doubt about it. I saw the brutality day after day but I was powerless to stop it. It was a stain on my life and I couldn't let it go.

Even there, as a prisoner of war, I was certain that our side would defeat the Germans and that one day *we* would force someone to account for this. I wanted the names of *Kapos* and SS officers responsible for the obscenity around me. I wanted to see as much as I could. I knew that there had to be an answer to all this and that one day there would be a reckoning.

So yes, there was something I could do; something I was driven to do. It wasn't much but if I could get in, if I could only see, I could bear witness.

There was something else, something not about grand causes but about me. I had always been a better leader than a follower; at least I thought I was. My dreams of becoming an officer had been stymied and my war had been cut short at Sidi Rezegh, but I was still on duty and now I had a cause. I could do this.

Chapter 12

Evening was approaching and I knew the British POWs would soon start to assemble fifty yards away from the stripeys for the march back to E715.

I could see that the Jewish work *Kommandos* were getting ready to form their own column for the trudge back to their camp and I made my move.

People were milling around so taking advantage of the end-of-day confusion, I strode purposefully towards the *Bude*, a wooden shed tucked away in the contractor's yard. I opened the door and stepped inside. I knew the stark interior with its small tables and a simple bench because we sometimes ate and sheltered in it. As soon as I was hidden inside I pulled off my heavy boots and got the coarse wooden clogs ready for a speedy exchange. Hans saw me go into the hut, and followed rapidly on my heels.

Suddenly he was framed in the doorway and without hesitation he pushed on in. He was clearly agitated; what we were doing was more dangerous for him than for me but he had come. For him the chance of a safer night and a bit more food was worth the risk. With a nervous glance over his shoulder as he dropped the latch, he darted across to me, his head down as if it helped to hide our purpose.

There was no time to talk. Speed was essential; this couldn't take more than a minute or we could be missed.

Hans pulled off his infested top and tossed it to me. In return I gave him my thick military tunic. I pulled on his blue striped outfit, the smell of filth and human decay rose from the weave and I was conscious of the creatures emerging from the folds and frayed seams, ready for new blood. I could cope with that, I knew how to live with lice. The desert and the Italian camps had taught me that. The thought of catching typhus never occurred to me then. For now, lice were the least of my problems.

I had left my army shirt in the barracks and was wearing just a vest under my military tunic. A shirt of any sort beneath this zebra sacking could have aroused suspicion even with my head shaved and my face smeared to look gaunt.

All the markers of my real identity had now been stripped away. *What a difference a uniform makes*, I thought fleetingly as I looked at Hans, now dressed in my clothes. I had been right; he was roughly the same height and build as myself and, like me, he was quite pale-skinned.

I had bartered for a pair of old shoes for him and stashed them away in the *Bude* in advance. Wooden clogs on a British POW would have been noticed. I had already hidden my army boots away before he came. I wasn't going to trust anyone with them, not even overnight.

Once the swap was completed I quickly talked Hans through the plan again. I told him he mustn't show any excitement or do anything to draw attention to himself in any way. His movements had to be calm and deliberate. Above all, I said, don't run. I doubt he had the strength anyway. He left immediately looking every inch a British soldier and headed off, as he had been told, to find Bill and Jimmy.

I waited a moment. Then I adopted the hangdog expression that I had observed, dropped my shoulders and with my eyes cast downwards I left the hut and hobbled towards the Jewish column which was forming up. There I edged myself into the middle of a rank, coughing as I went so I could hide my accent behind a croaking voice if anyone spoke to me.

It felt good, like I was calling the shots again. I wasn't merely a bystander any more. Just cheating their discipline meant I was putting one over on the enemy.

I was suddenly aware of new dangers. I ran my fingers furtively up the front of the pyjama-like jacket to check it was fastened to the top, bringing it tight around my throat. It had to be. I knew a missing button or an open neck could result in a clobbering by the *Kapos*. I would have no alternative but to take the beating or give the game away. If I was unmasked they would have shot me on the spot; that much I knew. Inside I was geared up for a fight but outwardly I had to feign weakness and compliance.

Adrenalin pumped through my veins as I listened to the rhythmic background drone of counting: '*Eins, zwei, drei, vier*.'

The living were counted with the dead whose corpses lay piled to one side. As long as the *Kapos* saw a head in the dirt they would count it as a body; as long as the numbers were the same morning and evening it didn't matter if that body was still alive. It made no difference to them.

If a *Kapo* made a mistake he had to blame the prisoners to save his skin. That meant at least a punch, a full beating or, if the SS got involved, a blow with a rifle butt or worse. They put pressure on the *Kapos*; the *Kapos* beat the prisoners. That was how it was. I'd seen it from the comparative safety of the POW ranks. I hated the *Kapos* all the more for it.

When the counting was over they did it again to be sure. There were SS guards, guns at the ready, standing watchfully at each side of the column, with a *Kapo* flitting along the ranks, gesturing with his hands and fingers as he checked the numbers. My attention had shifted to the route out of the yard. I tried to anticipate the next danger.

From where I stood in the middle of a rank, pressed between the curving shoulders of men who could easily be corpses tomorrow, it was hard to see the heap of today's bodies which had been dumped away to one side. It was if the mounds of grimy rags in vaguely human form were already being sucked into the earth.

For some, the end had no doubt brought release; suffering and consciousness extinguished together. The Jewish *Häftlinge* were always collapsing on the job, gasping their last breath unnoticed in the dirt as work continued around them or they were kicked and punched until they simply faded away.

I was startled by a sudden burst of activity, again focused on the pile of bodies. Their fellow prisoners were dragging the skeletal remains across the ground and dumping them on thin boards making improvised wooden stretchers. They showed no emotion. The dead were just another load, this time of skin and bone, and the limbs of those who lifted them quivered with the burden. There were not enough boards so some of the carriers had to pick up the remains in their own hands, grabbing at arms and legs or grasping a fistful of their worn-out uniforms. Dropping a body would mean a delay and a beating and an injury here meant rapid decline and usually death.

Those with boards shared the weight between two or more. Even here, even now, human ingenuity was hard at work: one man had rigged up a rope around his shoulders and under the timber stretcher to relieve the strain on his scrawny muscles. They all knew that further exhaustion would shorten their own lives.

With the cadavers loaded, their carriers rejoined the ranks. I was supported by adrenalin but emotionally I was closed down. My defence mechanisms were in play. I didn't have to think, I just had to do. Too much thought would dull my purpose and bring danger. If you want to speak a language fluently, you have to think in that language and so it was with me, there, in amongst those broken, shadow people. I had to accept what was happening to them as they did. I had to think and act as they did.

After weeks of plotting and running the scenario through in my mind the success of my plan was poised on a razor's edge. The cold focus returned. It was like all those desert patrols again. I had milliseconds to assess the situation and respond. I had to stay sharp or it was the bullet.

My pulse was racing inside a body that had to ooze hopelessness. Here there could be no fighting back. This was a different job but it was a job all the same. I had to bear witness and nothing must get in my way.

Looking forward in the column I saw that one of the corpses was about to slip off the improvised stretcher. Something had to be done or there'd be trouble.

Quickly and without fuss, one of his comrades flicked the body back into position. He splayed the legs roughly apart so that one dropped on each side of the thin timber and the feet dangled in the dirt. That simple adjustment stopped the stiffening corpse from rolling off the board as it bounced along. The dead man was holding himself in place. He was helping his feeble pallbearers on a journey without ceremony with no funeral at its end.

Finally, the column shambled awkwardly off. If there had been a time to abort my plan it had gone. I'd left my comrades behind, and all that was familiar and predictable receded rapidly behind me. The wooden clogs were loose and cumbersome to move in and I gripped hard with my toes to keep them on. The rags I'd used to wrap my feet helped a little but they still chafed badly. At least that helped me master the shambling walk.

We were soon outside the factory gates. Immediately there was a commotion somewhere in the column and we stopped abruptly. I tried to remain composed or at least like the others but I wanted to see what had happened without looking inquisitive. I heard shouting, the guards were beating someone in the line and a sense of suppressed agitation passed through the ranks. They had seen it all before and so had I, but this time I was not a spectator. I was one of them. In this garb I had already ceased to exist in the eyes of my captors. My life could as easily be snuffed out as theirs. In putting my plan together I had felt in charge because I was taking the initiative again but in reality I was as powerless as those around me. I knew I needed a lot of luck.

In time we were moving again. It wasn't an especially long march but it was painful and lethargic. To those around me, each step of that trudge was an effort. Think of a condemned man, shackled, weary and full of foreboding and that is how they were; that's how I tried to appear. I was entering the unknown.

Peering through the ranks before me as we shuffled along, I caught glimpses of the lolling bodies. An arm was flopping loosely. The leg of another kicked pendulum-like as with each step it caught the earth passing below. The body carriers were showing signs of fatigue, their backs were arching with the weight, gnarled fingers were weakening as they stumbled along. Without warning one man crumpled and the body he was carrying dropped to the ground. A burst of violence descended on him almost instantly. I heard the smack of fists, the dull thud of rifle-butts or clubs on frail bodies.

Another *Häftling* took over the carrying and we were moving again, the feet of each man dragging along the ground in that prolonged, hopeless shuffle. Four times we stopped in the course of that journey and each time I heard the impact of blows on ribs or shoulders.

By then I could see our destination – a sprawling overcrowded camp with low barracks buildings enclosed in an overhanging, double barbed-wire fence. And somewhere in amongst it all was a naked wire carrying a high-voltage current. Watchtowers placed at intervals kept constant vigil and SS guards patrolled the perimeter. We dropped off the main track and headed towards the entrance. This was where their short lives were played out, where they jostled for a crust or succumbed.

It was still light when we passed through the gate and I saw the sign bearing the cruel promise '*Arbeit Macht Frei*' – work sets you free.

I didn't know then that the irony of those words would scream across the decades. This was Auschwitz III-Monowitz.

Evening was slowly approaching and somewhere far above us

in the softening light was a clear sky. I sensed it, I knew it was there but it didn't fully register, not then. I never saw a blue sky the whole time I was a prisoner in that godforsaken place. I didn't look up. Just as I had refused to read my mother's letters in the desert, now even a glance at the beauty up above would have been a dangerous distraction. It would have blunted my purpose, reminding me of the vast expanse of the world and freedom.

From somewhere an order was shouted and we whipped the caps from our heads. I pulled myself upright just like the rest. I abandoned my hangdog expression. I knew we had to look to the SS like we could work another day. They were already pulling someone from the line. There was no begging, no pleading or protest. They were too weak. At the time I felt some of them had been brought so low they welcomed the end when it came. I never saw what happened to him but I knew he would be on the lorry to Birkenau and the gas chambers before long.

Once through the gates I began to take in the layout of the camp, with its sprawl of shoddy barracks buildings.

With the wind in the quarter it was then, the sweet, ghastly smell of the distant crematoria swept across the site, catching in my nose and throat. It was a sickly, stench that joined all the other smells around me produced by filth and decaying people.

Further into the camp a shaven-headed body was hanging motionless from a gibbet. His neck was broken and twisted, forcing his head to one side. If his hands were tied I couldn't tell. If there was a sign round the neck saying what he had done to end up there, I didn't take it in.

I was used to bodies by now but the torment that preceded death can be seen in the shape of a hanged man. His body had been left as a warning to everyone. '*Aufpassen*' – beware, it screamed. It shook me, that. Strung up or not, they had all of us by the throat. They could jerk the noose tight when they wanted.

The body carriers were on the move again. With fatigue carved on their sunken cheeks, they arched their backs for one final effort. They took the skeletal remains to one side and tipped them into the dirt. With barely a sound, one by one the corpses slid to the ground. Then the body carriers straightened their backs and rejoined the rest of us and the dead were counted once more.

I had no intention of trying to escape, that wasn't why I was there, but I surveyed the scene out of habit, taking in the layout, looking for exits I would never be able to use. To run was pointless. Once inside, there *was* no way out. If I was identified as an imposter I was dead. There was no Plan B.

The *Appelplatz* was raised slightly, and as our ragged column dragged itself into place, lining up alongside markings on the ground, I became aware of something strange.

From somewhere across the parade ground, above the barked orders, the shuffles and the coughs, I heard the prisoners of the camp orchestra playing classical music.

Chapter 13

I knew, standing there mid-column on the *Appelplatz,* that if I were betrayed there would be no witnesses beyond the poor devils at my shoulder. How many of them would be alive in three months? Not many. I'd have been shot or carted away with the orchestra providing a ludicrous soundtrack. I heard later they were forced to play at executions.

I kept my head bowed but my height meant I could watch the faces of the SS guards without straining. Any change of mood or attention on their part might signal danger. If a *Kapo* had turned me in he might have got a reward but he would risk falling under suspicion too. There was no eye contact. It didn't happen. I started to breathe more easily.

When the latest count and recount were completed and the numbers were agreed, we were dismissed and the passive ranks around me came to life. I scanned the rows of bony faces, looking for the men I had to follow in that mass of worn stripes. I couldn't afford to attract attention by looking disorientated. If I had gone to the wrong barracks I would have been revealed as an outsider. I was focused and my pulse raced but I couldn't let it show. I had to go on thinking strong and acting weak.

The inmates were already shuffling away when I got a glimpse of one of my men and, without saying a word, I headed off behind him towards his barracks. We entered into a narrow passage which led to the sleeping area.

I gagged on the foul air as I squeezed through. The men were sandwiched between the rough timber bunks which climbed up in three tiers around the dingy room.

Many climbed in and collapsed straight away. I followed my two guides and we did the same without saying a word. This was the cramped bunk they normally shared with Hans. I clambered in and hid myself away to watch and listen.

These were not ordinary bunks. Instead of lying lengthways as is normal, we were to sleep three to a bed, crossways to the frame. We lay head to foot but as the bunk was little over five feet deep I had to curl my legs up to fit in at all. It also meant that the middle person had a pair of stinking feet either side of his head.

I kept my head down towards the inside of the bunk with my feet towards the corridor so I couldn't be seen. Behind our heads was a tiny wooden divider and beyond that another set of bunks and more festering prisoners. For now my partners lay head to head and I got my first look at them close up. Both faces were drawn and weary, old beyond their years and yet they looked stronger than some.

One was a German Jew, the other Polish. The German was easier to communicate with. My knowledge of the language was basic but improving and he spoke a bit of English. The camps operated largely in German but it didn't mean everyone spoke it well so dialogue with the Pole was limited.

I could hear raised voices in strange tongues coming from the passageway near the entrance. It sounded like an argument. The nightly bartering that I had heard so much about had begun. Anything picked up during the day, anything that was a *thing*, anything that you could possess, however small, was traded here by the men squashed into the gangway. A button, a thread of cotton, if you needed one, all these had a value, even a nail. If it could be turned into something useable, if someone wanted it, it could be traded and re-traded for a few extra calories.

I had no watch but from the light outside when we arrived and the time that had passed, I guessed it was seven or eight o'clock in the evening. Most of those around me were already played-out and didn't move unnecessarily. They lay, trying to conserve energy.

I was startled by the crash of metal and another putrid smell filled the room. The nightly soup had arrived in a large vat. The barracks were crammed and airless but that pungent odour quickly overpowered all other smells. Everyone jostled into line, presented their bowls and then hobbled back to their bunks to eat it.

I stayed put. I didn't want to draw attention to myself and I couldn't have swallowed it anyway. It was ghastly stuff made of rotten cabbage and boiled-up potato peelings with God knows what else. The smell alone turned my stomach. I was still feeding on adrenalin and avoiding the soup was easy. The others had no choice. They had to eat it.

Each prisoner guarded his metal bowl with his life, they were even tied to their belts. Without a bowl there was no soup and without that ghastly soup there was no life. Later, as sleep took them, the bowls became a hard pillow that they clung onto, even when unconscious.

I never asked the names of my protectors but I remember thinking at the time that they didn't look especially Jewish. But then, what did Jews look like? I wasn't sure I knew. With the barracks lost in darkness it was easier to talk. It wasn't a flowing conversation. I put questions in German and English and we struggled in whispers. My bunkmates had the sunken eyes common to all but they seemed less traumatised by their surroundings than most. I had the impression they were new to the camp.

I told myself they were buoyed-up by the cigarettes I had got to them through Hans and by the thought of those they would receive when I was safe – cigarettes they would trade for calories.

I guessed there were between a hundred and a hundred and fifty people in that barracks hut. I was sure many had known comfortable lives; they had been professors, teachers, businessmen who had been stripped of everything and thrown together. Now I was gasping for air alongside them amidst the stench of faeces and sweat. It smelt of death in there and no mistake. It was sickly and overpowering.

Little by little in hissing tones, my bunkmates gave me a picture of life in Auschwitz III. They told me of the fenced-off hospital block, the *Krankenbau*, with no facilities where the seriously ill were sent. If they weren't back on their feet within a fortnight at most, they were on the lorry to Birkenau to be gassed.

They told of the women held in captivity in the *Frauenhaus* and used as prostitutes. There were sixteen or seventeen of them, I was told. It was usually the German *Kapos* that got to go there. It was payment for the punishments they inflicted.

The bestial torment of it flashed in grainy images before my eyes in the darkness. God almighty! Given the type of men the *Kapos* were, career criminals, possibly rapists and murderers – it was unthinkable.

I tried to memorise their names and those of the SS guards but I was frustrated. I had wanted to know more about the selections, the gas chambers, but now I understood that I was in the wrong place for that. The camps were separate but inextricably linked. These people were being driven on relentlessly; falter or weaken and they were sent on to the gas chambers. There were many parts but it was one machine.

As the hours passed, my Polish bunkmate dropped into an unsettled sleep. The German struggled on with my questions but the silences grew longer and his words less distinct.

I lay and listened to the wheezing and groaning of the others in the dark. Someone was rambling to himself, endlessly repeating the same locked-in phrases. He was not alone. There were the screams of people reliving by night the terrors of the day, a beating, a hanging, a selection. For others it would be the loss of a wife, a mother, a child on arrival. When they awoke, the nightmares continued around them. For them there was no escape.

When you give up, you don't even feel pain any more. Every emotion or feeling is cut away. That's how they were. That's how it was.

I struggled to breathe again. It was stiflingly hot and there was the putrid smell of ripening bodies. Auschwitz III was like nothing else on earth; it was hell on earth. This is what I had come to witness but it was a ghastly, terrifying experience.

I was hunkered down amongst those fading people but unlike them I had brought myself in here. I had plotted, angled and bribed to see this place and just as I had got in, I was going to get out, not to freedom, not yet, but to a better place than this.

I was going to leave those people to their fate and Hans would be back in that awful bunk. He would have those same anguished noises filling his head. He would try to swim above it all but lying there, six feet tall in an undersized bunk with my knees jammed into the bones of a stranger, I knew in the end it was inevitable. I drifted into a turbulent sleep listening to the broken-tongued words of a man I knew would soon be dead.

I woke with a feeling of utter desolation. The *Kapo* was storming through the hut kicking the timber bunks. He was barking orders that echoed off the rough concrete floor. The lights came on. It must have been about four in the morning.

I could hear a man being beaten because he was moving too slowly. Anyone too weak to stand, those who had deteriorated overnight or had given up in the darkness, were pushed to one side. I guessed what would happen to them.

Breakfast was odd-tasting black bread smeared with something I took to be rancid margarine. We passed between tables picking it up as we went by. There was no going back. I kept my head down, took it and passed on. I was hungry but I still couldn't eat it.

I thought of the cartwheels of white bread we had in the British camp, the eggs we could acquire by trade or barter. Even in our camp I dreamt constantly of food but there was no comparison to life here, none at all. On their diet death was certain, the only question was when.

I was already thinking ahead, preparing for my next ordeal – how I was going to get out of here. We shuffled out to the *Appelplatz* where we were counted and recounted again. When that was over, we were marched down towards the gates under the eyes of the SS. Again I pulled myself upright. They were looking to drag anyone too weak to work from the line. Once outside the gates we turned right onto the track towards the road that ran towards the IG Farben complex. I felt the first wave of relief. I still had to complete the swap but even with a groaning stomach, the long day ahead was welcome for once. I was out of that terrible place and looking forward to hearing English voices again, to getting my uniform back.

We marched into the construction site and after a while I spotted my British comrades. I hoped that somewhere amongst them was Hans. Moving around the site was more difficult for me in his rags; in my uniform he now had the protected status of a POW. As soon as the column fell out there was a brief lull before the instructions for the day were given and I took advantage of it to get across to the *Bude* and hide myself inside as I had arranged. I had told Hans he had to watch out for me. He saw me set off and followed quickly. Had one of the columns been delayed by a lengthy count we could have been in difficulty. As it was the exchange could take place before the work began. I could only plan so far, with the rest I had to play it by ear. I was good at that but it still required a lot of luck.

He was agitated when he appeared in my uniform but if he minded swapping back, he never said. He didn't want to talk. He was a decent chap and I had always known he would do the job. Still, I was relieved to see him. I knew that if he had panicked on the outside and refused to come back, that would have been it for both of us. When he emerged from the *Bude* it would be as a concentration camp inmate and he knew it. He wanted to get on with it. I had retrieved my boots from where I'd hidden them before he arrived and his clogs were ready.

I got his striped rags off and was relieved to slide my tunic and trousers on again. I was rejoining my tribe, taking back my protected POW status just as he was losing it. The symbolism was lost in the rush. I wanted to do it quickly.

I repeated the warnings I had given him before we had swapped: stay calm and don't run. I hardly needed to tell him how to behave like a *Häftling*. I wasn't sure he was taking it in. He was gone as soon as he was ready.

It was days before I was able to reflect on those hours in Auschwitz III and appreciate the utter desperation of the place. It was the worst thing you could do to a man, I realised. Take everything away from him – his possessions, his pride, his self-esteem – and then kill him. Kill him slowly. Man's inhumanity to man doesn't begin to describe it. It was far worse than the horror I faced in the desert war. Then I had an enemy before me and I did my duty. I was good at it and so I survived.

The swap had called for a lot of luck but I was disappointed with what I had learnt from one trip. There were many questions I still couldn't answer but I had seen it and that was a start. The feeling of the place preyed on my mind.

I rejoined the British prisoners and the daily grind began. There was a pile of flanged pipes to be loaded, and more of those screw-top valves. They weighed about sixty pounds apiece. Getting them on the trolley was the hard part but once the wheels were rolling it was bearable. Once I had got them across the site we stacked them ready for installation and so it went on. It was midday before I could eat anything and by then my appetite had returned.

It was a while before I could talk to Bill. I knew he would have done the business with Hans; I was sure of it. Jimmy had been less involved as it turned out, but they had managed. Bill had got him in rapidly and hidden him away in my bunk well out of sight in the back corner of the hut. They had both been sworn to secrecy. We never really trusted anybody so the fewer that knew the better.

Avey was ill, that was all they told the others. I had taken to my bunk and wanted to be left alone. Bill took Hans food and drink and he had kept his head down throughout the evening. None of us knew all the British prisoners in the camp by sight, there were too many of us, but the huts themselves were relatively small so they had to keep him out of view until the count. Fortunately people didn't take much notice of each other and it passed off without incident.

For Hans the subterfuge and risk had been worth it for the cigarettes that he could trade to his advantage. The extra rations available in the British camp should have given him a boost, some more calories. It wasn't until I talked to him sometime later that he told me the food had made him ill. After months of stinking cabbage soup, the extras had actually upset him. It couldn't have been anticipated but I was shocked to hear of it. It took the shine off the achievement somehow. He had been comfortable enough resting on my straw mattress under the blankets made from those strange wood fibres. It was better than he was used to and for one night he had been away from the people who wanted him dead.

As for the *Kapo*, I had to get the second lot of cigarettes to him now I was safe. It was some time later that I managed to pay him off. I engineered to walk past him and muttered out of the side of my mouth that I would be in a small building nearby in a few minutes. He turned up and I handed the remaining cigarettes over. He hid them away in his striped shirt and was gone. It was as if I had ripped a twenty-pound note in half and kept part of it back. He had to stick to the bargain.

The whole escapade was foolhardy. Looking back now from the comforts we enjoy today it appears ludicrous, you wouldn't think it was possible but it's what happened.

It was about this time that a new and somewhat ironic danger appeared. By mid-1944 the Allies had realised that the IG Farben Buna-Werke was now within range of the US Air Force Flying Fortresses and worth bombing. Jewish prisoners welcomed the raids despite the danger. They knew that the airmen far above were their friends and they were bringing freedom, but they were still terrified.

The warning on site was given by a large red and yellow painted basket suspended from one of the tall chimneys above the Queen Mary. It was supposed to rise as the bombers approached; the higher it was the closer they were. When it reached the top the planes were virtually overhead.

If we were at work when the bombers came we took cover where we could. We dived into slit trenches or crouched behind walls, while some hid in pipes. I once managed to get down an inspection hatch and into a massive culvert that which ran into the river and I found myself alongside about forty civilian workers and guards. I was allowed to stay. Around the site there were small concrete shelters for the individual guards so they could man their posts during an attack. They were both conical and comical, each one a sort of walk-in German helmet.

There was a giant concrete air-raid bunker on the site. It was taller than many of the buildings, grey, square and ugly. The Germans called anything that shape *klotzig*. It fitted. It could probably withstand a direct hit. I'm told it's still there.

The Jews had to make do with lying on their bellies in the earth and seeking what protection they could find from the terrain. Some gathered round us, thinking that as allied prisoners we enjoyed some special protection or knowledge of where the bombs would fall. We didn't.

20 August 1944 was a pleasant summer's day by Auschwitz standards. It was one of those rare Sundays when we weren't required to work and some of the lads had arranged what they called a gala. It was a desperate attempt to boost morale but it

wasn't up to much. There were a few improvised sideshows – with tin cans to knock over and that kind of thing.

I heard the air-raid warning and the mood changed. We left the huts quickly and went down into the field at the rear of the enclosure where the land dropped away. There was a drainage ditch that ran east to west and a small bomb shelter in the easterly corner. It was nothing like the huge bunker on the factory site but it was pretty solid. I didn't want to go inside. The rumours of the gassings – correct or not – were always in the front of my mind. The heavy steel doors had a large metal catch on the outside and that stoked my suspicions. It was dark and portentous. I took my chances outside in the ditch. I was not alone. Many of the lads heading into the shelter got as far as the walled ramp that ran down to the doors and stopped. They thought they were safe without going inside.

Smoke was already drifting across the camp, released from canisters to the south of the site. It was designed to fog the entire area and entice the planes away from the buna plant, making precision bombing impossible. At the altitude the Americans bombed from, accuracy was unlikely anyway.

I heard the fearful drone of bombers high above. They seemed to be coming from the south. I rolled into the ditch and heard the whistle of falling bombs. It was little comfort knowing that they were friendly. The ditch was waterlogged and my feet were soon soaked. I pressed my face into the earth banking and covered my head. There was a terrific explosion, about forty yards away. I felt the blast waves on the side of my face. It had come from near the bomb shelter. More blasts followed further away towards the factory site. It was about fifteen minutes before the raid stopped and I could check the damage.

I ran to the shelter to find a pile of concrete about fifteen feet deep where the entrance ramp had been. There were bodies and body parts scattered over a wide area. The spot where the lads had stood had taken a direct hit. Those inside the shelter had survived, they emerged through a separate entrance. There were a few wounded lads around, but most of those outside the shelter door were dead and their bodies were trapped in the rubble.

'Is there a miner here?' someone was shouting. One of the lads had started to pull away the masonry but he was making little impact. He was in shock and far too timid for the task. I called him to come out and took his place and began digging without pause. Every stone was moved carefully to prevent the larger concrete slabs from slipping and crushing any potential survivors below.

I shouted for ropes and they arrived after a delay. I tied one end around one large slab of concrete after another and the lads at the rim of the crater heaved them up so I could check underneath. As we dug down we uncovered one smashed body after another, some with limbs missing, others blown apart or crushed in the masonry.

There was one large piece of concrete impeding the dig. It had to be moved. If anyone was still breathing down there we needed to get to him quickly. I could rock it but it could only move in one direction. That meant rolling it across the head of a dead soldier trapped in the rubble. I knew it had to be done for the sake of any survivors below but that didn't stop one of the lads taking me to task. 'The poor feller's dead,' I argued. 'What would you do?' He backed down as he knew there was no alternative. I took a deep breath and began to push. Eventually I got that body out and the remains were passed up to those outside the crater. I returned to digging.

We dug on down and back towards the shelter doorway but our hopes of finding any more survivors were slipping away. Then there was a muffled noise and I realised someone was alive in there. I pulled away more stones creating a hole large enough to crawl into. When I got to him, he was semi-conscious. I asked him which part of his body was trapped. He couldn't answer. I called for some water and went back in with a tiny bowl to splash his face. Now he was conscious, angry and swearing. He gave me a dog's life but we eventually got him out. His life had been saved by a three-legged wooden stool that had deflected some of the fallen masonry and created a protective pocket around him.

Above ground, the lads had been at work dealing with the injured. There were now more than thirty sets of remains laid out. We reassembled them as best we would and they were sewn into blankets straight away. It was a grisly task. They were our friends.

Innocent people were dying around us all the time but it's different when they are your comrades. It was a massive blow to morale but we had to get on with it. There were claims later – which were believed by the Red Cross – that the lads had been killed because they had been watching the 'show'. It wasn't like that. They thought they were safe.

The bodies were to be buried in a cemetery belonging to the Church of the Ascension of the Blessed Virgin Mary in Oswiecim. I was sent on ahead with Bill Meredith – a lad from Liverpool – to help dig a mass grave to one side against the wall. There was a small chapel at the end of a walkway and it was the first time I had seen gravestones with photographs on them. They intrigued me.

We stripped to the waist and began digging. When it was finished a lorry arrived with the remains on the back. There were a few lads around but there was no ceremony or service that I remember. They passed the bodies down and Bill and I laid them in the earth side by side. It was like in the desert. For the first time in too long I thought about the men I'd left in the sand and about Les who I had left unburied.

There was no time to pay respects. We were sent back on the lorry leaving the bodies uncovered. I don't know who closed the grave. Three weeks later a bomb fell on the cemetery and their resting place was destroyed. After the war the bodies that could be identified and some that couldn't were moved to an official war cemetery in Krakow where they have been left in peace ever since.

Chapter 14

Months had passed since I had written to my mother about Ernst. I saw him around the factory site from time to time but I had heard nothing from home. I had no idea whether my mother had received the letter or whether she had contacted his sister Susanne in Birmingham – if she was still there. It had been worth a try but privately I thought it was hopeless. The Red Cross postal system was a lifeline but it was regularly disrupted and getting worse.

After some months a letter arrived addressed to me in an unfamiliar hand. It was followed by a parcel. The letter was written in English and I opened it without thinking of Ernst. I think it began 'Dear Ginger', and it was signed by Susanne. It was intended for him but written as if to me. She said she was sending cigarettes. It had worked.

A letter from my mother confirmed that she had contacted Susanne and told her that cigarettes were the only way to help. It was now up to her. I opened the parcel and there they were, two hundred English Players cigarettes. Those my uncle sent – on the occasions they got through – were the 555 brand. The Players cigarettes were for Ernst and there were more than I had seen for many months.

It was a miracle: Ernst's sister was safe and well. More to the point, she now knew that her brother was alive and in Auschwitz. I could only hope the name meant nothing to her.

We had made a human connection. It meant more than the

contents of the package, valuable though they were. The contact letter alone defied the evil of the place. I was overjoyed. Now I had to get the letter and the cigarettes to him and that meant smuggling them into the IG Farben site. There were sometimes searches but I was lucky.

Cigarettes were more valuable than gold in the camps. When I swapped with Hans, the *Kapo* had held our lives in his hands and I bribed him to turn a blind eye for fifty fags, twenty-five before, twenty-five afterwards. It was a princely sum in the camp and now I was about to give Ernst far more.

I never really knew what Ernst's job on the site was but he was able to move around more than most and he appeared to be spared the worst of the outdoor labour. I guessed he was a carrier or a messenger of some sort.

It was a while before I saw him again. I waited for an opportunity to get up close and whispered to him to meet me in a secluded spot in five minutes.

He appeared. I checked we were alone and then pulled the letter from his sister out of my pocket. He was beside himself when he realised what it was. I told him to take it away and read it, then gestured that he should rip it up. He had lost everything, they all had. Destroying a letter, probably his only personal possession at that time, was asking a lot. I knew that would be hard. But the safety of both of us depended on it and I trusted he would do it. He took the letter and hid it somewhere in his zebra uniform.

I double-checked no one was coming before pulling the first batch of the cigarettes and a bar of chocolate from my battledress. Giving the cigarettes in one go risked losing everything because there were probably too many to hide. I told him I would give them in instalments over time. In that place, at that time, it was a king's ransom and Ernst knew it.

I was surrounded by all those desperate people. They had been stripped of everything and wrenched from wives, children, parents and grandparents who were murdered on arrival. Those who were spared toiled on, starved and broken, knowing those they loved had been gassed and their bodies burnt. Eventually despair, disease, exhaustion or beatings would finish them too.

That was the context. Amongst all that I was giving Ernst a letter and a gift from his sister in England. It was all I could do for him. I had no idea how he would use those cigarettes; what food or favours he would trade them for. They wouldn't buy him freedom, but they might buy him advantage, a chance to survive. That was all. It was up to him now.

He had come so far already but none of us knew how this would turn out. The stench from those far-off chimneys and the corpses at the end of each working day were testament enough. Each life was subject to malign force or murderous whim.

I'd had a glimpse behind the wire of Auschwitz III-Monowitz, but he knew that world and how best to survive it. I had confidence in him, but I knew he was still likely to die. I tried not to show him I knew. I smuggled the rest of the cigarettes to him over the coming weeks. And he never told me what he did with them.

Apart from his sister in England I knew nothing more of his family. He never referred to parents or grandparents and he appeared unencumbered. It was easier to survive that way. I knew that from my own experience. It was true of my time in the desert and when the ship was torpedoed. It was true in captivity. It was easier to rely on number one, it focused the mind. Like I've said there is nothing without number one. That's maybe why I connected with so few people in those years.

Ernst had been different. Despite the despair in his eyes, there were mischievous traces of the lad he'd been, hints of the man he could become. I felt I'd recognised a kindred spirit. I always looked out for him and would give him more cigarettes when I could. Had the war lasted longer I'm sure we would have tried to get another supply sent over.

I was desperate to get out of that godforsaken place even for a matter of hours so when the opportunity came up to join a working party outside the Buna-Werke, I grasped it. Any opportunity to contact civilians had to be taken. We were ordered to go to the town of Katowitz by train to load up with supplies and come back. We weren't told what we were to carry or why they thought it required six of us. We were led out of the camp under armed guard and after a walk we arrived at a railway station with low platforms that looked out across an open marshalling yard.

From where I stood, I could see diagonally across the tracks. A number of cattle trucks containing prisoners had just arrived further down the line. They were being formed into long columns about a hundred yards away. The women had been separated from the men but they were all still in civilian clothes. We knew what we were seeing. We knew what would happen to those women and children.

One of the women was holding a crying baby in her arms. An SS guard was walking up and down the line. I saw him stop and remonstrate with the woman before walking on. The child continued to cry. He went on a few paces then turned, marched back down the line to the woman and then punched the baby with all his might in the face. There was silence.

I nearly vomited with shock and frustrated rage. Even at that distance I knew the child would have been killed. That horrific scene wiped out any relief at getting out of the camp for the day. The train arrived for us and we climbed in. I couldn't speak. We were used to seeing cruelty to adults but the killing of a baby in a mother's arms was unspeakable.

We arrived at a military-run warehouse with a large yard near Katowitz where we were ordered to begin loading a train carriage. Most of the load was comprised of large blankets that had been stitched together forming sacks. I couldn't say what was inside, it could have been bread. I never found out. I didn't much care after what I'd seen.

We returned in a normal civilian carriage with guards in the corridor to prevent us escaping. I had seen a baby punched to death. I replayed that scene again and again in my mind as I stared out of the window. Already I was starting to lock things away. There was nothing I could do. I had never walked by on the other side nor ducked a fight; that's not how I was brought up. Now I was having to do it all the time.

My swap with Hans had brought some names, some information. I had a better idea what went on in their camp but I had expected to learn more. I was disappointed. The selections took place there but the mechanised slaughter was happening elsewhere. There was still a lot I didn't know.

Weeks passed and winter was approaching, the weather was turning cold. Victory seemed to be coming our way but slowly. I still had no idea how this terrible saga of the camps would end. Who would survive to tell the tale; who would be left to bear witness?

Slowly over the months the idea took me to try again. Hans was still alive. Miraculously his two comrades were too. I suggested that we swap again and he agreed; his lot had not improved and it was worth the risk. Again the days of planning began. This time the swap would take place not in the *Bude* – the hut we used the first time – but in a *Bau*, a brick building going up on the site.

Just inside the main door there was a tiny room we sometimes used to rest in and we decided to make the exchange there. It had corners where things could be concealed ahead of the swap so it seemed a better place.

When the day came I felt better prepared than the first time. I knew how the march went, where the difficulties lay, but I would still need a tremendous amount of luck.

We swapped clothes quickly, this time feeling the chill as I got his zebra uniform on. Again he left first, anxious to get on with it.

My cheeks were smudged with dirt, my hair had been re-hacked and crudely shaved again. I paused, checked my buttons were done up before stepping out and prepared to feign the weakness of exhausted men. I got across to the stripeys without incident and readied myself for the count, lost in their number.

I hadn't reckoned with the plunging temperature. I hated the cold; I still do. I shuddered violently. This time the count was interminable.

We moved off on that now familiar march; the bodies of the latest dead were taken back with us, just like the first time I had entered the camp. And again, just like the first time, some were dropped, picked up and dropped again. After that prolonged trudge I passed through the gates of Auschwitz III-Monowitz for the second time. The order '*Mützen ab*' was bellowed from somewhere and we removed our hats and pulled ourselves upright. Then it was on and up towards the *Appelplatz* – the parade ground about halfway down the central walkway on the right. There were fences around us even on the inside. The orchestra was playing, just like before.

We formed up to be counted again. This time it went on for what felt like hours. The exertion of the march had not warmed me. There was nothing in those stripey rags to keep any of my body heat in. Evening was approaching. I didn't need to feign anything, I felt as miserable as the men around me. Then it started to rain.

I was sure there were more of us on the *Appelplatz* this time, not that I counted. When we were finally dismissed I followed my guides down towards the barracks buildings to one side of the square and nearer to the perimeter fence with its high voltage cables. Once inside I took to the bunk and stayed there. I knew I wasn't going to be eating their food.

My two friends had suffered in the months since I had last shared their bunk. I was surprised they had lived that long. I didn't tell them but they both looked thinner. The Pole was worse. His skin now had a sickly yellowish hue. He had the look of a man on the way out. The inmates gave it a strange name then. They called it the look of the *Muselmann*.

I sensed that the allied bombing and the progress of the war had given them a faint hope of surviving but it remained ethereal. My time was limited but I couldn't press either of them to talk, they were exhausted and the Pole collapsed into unconsciousness when he climbed into the bunk. I felt sure he wouldn't last the night. I managed to talk to the German a little longer.

I felt better prepared for the feeling in there this time; the moaning, the rambling, the odd screams. The German was probably in his early twenties but sharing that bunk they were bodies more than people to me already; thin bodies at that. They gave off little heat and I was shivering.

Death had a smell about it, and I had noticed it the first time. I can't describe it but it hung in the air in those barracks sheds, dank, dark and ghastly. The strain of the day had beaten us. I fell asleep to the sound of groaning and the distant rhythm of prayers.

The Pole made it through the night but needed help to get on his feet in the morning. He can't have lived much longer and I never saw him on the site after that. I was glad to be done with the count, to be through the gate and back on the road to the Buna-Werke, to the work I normally cursed.

The swap in the *Bau* was done quickly and without a word. I was relieved to be back and safely in uniform. I tried one more time some weeks later, again using the *Bude* to change in like the first time. I'd left the door on the shed open because a closed door suggested secrets. This time, a guard was nosing around in the contractor's yard and we had to abandon the attempt before it began.

In retrospect I should have noted mentally what I had learnt the first time and left it at that. That wasn't how I was. I'd got away with it once, I'd do it again. I had memorised some of the names of the *Kapos* and the guards back then but foremost I had seen it for myself and that mattered to me. Hearsay had no value. We didn't know how these camps would be wound up or who would be left at the end of the war to say that these crimes had happened at all.

Chapter 15

It was a wet and miserable morning. It had rained heavily and the ground had turned to sludge. I was one of twenty British POWs ordered to help lay electric power cables for a new plant. We were lined up and standing waist deep in a muddy trench with a fat mains cable between our legs. In the strange logic of the camps we were doing the job because the slave labourers were now too weak to haul the heavy-duty cable. We were unrolling it from a massive wooden drum and the longer it got the heavier it was. If we didn't pull in unison we couldn't shift it at all.

A young Jewish boy, perhaps eighteen years old, was standing by the cable drum above me. He was thin and weak like the rest but he had a pleasant face. I never saw what he'd done wrong; the guards didn't need reasons. An SS officer approached him and the boy did what they all had to do. He stopped work, whipped his cap off his head, thrashing it against the side of his legs and stood to attention.

It didn't stop him getting clobbered. The officer hit him in the face with something hard in his hand and within seconds the blood was flowing uncontrollably. The boy managed to haul himself back to attention mumbling something in a language I couldn't place. As soon as the boy was bolt upright he was struck again and knocked to the ground crying with pain. Again he pulled himself up and again he was hammered in the face. By now his striped uniform was covered in blood. I was watching a young boy being clubbed to death. I'd seen it all before but the suppressed rage inside me welled up and this time something snapped.

I shouted up at the SS officer in bad German '*Du verfluchter Untermensch!*' It was the worst I could muster. I had called him a damned sub-human, a term the Nazis used to describe anyone they regarded as inferior: the Slavs, Gypsies, the Jews. I knew they were explosive words. The beating stopped but I knew it wouldn't be the end of it.

It was a cold ten minutes before the officer retaliated. He let me finish the work first. I climbed out of the trench and I turned my back to walk away. He came from behind without warning. The instant he was alongside me there was a crushing blow to my face. I was knocked to the ground holding my right eye; he'd hit me with the butt of his pistol. I blacked out for a matter of seconds. When I recovered, my eye was already closing up with cuts above and below it. The officer had gone.

I never saw what happened to the boy but he can't have lived long. If those head injuries didn't kill him he had been marked out and would die soon anyway.

My eye was a mess and I'd had just one blow. There was a South African doctor in our camp, a chap called Harrison. The Red Cross visitors claimed he had the medical supplies he needed. What he actually had was aspirin and a 60-watt light bulb for basic heat treatment. He did what he could for me and I knew better than to report the injury.

The swelling disappeared and the cuts healed, but my vision was odd and it stayed that way for years. Sometimes I'd look at a broad building and it collapsed before me, appearing no wider than a telephone pole. Years after the war that eye turned cancerous and was taken out and replaced with a glass implant. I knew why.

That boy's powerlessness and my inability to help him haunted me. I had been brought up to challenge injustice and in Auschwitz I could do so little. I saw so many people beaten, so many killed.

But it's the image of that brave boy that looms up at me in the dark. His are the features I see when I wake covered in sweat. I knew nothing about him, not even his name, but that boy's bloodied face has been with me night and day for almost seventy years.

Many lads did what they could for the stripeys, a cigarette here and there and some food if they could get it to them. For others the trauma spawned fear. Some of the lads were afraid of their diseases, of being sucked under with them. We were all captives trying to survive after all. Generosity wasn't restricted to those who had been fortunate in civvy street.

Frank Ginn was one such soldier. I hesitate to say it but the poor lad was more or less illiterate. I would regularly read and write his letters for him and I got to know him. He struggled with German and you needed some to communicate in the camps.

One day he asked me to accompany him to a joiners shed north-east of the Queen Mary building. Inside, there was a big bench, tools and shavings everywhere and a couple of Greek Jews working alone.

They had a smattering of monosyllabic German and Frank thought I might be able to communicate better with them. The Greeks in the camp, those that had survived, were mostly from Salonika, it was said. They were adept traders, tough and wily.

These two were supposed to be making things for the construction site and they had landed jobs fitting their skills at home. For all the stripeys that was a real boon. They were out of the weather and looked better fed than most.

Frank had given them food when he could but now they assumed I was his boss – I can't think why – and I became the object of their interest. They smiled whenever I came in. It was during one of these occasions that the SS arrived.

I expected trouble but they didn't so much as bat an eyelid on seeing me there. There were no questions asked. I assumed the Greeks were making something for them on the side. They all had to seek what protection they could; turn their skills into a crust. The complex web of relationships made it hard to know who I could trust on the site. That's why I always kept names out of the equation. I never knew who was connected to whom. There could be spies anywhere. Information also was a commodity to trade for advantage.

One day, to my surprise, the joiners produced a tiny wooden cabinet for me and insisted I take it. It was handcrafted with tiny drawers and dovetail joints. It was the kind of mini-chest I could have kept toiletries in except I didn't have any. It was a bizarre item to receive in a concentration camp, especially when most prisoners were scrambling for buttons and cigarette ends to trade. I was baffled.

Frank had made the initial connection with them but they had become my friends too over the months. Now they wanted me to have the chest and I felt uncomfortable about it. The Greeks had a reputation for driving a hard bargain and it made little sense. They probably saw it as an investment in future favours but they never spoke of it like that.

Admittedly it wasn't an easy thing for them to trade. The camp inmates could have no use for it. Cigarettes were a better currency for them, they were portable and readily swapped.

The chest had to go to a civilian worker or an outsider of some sort. I suppose a POW fitted the bill. They never said what they wanted in return; it was enough perhaps that I was indebted to them. From then on I tried to give them food if I could so I suppose it worked.

Smuggling it out of the site proved easy on that occasion. There were sometimes searches and *Postens* to be bribed. It was a leaky place and the guards could easily be induced to turn a blind eye to smuggling if there was something in it for them. On this occasion I sailed through, got back to E715 and put it in my rucksack in the hut. It was a rare thing of beauty made in a place of ugliness.

By December 1944 the Red Cross parcels had dried up. Allied

bombing had seen to that. Their extra rations had kept us alive; without them we would have suffered terribly. Now we had to survive on the meagre rations the Germans gave us. There was less to pass on to the Jewish prisoners.

I don't recall the last time I saw Hans or Ernst. They were often on my mind but by January 1945 we knew the Russians were closing in. We could hear gunfire and artillery in the distance. The camp's days were numbered. I didn't know whether that meant liberation or further turmoil.

On 18 January 1945 the Jews were marched out of Auschwitz III-Monowitz for the last time. The camp, just a few hundred yards along the track from E715, was abandoned except for some of the sick who were left behind. The poor stripeys had been marched out at gunpoint in the depths of winter through snow and ice. Thousands of them were forced to leave. The death march had begun.

That morning, we marched into IG Farben as usual, expecting to work, and found it empty. The striped figures who had swarmed over the construction site and appeared to spring from the earth itself when I had first seen them were gone. It was still and eerie.

Rumours flourished. I thought we were being held back as hostages as the Russians advanced. That night there was a ferocious Russian air raid. We fled the camp as usual to take cover, leaving our things inside. I hid in a small depression in the field behind the huts as the bombs hailed down. There was no let up. It went on and on.

I spent the night in that dent in the ground and don't remember sleeping. I was close but I didn't see any of the individual blasts, my head was down and covered. When it was over, I emerged from my hole to find the camp all but destroyed. I sought out what was left of my block and I crawled into the debris to see what I could salvage. I found my watch, which had been hanging on a nail on the bunk, and a rucksack with a few things in it, including that tiny painted chest the Greeks had given me. I grabbed them and scrambled out. Some of the others were doing the same but there wasn't much time.

It was still dark and cold and I had no greatcoat – I don't remember ever having one. It was a necessity I'd have to do without. The Russian guns were clearer now, perhaps five miles away and getting louder. They gave us heart but filled us with foreboding in equal measure.

When the morning came for us to leave the Germans got us together before first light and ordered us into two columns. Some said later that Mieser, the German NCO, had given the lads the option of heading east towards the Russian front line on their own or going west with the column. That's not my memory of it. We were still being held at gunpoint. Heading towards the Russians in strange uniforms would have been suicide anyway. Years later I was told that two lads had taken the risk and had died at the hands of the Red Army.

Our column was the last to go. We were marched through the gates with the twists of barbed wire laced back and forth through the rungs and left what remained of E715 for the last time.

Chapter 16

We were marched a short way along the fence of the IG Farben site in the bitter cold and dark and I spat farewell at those diabolical towers and chimneys, the steel gantries, the gasometers and the miles of piping. Then we turned away towards the south-west, avoiding the town of Auschwitz and leaving the mounds of frozen earth and misery behind, never to return.

No one told us where we were going. I have no memory of passing through that community where so many of the civilian staff had lived. I thought of the Jewish prisoners I had known, of Ernst, whose sister in England had perhaps dared to hope he might survive, and of Hans about whom I still knew little. There were many others but they were faces without names.

We hadn't gone very far when I saw a roll of rags lying in the road and gathering snow up ahead. As we got closer I recognised the lumps of stripey sacking, now dusted white and hardened by frost. Then there was another and another. There was no mistaking them. We stepped around the stiffened corpses and kept on going. Some had been shot in the face and dumped in ditches, others lay on the track where they had stumbled and had been killed. What heat they'd had in their frail bodies had long gone. The bullet holes only told half the story.

I should have realised it wouldn't be over so soon, that there would be more to witness. Now I wasn't sure who would survive to tell the world. For weeks I had tried to second guess how it would end. Now I knew. The Germans had marched off their

Jewish prisoners, thinking they could wring some more work out of them. But if their slaves faltered, that was it. It didn't look like many had made it.

Their bodies had been left where they fell to stiffen in the ice. They had begun the march starved and exhausted and many had succumbed rapidly to fatigue and cold. Some had collapsed and never got up again.

'Death begins with the shoes,' Primo Levi wrote later of his time in Auschwitz III-Monowitz. It was true of the concentration camp where the chafing of crude wooden clogs caused feet to swell and suppurate, slowing people down, bringing decline, beatings and death and it was true out there in the snow.

He, I learnt later, was one of those who had been too ill to leave Auschwitz III-Monowitz and so he had avoided the death march and survived.

We were walking over frozen bodies for days. I knew then there would be few survivors. There were so many stiffening corpses. Ernst, Hans, and the rest were surely dead. If I got home to England I had thought I could perhaps find his sister Susanne, tell her what I'd seen, but there seemed little point now. For the moment, I put them out of mind, they were dead and that was it. Now I had to survive. Like I say, without number one there is nothing.

Our guards were Wehrmacht and not the SS but still we didn't know what they planned for us. There was one particular soldier I recall, a veteran from the eastern front. He had faced the Russians in action and had a false leather hand to prove it. He had every reason to head west. I couldn't resist the taunt. I got alongside him after miles of striding over corpses and in the best German I could muster I said to his face. '*Ihre Zeit kommt noch*' – your time will come. He went rigid. He knew what I meant.

He spat something back at me and I understood: 'I'll shoot you first.' He probably would have done too. Fears were fears and fingers were on triggers. After a while I stopped seeing bodies. I knew it wasn't because the murder had ceased. We were simply on a different route.

Food was very scarce and most of what we ate was stolen from the fields. Some nights we slept under guard in barns, on others we had no choice but to lay out in the snow. I was exhausted but with no greatcoat for warmth, to sleep at night was to die so I struggled to stay conscious.

After a few days I could see mountains ahead and we began to gain altitude. As we climbed the temperature slid further. We were told it touched minus thirty degrees centigrade. The snow scoured my face and ice froze into balls around my ears. It was a long miserable ascent. I began losing the sensation in my feet; frostbite was setting in. I heard later of lads pulling off their boots and leaving parts of their toes inside.

On and up we climbed until the route began to level out and then drop away into a long and winding descent. The snow stopped coming down and the drifts around us became shallower. Patches of vegetation began to poke through and as we struggled on, the snow thinned and began to disappear.

After many hours we were ordered to stop for a break in a field by a river that was in full spate. Then the sun broke through the clouds and the water was instantly energised, sparkling with a thousand points of reflected light. It was fresh, pure and beckoning, and I thought at once that it would cleanse me of all the filth, suffering and mental anguish. It was raging melt water from the icy hilltops and perilously cold but its beauty disarmed me. I knew if I plunged in all my trials would be over. It was a moment of destructive serenity and I had to struggle to resist.

We marched about twenty miles each day and the weather soon became colder again. We were usually in open country but we were under armed guard all the time and escape was impossible. Where would we go? What sustenance could we find in that wintery landscape?

The food situation was already dire. At one point a guard

allowed me to swap my watch for bread with a civilian during a rest stop. It had to be done but I resented the guard taking his share.

When we stopped I saw the soldiers setting up their machine guns on tripods. That always made us jumpy. We didn't know what they had planned for us. After all, we had witnessed Auschwitz. After a while we noticed the guns were facing away from our tiny column and we relaxed. We were in partisan territory and they expected an attack.

The guards had a vehicle carrying their packs, some of their weapons and what supplies they had to feed us. When it broke down they abandoned it, commandeered a horse and cart and transferred the entire load to that. The animal was knackered from the start. They were soon beating it mercilessly. After all the murders I witnessed in Auschwitz and all the corpses I had stepped over on that march, the plight of the beast still affronted me. The way it was being whipped it wouldn't live long. In my mind there was no lower being than one who mistreats a defenceless animal. People can rebel, animals can't.

I knew about horses from the farm. I could handle it better but I had to convince the guards. If the old nag died I told them, they would have to carry their kit themselves. If they let me lead the horse, I could keep it alive. They relented.

I took the reins and with the snow driving in my face once again I spoke gently into the horse's ear. Domesticated animals have no anger in them. Earn their trust and they respond. Treat an animal well and it gives nothing but help. I got it walking again and it did another fifty miles in the drifting snow for me. Then the guards shot it in the head and strung it up in a barn. By then it was the right thing to do. Its misery was over.

I picked up a blade and sliced a piece of flesh from the rump and ate it raw. The guards took the rest and I never saw what they did with it. They probably cooked it. I couldn't get any back to the lads.

We stopped there for a couple of days giving us time to rest. And then it was on with the trudge. On one occasion we slept the night in a normal prison with iron bars and the lot. It was shelter and better than a windy barn. On another occasion we slept in a malt house.

There was a small gang of lads that hung around me on the march. I guess I bossed them about a bit. Bill Hedges was one of them and Jimmy Fleet, of course. It's strange to say but I think Jimmy saw me as having more mental strength than the others. He suffered a lot on the march and I was able to support him. I still owed both for hiding Hans during the swaps but that was already history. We had troubles of our own now and I avoided the tangle of deep friendships, the desert had taught me that. Tomorrow I could easily be shovelling snow or earth over their bodies, why make it worse? I kept my distance but Jimmy and Bill had covered for me, and I would look out for them.

We operated as a unit and developed a system of our own – a modus operandi. At the end of a long, hard march we were shown a place to kip and left to it. Military rank meant nothing in captivity and less still on that trek. People gravitated to those who knew what to do. If there was respect, it was earned. I tended to give the orders and we fanned out rapidly searching for food, mangelwurzels if we were lucky. The others scouted out the best corners to sleep in. I checked out where the guards were and what their routine was, to see what we could get away with. That system got us through.

I remember us searching one barn but the hunt for food turned up nothing. I flopped down determined to enjoy the one thing there was in quantity, the piles of beautiful fresh straw to sleep on.

My weight compressed those pale yellow stalks that had once supported grain. I was obsessed with thoughts of the bread it had produced. On the march we thought of nothing but food and as we slept we dreamt of it.

Now I couldn't sleep or get comfortable. There was something lumpy beneath the straw. I dug down and found I was lying on a stash of potatoes. We'd struck gold. Someone was trying to help us, I was sure of it. I shouted the lads across. There were about six pounds of spuds in all. We lit a fire, cooked and ate what we could. It was a veritable feast, wonderful. We carried the rest with us when we moved. We never found anything like it again.

We had passed through Ratibor in Silesia and on into Czechoslovakia. As days turned to weeks we headed deeper into Bohemia, passing through Pardubice on the river Elbe and on through the outskirts of Prague to Pilsen. In parts of Sudetenland, where you might say this whole sorry mess began with the German occupation which started the war, local people – Czechs rather than ethnic Germans – threw bread to us as we passed. The guards stepped in and tried to stop them but we still got some. It was appreciated.

Hunger hurts. It had been a tough day. The lads were all bedded down in a small barn for the night when I noticed that the dividing wall stopped short of the rafters. It was eight feet high and after a few attempts, I managed to climb up and swung my legs over, dropping down the other side into a ramshackled outhouse.

I began exploring and found a bowl of solidified, rancid fat possibly for the animals. I considered it then gagged, put it down and shinned back over the wall and hit the sack. I thought about it all night. When the order came to leave the next morning I jumped up without thinking, leapt over the wall and found the bowl. I ate the lot without pause and managed to keep it down.

The mind conquers everything. I forced the most appalling things down my gullet on that march and each time I convinced myself that it was a Christmas dinner. It's how I survived.

From Pilsen it seemed we were being taken towards the Austrian border. By now I was desperate. We weren't getting any food. I wasn't going to starve to death as a captive. I might as well be on the run fending for myself.

I decided to go alone and never told a soul, not even Bill and

Jimmy. If I had said anything it would have put pressure on them to come along. If I died, they would die. I wouldn't take that responsibility. I operated better alone.

We stopped for the night somewhere south of Pilsen where we were ordered to sleep in a large barn full of straw. The guards made their patrols but they were growing sloppy, their hearts weren't in it. I watched and waited. I noted the gaps in their nightly routine and at the first opportunity I made a run for it.

I crossed fields and scrubland, half expecting the hue and cry, worse still the bullets. I kept going until I was a safe distance away. Then I plunged into a ditch and slept until first light.

There was no time for relief. I was in charge of my destiny again and I risked being captured and shot. Making a home run required a plan. I didn't have one. I thought that mattered less, now the war was grinding to a close and the western allies were approaching. I did have a simple map, it would have to do.

I still had to eat. I came across a house, watched for a while then approached and found the door unsecured. Fear evaporates when you're hungry. Had anyone got in my way that would have been it. They didn't. I got away with a wheel-shaped loaf about a foot across. I found somewhere safe, hid myself away and ate the lot.

I set-off in a south-westerly direction, using the stars and the sunset for rough navigation. I walked mostly at night and lay low during the day. I was still in my battle dress and I could have done with a coat to hide it at least but I never found one. I kept away from settlements and off the roads and crossed the border into Germany over wild, open country.

I stole what food I could and took anything from the fields that might be eaten. It was no worse than on the march. I was getting deeper into Germany all the time and after countless nights of walking I made it as far as Regensberg.

I stumbled across a sprawling rail-marshalling yard and began searching the labels on the wagons in the vain hope of finding one heading north. I had it in my head to try and get to the British lines.

It was then I heard the drone of large planes overhead and the bombs began to fall. I knew with goods and troops on the move a railyard like the one I was in was a strategic target. I began to run and managed to get out and across a cemetery and kept going and going. I could hear the flak going up, the whistle of bombs coming down. One fell in that cemetery soon after I left.

I skirted along a hedgerow and came up against a well-camouflaged flak position. I managed to get around it and out into an open field. I thought I was safe. I wasn't.

I heard planes overhead again and dived to the ground. I rolled over on to my back and saw an American Flying Fortress coming down in flames with one wing blown off. There was a whooshing sound above followed by a thud, I thought it was a bomb but there was no blast. Something from that bomber had smashed into the earth a short distance away. I went to look when the raid was over and found a baseball bat sticking out of the ground. I guessed it had been carried by one of the bomber crew, possibly for luck. It hadn't helped. There were no parachutes in the sky that I'd seen. I pulled it out of the ground. This was one souvenir I would bring home.

I didn't try the marshalling yard again and headed north instead on foot. I usually did things the hard way. That was just me. I reached the outskirts of a city, which I hoped was Nuremberg. I thought I might try my luck on the trains again and made one foray towards the town but the bombers had got there first. It was devastated. In some neighbourhoods there were hardly two bricks standing on top of each other. I retreated the way I had come and began to circle around the city before pushing on north.

I thought I was getting closer to the allied lines all the time but I had hardly seen any German troop movements so perhaps I was wrong.

I had almost got as far as Bamberg before my luck changed. I emerged from a copse of trees to find a tank unit deployed and ready for action with at least a hundred yards between each one. They were Americans. I approached carefully but in the open and trusted they had good binoculars to see me coming.

They wouldn't waste a tank shell on an individual and why shoot a lone soldier heading towards them? If I was the enemy they'd have another prisoner.

I got close enough to shout out that I was a British POW and someone popped his head out of the nearest tank and greeted me. He disappeared again and I imagined he was on the radio. Then he jumped out and said I should follow him. We headed across the fields and after about 200 yards we got to another tank where the commanding officer was waiting.

He was out of this world. He had a couple of pistols and a knife down his boot. He came straight to the point. 'Where are these goddamn Krauts?'

I couldn't really tell him, I'd tried to avoid them myself. I had come from near Nuremberg, I told him, and I hadn't seen much. He took another look at me, turned to one of his soldiers and said, 'Give this man food and water.' I'd been liberated.

I devoured the rations instantly. I have no idea what they were but they tasted wonderful. The tanks were soon on the move and I was ushered back down the line. Eventually I was put in a vehicle and driven some miles back in the direction of Nuremberg to a small airstrip in a field. I was told that a number of former POWs would be assembling there and that planes would arrive in a few days to fly us out.

I climbed out of the vehicle, and waved the Americans off as they left to rejoin their advancing units. It had been a brief interlude. I'd enjoyed their rations and now I was alone again. Had I really been liberated? The place looked abandoned. There were no other POWs. It was just a field. It was back to surviving again.

I circled the area until I found an abandoned house on the margin of the site and managed to get in. It was shelter at least but I don't remember any beds. I curled up under a blanket on the floor. I had travelled hundreds of miles across central Europe on foot and scavenged for food. Even in my darkest moments I had hoped for a more uplifting liberation than this. I searched the house for something to eat and didn't find much. There were no signs of planes. I sat tight.

As I waited, I wondered whether the other British lads on the march had been herded into another camp or whether they were still out there hiking cross-country at gunpoint. It was years before I learnt that the guards had marched them on until they too ran into the Americans. One of the lads then grabbed a gun from his liberators – the story went – and the German NCO Mieser was shot dead on the spot. He wasn't the worst of them but I understood. I suspect leather-hand just slipped away. As for the Jewish prisoners, in my mind the men I had known – Ernst amongst them – had to be dead. I had seen so many corpses. I stopped thinking of them.

I sat on a wall at the end of that neglected garden and watched the sky for planes. I waited and waited, but none came. Perhaps I had been abandoned. After a while a small group of German girls walked past. I took a chance and called out to them. To my surprise they came across to talk. The girl who chatted most to me was blond, about twenty-two years old and very beautiful. They recognised I was a foreigner straight away and they wanted to know where I was from.

I explained that I was English and a former POW who was waiting to fly home. I didn't tell them where I had been captive. Already it felt like Auschwitz was another universe. The experience couldn't be carried into normal life. Even in Germany my experience didn't apply.

We talked for a while as best we could and I asked if they had any food. They produced a sandwich of sorts, which I took gratefully and ate straight away. Looking back it was probably their lunch.

We were in allied occupied territory but there weren't many troops around. The war was not yet over and they took a risk in being civil to me. They were curious and after talking a while they came in to see the abandoned house that was my temporary home. The girl who spoke most gave me her address in Nuremberg and her name, Gerdi Herberich. I promised to write and thank her when I got home and to send a food parcel. I am sorry to say I never did. By then I had other things on my mind and my world was twisting out of shape.

The friendly atmosphere in my shelter was soon shattered by the arrival of a group of Americans including some former POWs. The girls left quickly and I never saw or heard from any of them again. It was a small thing – just a sandwich or *Brötchen* as the Germans called it – but a human gesture to an enemy soldier and not without risk. They never asked for anything in return.

The atmosphere became more boisterous, but the new arrivals told me I was in the right place. I had stolen four tins of food from another empty house nearby and I kept one for myself and let the Americans have the others. They had no labels on them so when the Yanks opened theirs and got meat I expected the same. When I prised mine open it was a watery vegetable of some sort. I couldn't have been more disappointed but it helped get me though. Nine or ten of us were kipped down there and all we could do was wait.

Chapter 17

It was two days before the roar of large propeller engines shook that desolate house and I ran outside to see an RAF Dakota coming in low over the field to make a bumpy touch-down. It had barely turned to the side of the green strip when a second plane came in, bounced a few times on its main undercarriage before settling back on its tail wheel to run along the grass.

There was no one in charge, no control tower and no ground support that I could see. I dashed back inside, grabbed what stuff I had and set off across the field trying to anticipate where the plane would stop. The Dakota was sleek for its time but a workhorse nonetheless. The first plane taxied slowly, turned and came to a halt with its nose tilted towards the sky and its twin propellers still turning.

More lads appeared from distant corners of the field and raced towards it. A hatch opened in the side of the plane and a man in a thick leather jacket leaned out and shouted something. I couldn't hear over the engines but from his gestures I realised they weren't going to stop for long. I was amongst the first to climb in. It hardly mattered where it was heading, I was going anyway. About a dozen lads got in before the hatch was closed and I sat down on the narrow seats along the side of the ribbed metal interior. I twisted around to look over my shoulder and saw through the tiny window that the other lads were rallying around the second plane hoping to get in.

By then we were taxiing towards the end of the field and

preparing to takeoff. Smiles spread infectiously across faces and I knew I wasn't the only soldier going home after a rough war. I heard later that a third plane coming for us had developed engine trouble and had crashed in flames on the approach. By then we were climbing up through the clouds and turning towards Brussels. I slumped down, fiddled with the baseball bat I had carried with me since Regensberg and dared to hope at last that I was homeward bound. Thank God. It was over. I was still hungry.

I stood up and walked around during the flight, checking the view from the tiny windows on each side. The war was not quite over but no one doubted that it soon would be. I gazed down at the miles of liberated European fields below and wondered what the post-war years would bring.

We touched down on a military airfield near Brussels. I was taken to an army camp close by and given proper food for the first time in weeks. I had a wash but no shower or bath. I stayed there no more than a night and spoke to no one about my journey or my time in captivity. We had all endured terrible things; we didn't go on about it and no one asked.

The next day I was taken back to the airfield and emerged to see a large four-engine bomber with a glass bubble for the bomb-aimer at the front below the cockpit and a smaller one halfway down the fuselage like a swelling on its back. There was a gun sticking out of it.

I knew it was a Lancaster bomber though I'd never seen one before. I had been captured before it was in common use but it was exactly as I had imagined it from the talk of fellow prisoners.

It was being readied for take-off and I clambered in with the other lads. There were no seats and it was severely cramped. I knew instantly where I wanted to be for the flight but the captain told me the bomb-aimer's position – that flying glasshouse up front – was out of bounds. I refused to give up; arms were twisted, favours were begged and eventually my wish was granted.

I lay flat on my belly in that vulnerable transparent nose and felt the heady vibration of the props as the ground rushed beneath us and we lifted again into the air.

We circled the field, the course was set for home and after a while land gave way to sea.

I had seen what planes like those had done to Nuremberg and I feared what state Britain would be in. As we flew low over the Channel what I saw didn't bode well. There were shipwrecks and debris all along the coast and slicks of oil as far as I could see. Then the water cleared and in the distance I saw the white cliffs of England in the haze and I knew they couldn't have destroyed everything. I would get home.

Soon I could see green fields bisected by country lanes below me and hedgerows racing in all directions. I lay there prostrate in the front of the plane and eventually a landing field came into view. We dropped lower and lower until the grass became a blur of racing green that loomed up into my face as we landed with a bounce.

We came to a halt, the door was opened and before we could stray the captain insisted we signed the fuselage with a pen before saying goodbye. He must have flown countless combat missions but bringing the lads back home meant something to him.

My ears were still ringing from the noise when I heard a strangely familiar sound and one I hadn't heard for many a year. They were the strange voices of Englishwomen and they were serving tea.

I was taken to a barracks and allowed a shower at last. They gave me socks, underwear and a fresh second-hand uniform plus a pair of heavy-duty black leather boots with studs on the sole and metal rims on the heels. I still have them today. I didn't stay long. I had been beyond military discipline for a long time and I didn't wait for permission to go. I left a note in the barracks, walked out of the camp and got a train towards London.

I arrived at Liverpool Street station, changed trains and went on out to Essex without paying a ha'penny and without seeing the damage to the city. I wanted to get back to the people I loved. It was a day or two before VE Day and I hadn't been home for almost five years.

I climbed out of the train at North Weald station and looked over the wall into the coalyard and saw a man with a cart shifting sacks of the stuff. I recognised him instantly as my uncle Fred the coal merchant who had once played football for Fulham. I jumped over the wall and his words on seeing me alive were unprintable. He finished unloading and said he would take me the mile or so home from the station and he talked all the way without pause. After all those years I arrived back at the farm as a passenger on a coal cart, which he turned around at the gate leaving me to go in alone.

I passed by the yellow privet hedge and began that thirty-yard walk through the flower beds and up to the double-fronted house where I had grown up. That place had lived on somewhere in my mind, though thoughts of home had been a burden in the desert and in the camps. I couldn't get there back then so why torture myself with the memory and feeling of the place? But now I could embrace it.

I hadn't warned anyone I was coming. I knocked on the large oak door. There was a pause before it was opened by a woman who, though familiar, looked tired and drawn. She gasped on seeing me and I said to her, 'Mother, you do look old.'

How I have wished over the years that I could take those words back. She hugged me at the door as if she never wanted to let go. I was home but what a sight I must have been. I had weighed around twelve and a half stone when I joined up. When I got home I was a little over eight.

My mother had been left to struggle on alone. My father had been taken prisoner too. They had told her I had been wounded in Africa. In my letters I said I was fine, but she assumed I was putting on a front. Then the irregular mail from E715 had stopped. The death marches and my long walk across central Europe had begun. She had no idea I was alive and feared the worst. She had her own declining health to wrestle with.

In the few years she had left to live she never asked me about my war, my captivity or that long march. The thinking then was, don't talk about it. Soldiers and their families were encouraged to forget.

I don't quite know when my father came home. He had lied about his age to join up and he had done so partly with the thought of looking out for me. He was wounded and captured when the German paratroopers dropped on Crete. He was taken to Austria and forced to build mountain railways, despite bouts of pneumonia.

I heard that he might be home soon but that could mean anything. Then one day I was occupying myself in one of the small rooms to the back of the house when I heard a shuffling noise outside. Someone was trying to get in the back door and having trouble. I opened it and there he was struggling with his kitbag. He dropped it when he saw me and embraced me for the first time since I was a child. He looked pretty haggard; I felt myself weeping and noticed he was too.

I remembered a time as a small child when I sat on his knee and he'd sing to me: 'There will come a time one day when I am far away, There will be no father to guide you from day to day.'

The thought of him dying upset me as a child and I would hammer on his chest when he sang it until he stopped.

I had never seen him as an emotional man but I heard when his own mother died he went out into the middle of a field all alone and sang his heart out. His homecoming showed me we had both changed, though his embrace was still brief.

I never saw him meet my mother for the first time. I can only guess how it was. They were alone and that is how it should be.

I am sure he regretted leaving her to go and fight when he didn't have to. I don't think he ever picked up the pieces of his life after the war but if he was suffering the way I was, he never showed it.

He lived until 1960 but we never talked about the war, or compared our experiences of captivity. Not once. I don't think he ever knew I had been in a camp near Auschwitz.

I wasn't back long before the traumas began. By day I was in the friendly Essex village I had known, at night, in my sleep, I was thrown back into the obscenity of Auschwitz. The nightmares began; that boy being beaten around the head whilst standing to attention as blood streamed down his face. Countless times I relived that baby being punched by the SS guard. I would wake up with the sheets soaked with sweat, convinced I had smuggled myself into the Jewish camp and was about to be discovered.

Through the desert, the years of captivity and Auschwitz I had told myself, 'You didn't have to think, you had to do.' It was decision-making by instinct and it had got me through. Now there was no danger and too much time to think. The dreams were starting to conquer me. I relived the powerlessness of seeing and not doing and I did it nightly.

There was no help for traumatised soldiers back then. It wasn't even thought of. I know now I was a mess, a complete and total mess. Many of us were.

If my mother never asked about the war, people in the village couldn't stop their questions. They didn't really want to know, of course, they just wanted a few heroic anecdotes. They knew nothing about the concentration camps then and if I mentioned anything at all, it didn't resonate with them. It didn't fit in to what they knew or even what they wanted to know. People were just uncomfortable hearing about it and their response was to go blank. I called it the glazed-eye syndrome.

No one at home understood what we soldiers had been through. Some talked utter rubbish. The question that insulted me most was, 'How many Germans did you kill?' We were forced to do the things we had done and it cheapened the whole thing to talk about it like that. They were inviting us to gloat about the things we wanted to forget. The enemy soldiers we had killed had paid the price and going on about it showed a lack of respect.

One chap – a butcher from Epping who hadn't served anywhere – told me bravely that he would have run his wife through with a knife to spare her falling into the hands of the Germans if they had conquered Britain. That clearly wasn't meant for her ears. He squirmed when I ran into both of them side by side on the train a short time afterwards. I didn't need to say anything.

Auschwitz was already a distant planet but the dreams brought back some of the faces. There was nothing I could do to enquire about Hans but with Ernst it was different. There were some things I would force myself to do whether I was up to the task or not. I had to find Susanne in Birmingham and tell her what I knew. I had managed to negotiate some official leave by now and I had some weeks to spare. It was a fool's errand and I hadn't thought it through.

I don't know now how I made contact, whether I wrote, found a telephone number or whether I simply turned up on the doorstep. I knew she was called Susanne and I had connected her to the surname Cottrell. Ernst may even have given me that name from the start. I assumed she had been adopted by the family that had taken her in before the war so in my mind she was always Susanne Cottrell. The story of the cigarettes was one thing Mother did talk through very briefly. She was pleased I had got some of them and that it had helped. She didn't need to know about the camps and I went no further than that with her.

My recollection is that I met Susanne in Birmingham, I can't be sure. I was in no fit state to meet anyone and I hadn't planned what I would say. What with the war and captivity I had none of the tact needed to break bad news gently. I didn't really know why

I was going to see her at all. She was on my list I suppose, along with Les Jackson's folks and others I traced later.

I think I went to the house but it's all very vague now. I have a feeling we went for a walk; I remember being outside. She was about twenty-two years old – pleasant but shy and small in stature. She still had an accent.

It was an anguished meeting. I wanted her to know that the cigarettes had got through, that Ernst had been overjoyed to have them and that it might have bought him some brief help and protection. I could tell her all that, if I could spit it out, but where would the story go then? There was no happy ending.

I had visions of the death march and those frozen corpses. We had walked over their bodies for miles. I knew the chances were Ernst had been murdered with the others. If he had survived the march he had probably been herded into another death camp and perished later. I couldn't bring Susanne hope, nor could I tell her anything of Ernst's death; I hadn't witnessed it or seen his body.

I was suddenly alongside a young girl who had lost everything, but now had a chance to rebuild her life. Why burden her with the bestiality of Auschwitz? I couldn't talk about it anyway. There were a lot of silences. I still partly thought in German. After losing so much weight I must have looked dreadful.

It was a traumatic meeting and I left wondering whether I had done more harm than good. The barbarity of Auschwitz had entered every pore. I was saturated in the memory but I couldn't get it out. Who would I tell? Looking back I was in a terrible state. PTSD they call it now – post-traumatic stress disorder. It took me years to get back to rational thinking. I was weird all right.

Sometime later I tried half-heartedly to get in contact with Susanne again. I failed and gave up. I had done enough harm; I had to move on.

Around then, on 3 June 1945 I was given a new address book by an old girlfriend called Jane, a concert pianist. It was small and covered in brown leather and I pencilled in the details I had for the girl I still thought of as Susanne Cottrell: 7 Tixall Road, Birmingham. There's also an address for Gerdi Herberich in Nuremberg – it must have been a good sandwich.

Les Jackson's relatives are scribbled in there too. His folks were the next on my list for a visit but my experience with Susanne had shaken me. It took me months to go back to Aspen Grove in Liverpool and face them.

Eventually, I drove up to meet his father and we went to the pub and both drank too much. He had lost his son and I knew exactly how. I was there to fill in the gaps but I spared him the details. He didn't need to know that Les had been blown apart. I said what we all said in those circumstances, that I was with him when he was killed, that it had been quick. I hope it helped. Mr Jackson wasn't emotional about it, the sherbet saw to that. Dear old Les, he's still out there somewhere in the sand.

We were slightly the worse for wear when we got back to the house, then in walked Marjorie, his sister. She was as beautiful as ever. I'd danced with her before embarkation and had her picture stuck on the cabin wall. She was with a feller called Evans and I realised she was married. To ease her embarrassment in front of her husband I pretended not to know her and introduced myself as if we were strangers; I was also protecting myself. Marjorie had been special, she moved beautifully in the ballroom, but I had been away a long time. Life had moved on and another door had closed. I slept at the house and left early next morning.

Les's story is not quite finished. He had a wife who lived in Southampton and when I was back in barracks at Winchester I went to see her unannounced. I should have known better. I wasn't thinking straight at all then. I introduced myself at the door and she was flustered and asked me to wait outside. After a few moments she appeared with her coat and suggested we go to a pub to talk.

I guessed straight away she had a new man. There was nothing wrong in that, Les had been dead a few years, but it was strange for me. I had come to bring comfort, pass on what details I felt I could, but she wasn't that interested. I don't know what I expected. I thought she would want to know what happened, to hear some of the escapades we had been through. She didn't have much time and she seemed distracted and anxious. I told her what I could and we said goodbye outside the pub. I didn't go back to the house.

It upset me, that meeting. The soldiers had gone away to fight and many had paid with their lives. The war had just ended and they were already lost and forgotten; the water had closed over their heads. It all added to my swelling mental turmoil.

I hadn't been back long when I got a mysterious phone call at home in Essex. It was from a man who said he had been a Jewish prisoner in Auschwitz III-Monowitz. He wasn't someone I knew all that well from the camp, he had never asked for my help and I had never to my knowledge given him anything. We knew him by the nickname 'Mops'. Somehow he had got hold of my real name and made contact through the Red Cross. I was intrigued, I had been so careful. He wasn't even a prisoner I'd had dealings with and now he was calling from Paris at a time when international phone calls were rare.

He told me all about the Jewish death march. He said he had counted hundreds of gunshots each day they walked and that many had been slaughtered. Miraculously, he had come through. It confirmed what I had seen but it was the first indication that anyone had survived. I wrote his name down in my little book as 'Merge' with an address in Paris. I never heard from him again but two or three weeks later four Jewish boys arrived at the house unexpectedly. 'Mops' had sent them. The oldest was eighteen, the other three around fourteen. They were polite lads who had come across from Ilford. They were not camp survivors but had lived out the war in Britain. Perhaps they had escaped on a similar *Kindertransport* as Susanne. They never asked for anything and I couldn't really help them. We chatted a bit, my mother gave them a meal and they set off again, leaving us mystified.

Chapter 18

The officers back at Winchester called me in, wanting to know if I had anything to report from my time as a POW. Too right I had but where would I start? I struggled to tell them about Auschwitz and sensed straight away that they couldn't take it in. They knew so little about the concentration camps in 1945 and for me that door had slammed shut. I couldn't prise it open again.

I told them what I could about the slavery, the beatings and random murders, the gas chambers and the crematoria but back in England it all sounded so far-fetched and words failed me. If they knew about the labour camps, they certainly had no idea that allied soldiers had been put to work alongside them. Their body language suggested they were uncomfortable hearing about it. Like the people in my village, they just glazed over.

Many former prisoners were made to feel they had let the side down by being captured at all. No one ever said it straight out, but we felt under suspicion. Instead of being victims of Nazi forced labour programmes it was as if we had unwittingly helped the German war effort. We weren't treated as returning heroes at any rate. I gave up and walked out.

I never spoke about Auschwitz officially for decades after that. I think they handed out forms to the lads coming home later asking for their experiences as prisoners. It probably spared the officers the embarrassment of talking about it. By then I had moved on. We had done what we could to sabotage work at IG Farben and had suffered as much as any who served. We had also witnessed humanity's darkest chapter and come home with nothing we could talk about. Nothing anyone could understand, at least.

I fulfilled one promise to myself and wrote down what I could remember about Auschwitz III-Monowitz. I scribbled down the few names that remained in my mind and the details I had gathered about camp conditions as I had seen them and then I put it away in an old leather briefcase and tried to forget about it. I tried to tell myself it was over.

It wasn't. Things were starting to happen which I couldn't fully explain. I still saw Jane from time to time. Her husband had died during the war and she was now working as a PA to a US Admiral stationed at the American Embassy in London. She kept up the piano playing all the same. We'd always had a fiery friendship, Jane and I. Even before the war we argued quite a lot but that never spoilt things. I was invited to join her and a large group of friends for dinner in London. It was a pleasant evening after which the party transferred to her apartment in Beaufort Street, Chelsea where the entertainment continued, or at least I think it did. I'm not sure what happened.

Some time later I walked into a police station far away in the East End on the other side of London. I was dazed and confused and desperately scared. It turned out I'd lost three days of my life. They said I wasn't drunk and as far as I could tell I hadn't been unconscious but I still couldn't account for the time.

On top of that I had a US army staff car with me. I don't know how I got it but I guess it came from one of Jane's party guests. At least the car wasn't damaged so that was something. I was worried, very worried both for myself and others. I had been so jumpy since I got home. If someone caught me unawares or touched me on the back I spun round expecting to have to fight. I got angry easily. I had been beyond the rules for so long that anything was possible. If I had been in trouble or hurt anyone during those missing three days I had no recollection of it. The memory loss scared me.

I handed myself in at the police station and told them what I thought had happened. It was all a bit silly, really. They didn't know what to do with me. They checked whether anyone matching my description was wanted for anything. I imagine they had a lot of weird behaviour to contend with from returning soldiers at that time. I left the staff car with the police and headed home alone both chastened and shaken by what had happened.

I was demobbed in early 1946. I returned home to the village only to be pestered by people asking the same mindless questions about the war. I couldn't give them what they wanted. People were fascinated by the strangest things, like the baseball bat that fell from the sky. I left that on the back seat of my open-topped car in Leytonstone while I went to get some food. When I came back it had been pinched. I'd always fancied I might find out who its owner had been and return it to the family. I wasn't thinking straight. The bat had survived but its owner was certainly dead. It would hardly bring his loved ones peace and comfort.

Few of my friends had returned to the village after the war and I felt the loneliness more in such a familiar place. The innocence and joy of life there had evaporated. There had never been enough hours in my day before I left. Life had a swing to it then. Now it was empty. I was restless, and feeling increasingly weak, I began to suffer stomach cramps. Something was wrong but I wasn't sure what. I hit on the idea of going up to Manchester to track down Bill Hedges. I thought I might even stay in the north and look for work.

I found Bill eventually and it was good to see him. He was married and if he was going through similar traumas to me he didn't say. We couldn't bring ourselves to talk about Auschwitz, in any detail. It didn't fit into our lives any more. He had survived the long march and got home, that was something but we both wanted to move on, find our places again in a world that couldn't comprehend us.

My stomach pains were getting more acute all the time by then.

When they struck I was forced to my knees, writhing in agony and I was getting crushing headaches along with it. I had chronic fatigue and I felt like I was falling apart. My tongue was as black as the ace of spades. I needed a doctor quickly.

He didn't hang around. I was whipped straight in to the Manchester Royal Infirmary where the doctors were equally mystified. I had had malaria and sandfly fever in the desert, dysentery and scabies in Italy and God knows what I might have contracted in Auschwitz. The talk there had been of typhus but it certainly wasn't the only disease incubating in the camps.

They checked my lungs and everything else before one of the professors got to the root of it and diagnosed systemic tuberculosis. He said I had it in my throat, my lungs, my stomach and intestines. I knew it was serious but it was hardly surprising after working alongside the slave labourers for so long. The professor told me it would be a major operation and I would be laid up for months, possibly years. I insisted on having the whole procedure explained to me properly before I approved the operation, so the doctors gathered around my bed and went through it in minute detail.

I found it easier to understand it in engineering terms. They were going to remove a lengthy piece of my intestines and reconnect the piping. It was a major re-plumbing job.

I woke after the operations to find a six-inch scar across my abdomen. I had expected it to be large but I was still shocked. They sewed me up but the wound was gaping open again very soon. They stitched me up again and again but the flesh refused to knit and the gash was sometimes two inches wide. My body was exhausted. It took half a year to close properly.

Bill never came to see me. My father managed the journey once. I had gone to Manchester for a new start but mainly to get away from people and that terrible question, 'What did you do in the war?' Now I was fighting for my survival and I was grateful to be alive. I hadn't realised how long it would take to get back on my feet. At least in hospital I had the anonymous solitude I craved.

Thoughts of Auschwitz were receding further all the time. I took no interest in the first wave of war crimes trials in Nuremberg of men like the Reichsmarshall Hermann Göring, the other military leaders Alfred Jodl, and Wilhelm Keitel and the rest.

The head of the SS, Heinrich Himmler, had already evaded justice. He committed suicide soon after being captured by the British in May 1945 just a few weeks after I got home. He was the man most responsible for the crimes I had seen, the death camps and slave labour. His death, like everything else around then, passed me by.

The trial of the Directors of IG Farben for their part in the slave labour programmes was still being prepared whilst I was fighting my way back from TB. By the time I was back on my feet that trial was well underway.

Some of the allied survivors of E715 swore affidavits during 1947 that were used by the prosecution. No one managed to track me down. I was still very ill, away from home in hospital and disconnected from all that was happening. I was in no condition to give evidence physically or mentally.

After many weeks in the Manchester Royal Infirmary I was moved to Baguley Sanatorium to rest and recover. TB hospitals were brisk places in those days and fresh air was the remedy. I had a room of my own with doors at either end like the ones we had in stables on the farm, where the bottom and top open and close separately. The upper half was always wedged open and it was the same with the windows, whatever the weather or season. At night they narrowed the gap slightly but it made little difference. There was a rubber cover over the blankets to protect against the rain and in winter they regularly swept snow from my bed with a dustpan. The room was really a roof without substantial walls so the wind and snow howled right through it. The blankets were supposed to keep me warm but even under the covers it was chilly and no mistake.

Being there was the easy part. What I really hated were the twice-daily injections into the muscles of the backside. When that was done there was an oral medicine to take that could strip the paint from the walls. Perhaps that's why there weren't any walls.

It was late 1947 before I was fit to leave. I had been in hospital for more than eighteen months. Soon after that, on 8 December, my father got in contact with me to say that Mother was seriously ill and I should come home immediately. I went straight to Manchester Station and was distressed to learn I couldn't get a train to London for six hours. When it finally left it was still a long slow journey. Then I had to change in London and get another connecting train out to the village. I arrived exhausted and too late. My mother had already died.

I had sensed on my return home from the war that she wasn't well. Her golden hair, which gave her the appearance of a woman in a Titian painting, had turned grey. She had paid the price for our war.

Father had been taking her to Epping on a shopping trip. She had sat down to change her shoes and fallen off the stool. He took her straight to hospital but there was little they could do. She died within a few hours. She had suffered a cerebral aneurysm – a bleed on the brain. She was a wonderful, loving person and only fifty-nine when she died.

After the funeral I realised there really was nothing left for me in North Weald and I left the village of my childhood for good, returning north to Manchester, determined to try and build a future for myself there.

It was a while before I got a job. Many firms said I was overqualified and of course my southern accent marked me out. There was a fair bit of prejudice against southern lads in the north in those days and vice-versa.

I had always been practical. I had kept the carrier rolling in the desert and I was used to fiddling with cars and motorbikes before the war so I bought myself some tools and got a job as a maintenance fitter at a firm with a quaint name. It was called the Winterbottom Book Cloth Company based in Weaste, Manchester. It was a start. They produced – as the name suggests – material for binding books and a peculiar starched fabric used for tracing technical drawings, known as Imperial tracing cloth.

Soon after that I met a girl called Irene. She was a real party animal, both outgoing and excitable. We married quite quickly and we moved in with my mother-in-law in Burnage, south Manchester until we could find somewhere to live.

Eight months later I got a lucky break at work and a chance to shine. The steam engines that operated almost everything at the Winterbottom factory had broken down and the future of the firm was in jeopardy. The Works Manager, who was omnipotent in those days, called for the steam service engineers from Bolton but it was going to be days or even weeks before they could come.

I said I could fix it given half a chance. I was well liked but regarded as a bit unusual. It was a fair description then, I still wasn't myself. The works manager said it was ridiculous to think I could repair such a complex piece of machinery. What they didn't know was that pre-war I had helped Sir Oliver Lyle on his experiments to improve the efficiency of steam engines whilst working for the sugar company, Tate and Lyle. I had picked up a thing or two.

I had good reason to chance my arm but it was a gamble. They knew I was handy with tools and in the end they decided they had nothing to lose. I knew it was a huge job. I had to lift up a fifty-tonne crankshaft on hydraulic jacks, get the bearings out, roughly remould them and then finish them on a lathe. I put them back in position and scraped them smooth. After thirty-six hours without pause or sleep I got the engine running again. They were jubilant; I was relieved.

I had saved them tens of thousands of pounds. My success was noted by the head office and I was offered promotion and a new job with a firm owned by the same holding company.

The firm was called UMP and I was to be its chief engineer. My luck had changed; at last I was using my skills, making up for the education that had been cut short by conflict. The successful post-war years had begun.

At home I was less happy. Irene's lively temperament might have suited me before the war but I soon realised that I had changed. We weren't well suited. By day I was working and becoming more successful and at night I was still suffering terribly. In those troubled years the nightmares which had hovered over me in the hours of darkness, descended like a thick and noxious cloud.

I couldn't talk about it to her or anyone else. She could never understand; in those days no one understood. When my head touched the pillow the ghosts returned. Sleep became something to fear. That boy being beaten wasn't the only recurring nightmare. There were the faces of other tortured Jewish prisoners – disjointed images looming and melting before me. Countless times during the night I would surface into consciousness like a diver emerging from an underwater cave, confused and gasping for breath. My heart would be racing and I was drenched in sweat.

There was nowhere to go for help and in those days I wouldn't have admitted to myself that I needed it anyway. None of us did. My poor wife was unable to understand, no one had prepared her or me for anything like that, and it was a lot to ask of her.

The memory of Les's death never haunted me, neither did the countless other killings I had seen. I didn't dream of the man I killed with my hands in the desert, though the feeling of all those moments was always with me somewhere. Instead I dreamt constantly about the Jewish prisoners. Those memories saturated everything.

Worse, I dreamt of those hours in Auschwitz III. The ghastly smells flooded the bedroom around me, I heard that perpetual rambling of voices in the night, felt again how it was to lie there in those bunks. I was hidden in that dark and terrible place from which there was no escape. I knew the slightest noise would give me away. I couldn't move or breathe, I had to be still; my life depended on it.

I'd had that dream before but this time it was more terrifying. I was facing imminent discovery and only silence, absolute silence, could prevent disaster. As the dream reached its horrendous climax, Irene, lost in her own slumbers next to me, called out in her sleep.

I had to stop the sound or I would be caught and killed. Still asleep, I jumped on her, desperate to stifle the noise. It was seconds before I woke and realised what I was doing: I had my hands on her throat. I sat there on the edge of the bed with sweat dripping from my face and I knew she was hurt. She could barely speak, and she had red weal marks on her neck for days. It was a terrible, terrible moment. I had reached the bottom.

Something had to change. The next day I went to the doctors and the police station to report what had happened. It had shaken me deeply and it had to be done. I knew when I lost my memory in London that I was a loose cannon and I had gone to the police that time. This was worse, far worse.

I thought I was becoming dangerous and I wouldn't have minded if they had locked me up. Part of me wanted them to. It would prevent anything worse happening. They listened but they were very negative. They never took it seriously.

The doctor wasn't much help either and he sent me packing with some pills. I don't know what they were. Long before anyone spoke of post-traumatic stress disorder I was living in its grip. I felt alone with it. I had no idea that countless others were suffering too. I had never allowed myself to be a victim, so being a victim of my own mind was something indeed.

I knew I had to channel the pain and despair somehow. I had to cure myself. Strength of mind had got me through the war, the camps and the long march home. I had told myself then that they could never capture my mind, but now it had captured me and I was being destroyed by it. I had to take control again.

I took up judo because the discipline fascinated me. It was a bridge from the martial traditions I had grown up with, the boxing and the military life, to something more interesting. Boxing had certainly been about tactics and agility but now I was learning how to use an opponent's strength and anger against him. I didn't have to duck and punch, all I had to do was to find his fulcrum and he would fall. I trained until I became a black belt and the philosophy attracted me. I liked the idea of transcending the pain threshold. The mind is a marvellous thing. It had allowed me to do the things I had done, but could I heal myself?

I would have loved to study Buddhism and explore eastern religions but we didn't do things like that back then. My day job was pretty demanding and it probably wasn't my sort of thing anyway. The journey back to better health took years, decades even. It certainly wasn't a talking cure I went for, quite the reverse. I retreated further into silence about the war and all that I had done and seen. It was past and buried and it had no place in my life. I had to move on.

Our experiences as prisoners didn't chime with the popular mood. People wanted to hear of brave escape attempts, not forced labour programmes. So the prison camp movies focused on the officers who had not been compelled to work. The experience of the majority of ordinary prisoners was buried and lost. They wanted combat heroes and battles won, not defeats or ignominious capture. They wanted moments of glory not drawn-out stories of endurance, however hellish. We had played our part and then, in those early post-war years, we had become invisible.

Gradually I got the worst of the nightmares under control somehow. I could never beat them but at least they weren't beating me any more. I had always liked fast cars and now I took to motor racing in search of that life-affirming adrenalin rush. I joined a club that met at Oulton Park track and we raced our own souped-up Jaguars regularly. Life began to feel sharp again. I always drove at great speed even on the normal highway and regardless of the weather, I'm afraid. Normal life was slow and mundane. I needed the intensity of the rush and it helped dilute the memories.

As the years rolled by and foreign travel became more common I headed to Spain. Four times I ran with bulls through the streets of Pamplona during the San Fermín Festival. I entered into the spirit of it and dressed up for the event in a white shirt and trousers, all set off by the traditional red neckerchief and waistband. I had always been a terrible show-off but it was a great thrill. I went scuba-diving in the Red Sea long before that was fashionable too.

Not all my activities were so risky. I took to riding again and bought myself four horses and became a regular three-day event competitor, mastering dressage, show jumping and cross country. I managed to fit in a number of horseback safaris in Africa. So yes, post-war, I had a good life. I couldn't have squeezed more in. I never thought for a minute that I was hiding from anything in those years. I thought Auschwitz had been purged and forgotten, that I had moved on, but all the time it was still there.

I could never sit with my back to a door; I still can't. I am always alert and ready. I hate being cold or wasting food. It all stems from those years. The nightmares were not as extreme or as regular by then but they hadn't gone away.

Outwardly things were going well. I had a large house in Bramhall, Cheshire, a large garden with a tennis court and a thousand roses in the flowerbeds but I wasn't really happy at home. Irene and I shared few interests. I respected her but we were incompatible. We developed a largely separate social life, began to drift apart and that ultimately ended in divorce.

My father died in 1960. His pride and joy was a huge library of beautiful leather-bound books on every subject that he had collected over the decades. I couldn't get them home to Manchester, that was a serious journey in those days and I had no space for them anyway. About a week later a couple of cockney traders came to the house in Essex. They wanted to make an offer for the contents.

They mooched around, scoffed and then named a derisory figure for his book collection. That was it. I sent them packing. I piled the books up in the garden a good distance from the house and burnt the lot along with his splendid mahogany desk. The books belonged to him and they belonged there, where they had always been. No one else should have them. The fire burned for three day and three nights. I pulled one volume from the flames at the last minute and threw it in the back of the car, then I drove home.

Around that time we had a burglary at the house. A lot of valuable stuff was stolen, clocks, watches, silver cups and amongst it all the old leather briefcase with my scrawled notes about Auschwitz. I hadn't thought about them for years and I had never reread them since they were written. The case was heavy and always locked so it looked important but it had no value to anyone but me. Back then I was too concerned about the pricy items that had gone to care much for the battered case and my handwritten notes.

As chief engineer I had become quite a big wheel within the firm so when it was taken over in 1961, the new bosses at Venesta wanted to get rid of me. I turned down an offer of a job in London and became a group engineer for the Cheshire Sterilised Milk Company instead. I was making up for all those lost years. I had found another way of staying in charge, despite what was going on inside.

Things changed when I met Audrey. I knew then what I had been missing. She filled a hole in my life and has done so ever since. In work I felt I was taking responsibility, making decisions, driving life forward and generally running the show. I look at pictures of those years and see a confident-looking, middle-aged man with all the trappings of success, the fast cars, a spacious home, the large dogs, the horses.

Audrey describes meeting a very different person. She said I looked permanently lost as if searching for something. She detected a sadness which I hadn't admitted to myself and I hoped no else had noticed. In her memory, I was lean of face and my eyes were always fixed on the floor. She knew something was wrong. She was right, she usually is. I wasn't really normal. She had an inkling that it had something to do with Auschwitz but that was all. I was surprised she knew that much. Audrey helped me win my sanity back. She has been my life raft ever since.

There was another reminder of the war years. My injured eye was getting worse all the time. It had been trouble since I had been hit in the face after challenging the SS man. My vision would distort without warning, large objects would fold away to nothing before me, or worse there would be two of them. I had to abandon cricket and tennis. I couldn't judge where the ball was any more worse still, I couldn't see the engineering drawings in meetings. It was getting serious and it had to be sorted out.

Audrey and I were not fully together at that point but it was Saturday and I had arranged to take her shopping, after I had seen the eye specialist. It wasn't to be.

The professor did a series of tests, shone bright lights into my eye and looked into it using a series of optical gadgets. When he finished, he gave the verdict. It was not good.

The eye injury had turned cancerous and it threatened more than my vision. If they didn't operate within forty-eight hours the cancer could spread to my brain and I would die. At one o'clock I called Audrey to break the bad news to her. I wasn't coming out of hospital and they were preparing me for an operation on the following Monday morning.

My eye would have to be removed and replaced with a glass one. Once I was over the shock, the professor asked if I might be part of an experiment that would further their understanding of the workings of the eye and its connected nerves. The professor said he had asked a colleague to fly over from Sweden to take part. They were to sever the nerves of my eye under a local rather than a general anaesthetic. I was to talk them through what I was experiencing as it happened.

The day of the operation came. I closed my good eye and looked at the clock with my impaired right one for the last time. It was exactly eleven o'clock in the morning as they wheeled me into theatre fully conscious, but a little dazed.

I was laid on a table with bright lights overhead and the experiment began. I don't recall any real pain, but I do remember the professor probing ever deeper with his fine blade into my eye questioning me as they went. 'Do you see anything when I do this?' he asked.

'No, no different,' I said.

He probed a bit more. 'What about this?' he asked and on it went.

There was another fine movement of his hand, as delicate as a watchmaker's, and my right eye went dark. It was as if a weighty coin had been placed over it. The sight on my right side had gone for good and I had given a stilted commentary on it as it happened. I don't recall much after that; I was probably placed under a general anaesthetic so they could remove the eye altogether.

I came around and was relieved that I could see with my good eye. I had come through so much by then I don't recall feeling especially morbid about it, though Audrey had been very upset.

As a trade-off for assisting with their research, I would benefit from another experimental procedure. I was to be the recipient of one of the first moveable glass eyes. The muscles would be attached to a washer at the back of the socket and they in turn could fasten onto the false eye, allowing it some limited movement.

It was wonderfully futuristic then. What followed wasn't. They bunged my eye full of plasticine to make a cast and gave me a temporary glass eye, which didn't match. Sometime later I was sent to a small artist's studio. A young woman appeared, we exchanged a few pleasantries and then she sat me down as if she was going to paint my portrait. She looked long and hard at me then produced a blank glass eye, some mini pots of paint and tiny brushes. Like an artist working on a cameo, she mixed the colours to capture every fleck and hue. She did a wonderful job and it was a better match than many produced later by more hi-tech methods.

Most people are unaware that it is a glass eye until I tap it with a teaspoon to underline the point. I still remove it occasionally and I have been known to leave it with my hearing aid on the dressing table. Audrey says there are so many bits of me laid out there on some nights that she'd be better off sleeping over there. She usually throws in an imaginary wooden leg to enhance the joke.

Then in June 1966 a letter arrived with a cheque offering compensation for what the attached slip called 'Nazi persecution.' It was made out for the grand total of £204 and signed by the Paymaster General. I was appalled and disgusted. We never thought the government had treated us right and this just confirmed it.

It was some time before the years of fast living came to an end and it happened with a jolt. I had designed a revolutionary new compact extrusion process capable of making aluminium toothpaste tubes and food containers more efficiently. It was my own venture and I put all my money into it. I was fascinated by the challenge but took too little care of the contracts and the small print. It turned sour and I lost almost everything. Around the same time my share portfolio took a nosedive and the good times were over. I was always hopeless with money.

There was still one big project left in me. Associated Dairies, which became the retail giant ASDA, asked me to build a factory near Newcastle to produce and bottle long-life and sterilised milk. I agreed to do it. I bought the land, negotiated with the local authorities, then designed and built what became the first fully automated plant of its type in the country. It was opened by Prince Charles and it was a fitting, if not prosperous, end to a career of which I was proud.

I had begun to reassess life before retirement. Audrey and I didn't want to owe anybody money so we sold up and moved away from Cheshire. We bought a smaller house on the edge of the village of Bradwell in Derbyshire surrounded by fields. It's a place where ancient dry stonewalls climb the green hills and divide the valleys. They enclose the lane behind the house, which tumbles and twists past a gaping cavern, winding onwards until it reaches the main road outside the village. It is a place where we live the seasons rather than witness them. It is in turn both splendid and bleak. It is the best and the happiest home I have known.

Chapter 19

The silence continued. Audrey knew none of the details of my time in E715, of the Auschwitz swap or even about Ernst. If I was asked, I refused to talk about any of it. It didn't belong in our post-war lives. It remained locked away.

There weren't the people demanding to know and there were few occasions to talk about it. If I was asked I couldn't respond. Mine was not the experience of a real Holocaust survivor. I had witnessed some of humanity's greatest crimes, but I had not been subject to them. So what could any of us say? Where did we fit in? By then Ernst's was one of many gaunt faces in my mind, men whose moment of death might never be remembered by anyone.

But something was stirring. Not in me, not yet, but outside. The public were well aware of the Holocaust, the gas chambers and crematoria by now. Those terrible images of the concentration camps had begun appearing in the documentary programmes years earlier. Viewers had grown used to the pictures and had stopped seeing the victims as individuals, as people.

Now it was different. The attention started to shift from the gas chambers to the Nazi slave labour programmes themselves. I knew the victims I had seen had been less than slaves. A slave had a value to the owner, whereas the work these people were forced to do in places like IG Farben's Buna-Werke was mainly a method of murder. Radio and TV reports started to appear focusing on their experiences.

In September 1999 I saw an article in *The Times* about a Jewish survivor of the Auschwitz *Buna* plant called Rudy Kennedy but originally named Karmeinsky. He had appeared several times on radio and TV, campaigning for compensation for the victims of the Nazi slave labour camps. Strange though it was, I was seized by the possibility that I might know him and that we could have worked close together at IG Farben. I tried to contact him through the paper but nothing happened.

A few of the survivors were now making their anger known as never before. It was starting to have an impact. In August 2000, after years of wrangling, the German Government and leading companies set up the Foundation for Remembrance, Responsibility and the Future with ten billion Deutschmarks to compensate the slave and forced labourers and other victims of the Nazis.

We were persuaded to apply and I got the application form in on time to the International Organisation for Migration, one of the groups administering the scheme. It took them almost two years to reject my claim and all the others submitted by the allied prisoners of E715. The money didn't bother me, it was the lack of recognition for what had happened that irked. Again our experience went unrecognised. I lodged a passionate appeal and encouraged the other lads to do the same.

I launched into a period of intense activity and angry letter writing. I bombarded MPs, the Ministry of Defence, even the then Prime Minister Tony Blair. I was determined that people should know that allied prisoners had been forced to work, sometimes in terrible conditions. It hadn't been a question of sitting out the war and waiting to be liberated. We had been forced labourers too.

I particularly wanted the British Government to know about E715, a camp so close to Auschwitz that we had been part of its labour force. I felt that at least we deserved a payment similar to that received by the Far East prisoners of war who had suffered at the hands of the Japanese. Sometime later a cheque arrived for around £5000 from the IOM. I was pleased that my appeal to the German scheme had succeeded, but many of the lads had been rejected again. It didn't seem right.

I was engaging with the war properly for the first time since 1945 but I still hadn't really explored my own memory of what happened. The Imperial War Museum sent someone to talk to me. I don't know how she managed it but she did a first-rate job. Somehow she got me to talk. It can't have been easy. I rattled through it all so quickly. I was struggling for the first time to bring it all back. There were things I had never really spoken about before and I am sure I got some of it tangled now but I had taken the first step. I was talking about it. When the interviewer had gone I realised she hadn't heard the half of it. I had barely scratched the surface.

One day a stranger arrived at the door. It was a fine day, which in Derbyshire means it wasn't raining, and I was pottering around the house. The doorbell rang and I answered it to find a man who introduced himself as a military officer, though he was wearing civilian clothes. He came in and sat down on the sofa. He said he worked for the ex-serviceman's organisation Combat Stress, then he knocked over a cup of tea that Audrey had made him and it went all over the new carpet. I put him at ease again and he began to explain that his organisation tried to help former soldiers cope with war trauma. He wanted to know if I needed any support. My answer was brief: 'You're sixty years too late, mate,' I said.

I looked at the rank on his business card and then tore another strip off him. He hadn't been through a war as far as I could tell so what did he know? I was very direct. I hope I wasn't too harsh. We soldiers had been demobbed with a cheap suit and not so much as a thank you. I had survived the years of nightmares and mental anguish alone and then, in my eighties, someone was offering to help. Most of the lads were already dead.

Neither the government nor the military had cared after the

war. That's how things were then. Either families picked up the pieces or they didn't. I couldn't stop the nightmares completely but at least they didn't control me any more. The man from Combat Stress represented neither government nor military and he was trying to help, poor chap. I felt sorry for him afterwards. They do excellent work.

Things really started to change in 2003 when I was asked to appear as a live guest on a local radio show to discuss war pensions. I was sitting there in the studio briefed to talk about the War Pensions Welfare Service. The 'On Air' light was lit. The programme was live. There were two other guests alongside me, my microphone was open and I knew what I had come to say. Then the presenter asked me an entirely unexpected question. He asked about my own war service.

As I tend to do, I began at the beginning. Suddenly I was talking about the war in very personal terms for the first time. I started slowly but still found odd German terms cropping up as I remembered it all. At one point the presenter had to ask me to translate a German phrase I had used so the audience could keep up.

Soon the memories were flowing and the words were tumbling out. I would never be silenced again.

I ran through the story much as I have recounted it here until I began to describe Auschwitz and working alongside the Jewish prisoners from dawn to dusk every day. This was different. My voice started to break, the feelings welled up inside me and I ground to a halt. There was a long pause. I was back there again and struggling for words. I picked myself up and resumed with a safer part of the story and gained a moment to compose myself. Then I plunged back into it all again. I was describing the ghastly smell of the crematoria chimneys. I could taste it as I spoke. Again I was struggling. The other studio guests were silent, the presenter hardly needed to ask questions. I told him how I had grown used to seeing men kicked to death each day. This time something had really unlocked. I was able to talk about it all as never before; this was new for me. That show led to other interviews. Old memories were coming back all the time, there was no bottling it up now. I was off.

I wrote to Les Allen, the Honorary Secretary of the National Ex-Prisoners of War Association, and put him in the picture. Soon after that, Les sent a BBC reporter, Rob Broomby, up to see me. He had been investigating the story of the British prisoners held near Auschwitz. He had also worked on a lot of those early reports about the Jewish slave labourers and the German firms. He had returned from Berlin not long before, where he had been the BBC Correspondent. I liked Rob's approach. He was down to earth and respectful. He understood.

Rob was to become part of this story in more ways than one. He was looking at the case for compensating British prisoners who had been forced to work for the Germans. I told him about the Jewish prisoner called Ernst with the sister in England, who I had tried to help by smuggling cigarettes. I told him about the swap with Hans and described the nights in Auschwitz III.

I wasn't entirely surprised to learn when the broadcast went out that the full story of the swap didn't really fit the bill. I learnt later that he had attempted to do something else with that section of the interview but it hadn't worked out and he had abandoned it.

A few years went by before Rob, now working with a BBC producer called Patrick Howse, got in touch again. It was autumn 2009 and they wanted to record an interview about my story for radio and television. This time the focus was to be on the Auschwitz swap and my attempts to help Ernst.

In the weeks that followed, Rob telephoned again and again to ask more questions. He had the wild idea he might be able to trace Ernst's sister, Susanne. If she was still alive, he said, they might find out how Ernst had died. I had not spoken to her since 1945 and I had no way of knowing what path her life had taken since. If she was indeed still alive, she would be getting on in years by now, we all were.

I went back to my little brown leather address book from 1945 to dig out what I could. It was old and faded but still clearly legible. I had written down her name then as Susanne Cottrell of 7 Tixall Road, Birmingham. I guessed this was probably an adopted name.

Rob kept me updated on the search to find her but I could tell it wasn't going well. Weeks went by with no word.

The Association of Jewish Refugees had told him that Cottrell didn't sound at all like a Jewish name and their specialist on the *Kindertransports* couldn't trace anybody from a first name alone. His attempts to dig out the records from the Birmingham Council of Refugees for the period had been equally fruitless.

The first bit of luck for him came from the electoral register of 1945, which listed three voters living at the Tixall Road address. The good news was they all had the surname Cottrell, the bad news was none of them was a Susanne. There were three women listed, Ida, Sarah and Amy. He asked me whether one of them could have been Susanne listed under a different name. I had no way of knowing.

It was hopeless. I knew Rob was involved in daily news at the BBC and the hours of research were getting in the way of his other duties. I thought he would give it a few weeks and then throw in the towel. That's usually what happens. At that stage it was only going to be a four-minute TV news item and a slightly longer report for BBC Radio. It wasn't exactly a major documentary investigation.

Then he called me with a breakthrough of sorts. He had managed to contact the people who now lived at 7 Tixall Road. In a country where houses change hands at very regular intervals he was amazed to find an elderly couple still living there who had bought the house in the 1960s from a lady named Cottrell.

They recalled hearing the story of the German Jewish girl the

Cottrells had sheltered during the war. Rob was elated but of course it only confirmed what I already knew. He hadn't gleaned any more information. It gave him a temporary lift but it didn't mean she was still alive. The trail went cold. I wracked my brain for more details of that traumatic meeting to help him and came up with nothing. That period was largely a blur.

I wasn't certain that she had been formally adopted at all and if she had, those records would be private. The electoral register, census returns and even the phone book turned up a number of Cottrells scattered around the country but the hours spent on the phone had turned up nothing. His colleagues were starting to wonder whether it was a waste of time. There were plenty of easier stories to chase.

There was only one more thing for him to do. In desperation he started calling some of those he had spoken to already.

He picked up the phone to the family at Tixall Road again. Since the original inquiry they'd had some time to think. They had spoken to their son Andrew who lived in nearby Solihull. Not only did he remember hearing the story of the German girl who came to Britain as a child refugee at the start of the Second World War, but he was also sure she was still living in the Birmingham area. He thought she had married and taken the name James, and that she had a son called Peter. It got better. He was convinced he had seen her in the last year or two having dinner at a local pub restaurant.

It was great news. Rob was now looking for a Susanne James with a son called Peter who he believed had moved to the United States and might be a successful accountant. Now the search began on both sides of the Atlantic though James was a relatively common name.

But Andrew had supplied another lead. He was convinced that Susanne had lived until recently at an address on Warwick Road in the Acocks Green area of Birmingham.

It was a very long road. So long, in fact, that there was more than one person called James registered as living on it in recent years. One number worth chasing appeared to be a takeaway but they were more interested in orders than tracing missing people.

Another listing was intriguing. The electoral register for 2001 showed a Susanne E James at a Warwick Road address. The mystery was that there were two other names registered to vote at the same place, one of which sounded eastern European. The woman who picked up the phone was obviously too young to be Susanne and was confused by the call. No wonder, there was a complete stranger on the line asking weird questions about an elderly lady she clearly didn't know. Eventually she recalled being shown around the house as a prospective buyer by a small elderly lady with grey hair. It was promising but she couldn't remember her name.

More frustration. Rob called me to say he was almost ready to give up. He had invested weeks in the search by now and had little to show, so Rob and Patrick fixed a date to come up and record my story for TV and radio as it was.

He said they had built into the schedule one last day of knocking on doors in Birmingham as a final throw of the dice but then they would be cutting their losses. Such was the pressure of news. I was sure when I heard that they would never find the woman I had met sixty-four years ago as a young girl. Her brother Ernst was just one of millions of victims. I guessed what had happened to him and I didn't need to be told. It had been a hopeless quest but a nice thought while it lasted. They would have to rely on me alone for their story.

The TV crew arrived in good time. I remembered Rob from last time and I was introduced to Patrick. He had made a good impression on the telephone and he was, as I had imagined him, thoughtful and concerned. I was glad to see they were both wearing poppies.

They moved the furniture around and set up the cameras so

that they could capture a glimpse of Hope Valley through the picture window over my shoulder. They had brought two cameras and though one was considerably smaller than the other, it made the sitting room into a mini studio. I showed them the shotgun my father had given me as a boy which is still on the wall and the pictures of me in my horse-riding days. Audrey served cups of tea and put everyone at ease.

I settled into the armchair with Rob opposite me putting the questions. He started the interview in the western desert. We skimmed rapidly over the fighting, my capture, and escape from the torpedoed ship. Then it was on to the Italian POW camp and my transfer first to Germany and then eventually to E715 to work with the slave labourers from Auschwitz.

He quizzed me about the swap with Hans, my nights in Auschwitz III and then I began to tell the story of Ernst and the smuggled cigarettes. Compared to those early, stilted attempts to talk about it all, it was getting easier. I got to the end of the story of Ernst and the cigarettes and they paused to change tapes.

I remained in my seat with the lapel microphones connected and looked out of the window and across the valley to Bradwell Edge. I had ridden my horse, Ryedale, along that ridge on countless occasions in earlier days and I knew every step of the way. Ryedale was a fine stallion; a Hanoverian-Arab Cross seventeen hands high and the most intelligent horse I have ever known. I even bought a miniature Shetland pony called Copper to keep him company. He was small enough to walk under Ryedale's legs when he stood still. When they died, I dug a deep hole and buried first one and then the other in the field below the window. I had retreated from riding as the years advanced. Now, for me, the hill where I once rode is a view only and in most seasons a dramatic one.

On that day, as the TV crew fiddled around, it was as if all colour on the hill opposite had drained from the scene. The trees and bushes that give the fell its texture looked drab and tired.

Autumn had yet to inflame the broad leaf trees lower down the valley.

The TV lights were on again and we were ready to restart the interview. I had to gather my thoughts quickly. Rob was asking about Ernst again and what I thought had happened to him.

My mind flashed back over the frozen, whitened corpses on the death march, the striped bodies we had walked over for mile after mile sixty-four years earlier. I could feel the cold again. There was not a shred of doubt in my mind that Ernst would have died like so many others. I was about to retell the story of that march and what I'd seen when I was interrupted.

'We've done some research, Denis,' Rob was saying. He was leaning forward in his seat and handing me something. 'Ernst didn't die.'

My mouth fell open as I struggled to understand. Rob was saying that Ernst had survived the death march. Pictures were being thrust into my hand. I groped for the monocle on a red cord around my neck. The face of a handsome young man came into focus. There were the features I had known. His hair had grown back and he wasn't as thin as I remembered but it was him, all right. The boy I had known all those years ago was smiling back at me.

'Good heavens above,' was all I could manage.

Ernst had survived against all the odds. Rob told me that somehow he had struggled on when so many had perished. He had got to America and built a happy and prosperous life there for himself. He'd had a family and lived to be seventy-seven. Rob reached across and put an outline of Ernst's life story in my hands.

'Good heavens above,' I repeated, 'that is bloody marvellous.'

There were pictures of him as a child alongside a little girl. It had to be Susanne. There were photographs of him in later years looking as mischievous as only a fun-loving man in his seventies can. In one photo he was with an attractive woman with distinguished grey hair and a sympathetic face. You could have knocked me down with a feather.

I felt lifted and dashed in an instant. He had died only seven years earlier. I felt so close to him at that precise moment and yet I realised we would never meet. But the question was already forming in my mind. How could he have survived the death march?

Chapter 20

The TV crew wanted to film me outside so I put a warm jumper on. I walked in and out of the shot several times, opening and closing gates and repeating the movements from different angles. I fed mints to the two Shetland ponies, Oscar and Timmy, that we bought to prevent them going to France for meat. I can't bear to see animals suffer. The filming took forever. I still couldn't quite believe it. Ernst had survived the death march but how had they unearthed his story?

Twenty-four hours earlier Rob and Patrick had been no closer to a breakthrough. They had arrived in Solihull on a damp and dismal day and stopped the car outside a comfortable suburban home. They had gone to meet Andrew Warwick, whose parents still lived at the house in Tixall Road. They were shown into the kitchen and, leaning against the units, he repeated the story of his chance meeting with a lady he was sure was the Susanne they had been looking for. To save them time he drove them to the spot.

The Plume of Feathers was a large, comfortable pub with a dining room. It was a busy city establishment, not the kind of place where the staff knew many customers by name. One woman behind the bar had a vague recollection of an elderly lady fitting the description who came for lunch there with a friend. She usually chose the window seat but they hadn't seen her for a long time.

It wasn't a great lead. As midday neared, the queue of smartly dressed elderly people waiting to order lunch wound round the pub as far as the door. Most of the women in the line fitted the description.

Rob and Patrick went round asking what seemed a hopeless question. Had anyone heard of an elderly lady called Susanne who had escaped Germany as a child before the war, they asked? It was becoming farcical. They left phone numbers behind the bar and stepped out into the desolate car park feeling deflated. Patrick suggested finding a public library and checking the electoral register once more. But instead they set off for Tixall Road to thank Mr and Mrs Warwick for their help and to film the house. Their spirits were flagging. The listing for a Susanne James who had lived in Warwick Road eight years earlier was now the only lead left.

They set off again. Rob was struggling to see the map without glasses and rotating it at arm's length. Patrick pulled the car over to the side of a broad tree-lined road. 'This is getting silly,' he said, leaning over to see the map, 'I think we want to be there.' His finger did a swirl taking in half of Birmingham. He mumbled something about needles in haystacks and swung the car round and after a few miles the road signs started to make sense again. They were back on track.

Even if it had been Susanne listed at Warwick Road, there were endless reasons why she might not be there any more. She might no longer be alive or she could be in a care home. If she had a son in the United States, she could have moved there.

They stopped the car round the corner from the Warwick Road address and set off on foot. It had been a pleasant, residential street before the traffic had overwhelmed it. Now it was a busy arterial road, the A41 connecting Birmingham to Solihull. The steady stream of cars had produced a cleft in the neighbourhood. The residents on one side of road were unlikely to have much contact with those opposite. It didn't bode well. The dust and smoke from the exhausts coated the paintwork, even the leaves on the shrubs. Some of the houses around had small gardens to the front that no one could enjoy because of the traffic.

They checked the address one last time, headed for the front door and knocked hard. There was no response. They tried again, still nothing. They stepped around to the next house and did the same. No one was in; it was the middle of the day. They went along the street without getting a single answer. It was the kind of door-knocking journalism that no one does any more and you could see why.

There was one last door they hadn't hammered on and this time someone was at home. There was the sound of several locks being unbolted. The door opened to a crack and a middle-aged man peered cautiously around the edge. It wasn't the kind of neighbourhood where people turned up unexpectedly.

They smiled and began to explain. They were journalists and they were looking for an elderly lady named Susanne, possibly Susanne James, who had escaped from Germany before the war. He said little at first but his body language relaxed slightly and the door opened a little wider.

They showed proof of identity and kept him talking. The man was intrigued by the unexpected visitors. He said he did remember a neighbour called Susanne James but she had left some years ago.

'Do you think she's still alive?' they asked.

'Yes, as far as I know,' he said. The two men on the doorstep took deep breaths. 'What do you want her for?' he asked.

They explained the story briefly and assured him she would want to be found. It had to do with her brother and the war. There was a pause, he was weighing them up.

'You had better come in,' he said. They entered into a narrow hallway. There was a computer waiting to be unpacked on the floor and cables and wires for it spread around. It was clearly a bad time. Shelves of books darkened the staircase. The man's name was Michael and he was warming to Rob and Patrick. He had a wry smile on his face as if he was dealing with a couple of mischievous schoolboys who he might either choose to humour or send packing. They kept talking to smooth the atmosphere. And then he showed his hand.

'Actually,' he said, 'I know Susanne James quite well. Our families were neighbours for many years.'

Patrick almost managed a smile. There was another silence. Michael looked at the carpet and bit his lip for a second. He seemed unsure which way to jump. Rob pushed gently. 'How might we get in touch with her?' he asked. There was another pause before he came to a decision.

'I could pick up the phone,' Michael said.

It didn't need a response. Michael checked the number before dialling. Someone answered and he started to explain. He was soon in difficulty so he turned to Rob and said, 'Why don't you talk to her yourself? I'll put her on.'

He passed the phone over. On the end of the line Rob heard the delicate, friendly voice of an elderly woman. They had found the girl I had met sixty-four years earlier at a time when I was fighting for my sanity. She had arrived from Germany with the *Kindertransport* in June 1939 aged just fifteen. An unexpected phone call on a damp day in Solihull had begun to unlock the story.

Michael warned them she was quite shy but she leapt over her own shadow that day. Susanne gave them her address there and then and told them to come straight away. Rob suggested a meeting in a couple of hours so that she had time to think. He didn't want to rush it.

They drove a mile or two down the road to kill some time, and found a Middle-Eastern café with chipped Formica tables. They ordered falafels with salad and Rob had a mug of strong builder's tea. He was already grinning wildly and finding it hard to stay in his seat.

Patrick, solid and dependable, was thinking about logistics and trying to pretend it was just another job. That was how he avoided disappointment. Should he film the meeting or would that scare an elderly lady who still didn't know what they wanted? Neither of them was ready to trust their good fortune. Rob was starting to babble, 'I think we might have crackled it. Do you think we've cracked it?'

Patrick, who had been a top producer in Baghdad until recently, was wary of premature euphoria. He has a warm Blackburn accent and he chooses words carefully. 'Let's just see, shall we?' he said.

The car pulled into a quiet residential neighbourhood with tidy gardens. And there she was. A short pensioner with neat white hair and an open face was coming down the path from her house. Rob adjusted his recording kit, hoping to capture the greeting but decided the moment was too precious and introduced himself instead.

'I can't tell you how glad we are to have found you,' he said once they were inside the house and settled on the sofa.

I don't think he really believed they would find her, but he hadn't given up. The phone call had surprised her, but without too much time to worry she took it in her stride. Cups of tea arrived, they sank into the sofa and her story began.

Susanne was born in 1923 in Breslau, a beautiful medieval city, then part of Germany. Her original name had been Susanne Lobethal and she had lived on Goethestrasse 45–47.

They had been a prominent Jewish family but her father had deserted them and times had been hard. Then, on the eve of war, Susanne got a place on the *Kindertransport* to England but Ernst was unlucky. He remained in Germany and was deported to Auschwitz in January 1943.

Now they were starting to understand why Susanne had been so hard to trace. It turned out that she had never adopted the name Cottrell in England. That was a wrong assumption of mine though she had regarded Ida Cottrell, who had taken her in, as a mother figure. Susanne had been naturalised as British after the war and cut her name in half becoming Susanne Bethal, a name which had never shown up at all in any of the research. A vital link had been missing. Without the Warwick family tip-off that her married name had been James, all would have been lost. To confuse things still more, her first husband died in 1994 and she had remarried changing her name again. Her new husband Richard, who sadly died about a year later, was sitting in his armchair bemused by all the activity but enjoying the company.

She couldn't be persuaded to record a TV interview, she was shy after all.

'Oh, I look terrible in pictures' she told them. It wasn't true. She looked like the ideal grandmother.

Sitting side by side with them on the sofa, she confirmed what they had only dared to dream. Against all the odds her brother had survived. He had come through Auschwitz and the death march. 'Ernie', as she now called him, had endured great hardship and made it through and it had something to do with the cigarettes. They hadn't seen each other for many years after the war and then very rarely. He took on American citizenship and, like Susanne, he also cut the family name in half but where she became Bethal, he became Ernie Lobet.

She recalled the letter to Auschwitz and the cigarettes sent off in uncertainty during the war but few details.

She knew they had helped him survive but not exactly how. She remembered meeting a tall British soldier in 1945, a strange man who had come back from captivity and sought her out to say the cigarettes had got through. That was me.

I'd had a rough war, a tortuous captivity and I had survived the march across central Europe to get home. By then I had lost a lot of weight and I was in danger of losing my mind. I am sure now that I made a terrible impression and had done little to ease her anguish. Sixty-four years earlier I had walked into her life and walked out again without leaving a trace.

* * *

After the filming there was a long lull. I never heard much from Rob or Patrick and I began to wonder what was going on. At this point, Susanne's son Peter, who lives with his wife in the United States, became central to the story. Susanne had told them that Ernst had recorded his life story for the USC Shoah Foundation Institute, which collects the video testimonies of Holocaust survivors. Over the years it has grown into a vast archive of the darkest memories of the century. Peter had a copy of the interview that Ernie – as I will call him from now on – had made in 1995.

Rob called Peter in America only to find that Susanne had got there first to pass on the news of the visit with great excitement. Rob told Peter the story as he knew it at the time and asked him if he would check Ernie's interview to see if he had made any mention, however fleeting, of a British POW who might have helped him when he was in Auschwitz.

I had told Rob that I would not have used my real name. If I had identified myself at all it would be with the nickname Ginger. Rob passed that on to Peter, who remembers his uncle with great affection. He agreed to look at the interview, which was many hours long.

A couple of days afterwards, Rob was making his way home from work, later than usual via London's Blackfriars railway station. It was already dark, winter was approaching and the breeze had a damp edge to it. To kill time he walked to the end of the platform, which extends over the Thames, to take in the view. He was looking across the black reflective water to the dome of St Paul's Cathedral when his mobile phone rang.

It was Peter's voice on a crackly transatlantic line. 'I've looked at the video and it's incredible,' he said. 'Rob, you're going to want to see this.'

Chapter 21

After all those years I was desperate to speak to Susanne. I had to know what had happened to Ernie and how he survived. I also wanted to explain my odd behaviour all those years ago.

Rob had said he didn't want me to talk on the phone. He said he was arranging a reunion and they wanted the first spoken words between us to be captured on camera. They had done the work to get me this far so I agreed.

Then Rob called me to say there would be a delay. Susanne wanted to wait until her son Peter and his wife Lynn were over from America in a few weeks and then the three of them could come up to Derbyshire together. It seemed like a good plan. A few days before the scheduled meeting, Rob called to suggest we all went out to a pub for lunch after the filming. I didn't see the need and I didn't want our meeting to be in public. Audrey would make some food for us – what could be better? He told me later they had wondered whether we would have much to say to each other after all this time.

I could understand their concern. It wasn't as if we had been real friends in 1945. I had gone to see her out of duty and then realised there was nothing I could say to help. After sixty-four years even close friends would have to get to know each other again but we would be starting from scratch.

The day arrived. I wanted to make an effort so I put on a blue and gold silk cravat with a patterned waistcoat. I never really thought much about clothes but they were driving a long way to see me and none of us were getting any younger.

Rob, Patrick and the cameramen arrived early. Audrey made them tea and we stood around chatting. They were more nervous than I was. Rob's mobile phone rang and he stepped outside to get a better signal. It had rained overnight and the air was damp. He came in again to say the car had arrived then went back to show them the way.

I wasn't going to wait for the doorbell to ring so I went outside to look and there she was, wearing a grey coat with a fur collar and a red scarf. Six decades is a long time but she was walking briskly along the garden path with her son and his wife Lynn. She turned to climb the steps to the house, looked up smiled and said 'Hello.' I took her by the hand as she reached the door and I got the first chance to see her clearly.

'Susanne,' I said, leaning forward to kiss her, first on one cheek then the other, 'how are you, my love?'

'It's lovely to see you,' she said, 'lovely to see you.'

I was holding both her hands now so we could get a decent look at each other, 'It's over sixty years,' I said, 'over sixty years.' I led them into the house.

'It's a gorgeous place you have here,' Susanne said, admiring the view from the window. 'I am so pleased for you.'

I had been warned she might be shy but she didn't appear to be. She said later that the gentle hills of the Peak District had lifted her spirits and put her at ease as they approached in the car.

'You were taller when I first met you,' I said cheekily.

'I have shrunk a lot,' she said.

'Oh, join the club.'

'You were very tall,' she added. 'It's the only thing I remember about you.'

Heavens above, after all that time it was wonderful to see her but I was reliving it so quickly. I felt that strange meeting in 1945 was still between us and I wanted to get it off my chest.

'I have been trying to remember what I said to you, it must have been terrible because I was so screwed up that I couldn't explain anything to you at all or what my feelings were.'

She nodded.

We talked about the letters to my mother, the cigarettes she sent to me for Ernie, everything. 'You did a marvellous job,' I said to her, 'those cigarettes were a gold mine for Ernst.' I was still using his original name then.

'It was the least I could do with the war on,' she said. 'My brother was lovely. He had a heart of gold, you couldn't help but like him.'

I told her the story of the time he was almost caught in the *Bude* – the shed on the IG Farben site. I knew he was an intelligent chap. He kept his cool.

'Well, it's wonderful,' she said, 'and all those years and you didn't know that Ernie survived?'

'I didn't know he survived at all,' I said.

'All those years? Goodness me,' she looked up at me and added, 'I only wish he was here today.'

'Oh, so do I,' I said.

It took a second or two for her words to sink in. He had been in America all that time, we could have met so easily. I was halfway through my next sentence when it struck me. I pulled myself upright and tried to push on. 'I'd like to have a photograph of him,' I was saying, 'and the chance to talk to his family.'

'They'll be very excited,' she said but I wasn't able to hear any more. It all came over me at once: the news about Ernie, the dreadful memories and the pent-up emotion of all those decades. My throat blocked, I covered my face. I was bent double as if winded, bowed down in front of a woman I barely knew and I felt the tears I had never been able to shed welling-up.

'I'm sorry,' I said and my voice cracked. I was still bent over when I felt Susanne's hand on my shoulder.

No one said anything for some time. Then someone broke the silence and suggested we sit down and relax. Someone mentioned tea. It gave me something to do. I was the host again. I took some deep breaths, pulled myself together, arranged the sofa and got everyone sat down.

It was easier now. Lynn began to talk freely. She said she had known of my existence from when she first met Peter many years ago. Ernie had told them about the English POW called Ginger.

'I have always known of your existence,' Lynn said, 'but we didn't know your name was Denis.' She described hearing the story during a weekend spent with Ernie. 'I can't tell you how much it meant to him. I heard the story about you forty years after the fact. It was so important to him that Susanne knew he was still alive.' She went on. 'Nobody enjoyed life more than Ernie; he was so much fun, a real story teller. He went on to have a wonderful life.'

Susanne had been trying patiently to give me something. Now, with a little prompting and speaking quite formally as if she had rehearsed it, she took the chance. 'I am delighted to give you this tape that Ernie made in 1995,' she said, handing me a DVD recording.

It was, Peter explained, a short extract of Ernie's life story as recorded by the Shoah Foundation. 'Denis, you will want to see this,' he said.

We climbed the spiral stairs to the mezzanine floor where we open presents at Christmas and enjoy a sherbet or two with friends and family. I collapsed on the sofa next to Susanne and they slotted the DVD into the machine.

It took a moment or two before the picture appeared and there he was in a freeze-frame on the screen. He was about seventy years old then and looked fit with it. His strong grey hair was swept back from his forehead and he was wearing a smart, open-necked blue shirt. I recognised the same sympathetic face I had seen in the photographs and also flashes of the boy I had known. He was sitting in a room with book-lined walls and there was a small table lamp over his right shoulder.

I guessed he was in the middle of the Auschwitz story as he

wasn't smiling. 'Oh there he is,' Susanne said on seeing his face. It would be the first time she had seen any of the interview and I thought it might not be easy for her. This was her brother but we were going through it together. Suddenly the frozen image animated and Ernie was talking directly to us.

He was telling another remarkable camp story about two Czech Jews from Prague who befriended a civilian who smuggled food in to them from their girlfriends outside. It was a fascinating preamble.

Slowly his story began to turn into something more familiar and I had the feeling I knew where it was going. 'I had another stroke of luck,' I heard him say. He said he had been delivering soup to the German civilian workers. It suddenly made sense. I had thought he was a runner of some kind so that fitted. That was how he managed to move around the camp more easily than the other prisoners.

He described looking out for the English POWs. He wanted to tell them that he had a sister in England. He said he had been watching one particular prisoner in his khaki uniform for some time. I realised he was describing me.

He said he thought I was welding and he was waiting for me to drop a cigarette butt. It all fitted. I was reliving that moment as he spoke. He was describing that first stilted introduction a lifetime ago.

Ernst had given his name and then asked mine. I grasped Susanne's hand. The reply was 'Ginger'.

'Gingy,' I echoed, hearing it as it had sounded to me on his lips that first time.

Ernie's face lightened as he spoke. He looked into the middle distance with his head to one side as he described my red hair. The corners of his mouth lifted into a fond smile as he recalled the young soldier I was.

His memory differed a little in the detail. He thought I wrote the address down. I was sure I had memorised it but there it was as clear as day. He had remembered me and that's what mattered.

He told the whole story much as I have related it here. He recalled me giving him the odd cigarette when no one was looking and then some months later he related how I had called him over. He paced his words as the story reached its conclusion. 'He gave me a letter,' he said exhaling sharply and swallowing to retain composure, 'and ten packs of cigarettes and a bar of chocolate, from my sister.' There was a glint in his eye.

And there we were: Audrey, Susanne and I with Peter and his wife listening to Ernie tell the story in my Derbyshire home sixty-five years after it happened. It was like a message from beyond the grave.

He said he wasn't sure if he was the only one to have had such luck because he would never have related it to anybody. He knew to tell would have risked my life and his so he had kept quiet. I was touched.

What I had done had been such a small thing compared to the crimes that Ernie had endured but I knew, watching him that it had meant a lot to him. 'Ten packs of English cigarettes,' he said as if to underline it, 'it was like being given the Rockefeller Centre.'

He had been in Auschwitz III in 1944, a heartbeat away from the death camp itself, and I had got a letter to him from his sister in England. He seemed as amazed repeating it then, fifty years later, as I remembered him being at the time.

But how had he survived the death march? He still hadn't explained. I adjusted my hearing aid so as not to miss a word as he began to say what he had done with the cigarettes.

He had traded many for what he called 'future favours'. Even in Auschwitz Ernie had retained his generosity. He gave some to a friend he called Makki, some to a man who had come from Breslau on the same transport to ease his life and some to his *Kapo*, no doubt for protection. And then he came to it.

'The soles of my shoes had started to wear very, very thin,' he said. 'Of course, there were also shoe menders in the camps and I had new heavy soles put on my boots for two packs of English Players cigarettes.' It was all falling into place. 'That,' he said 'came to save my life on the death march in 1945.'

There it was and it was so simple. It was the shoes. I had walked over all those bodies. People who slipped and were shot, got frostbite and were shot, people whose wooden clogs bit into their swollen feet until they fell behind and were shot. Ernie had used the cigarettes to get the one thing that made the difference between life and death: strong boots.

He explained how, compared to some in the camp, he was enormously lucky. When the Russians approached and the SS prepared to evacuate Auschwitz he had been in better shape than many. He spoke German, he had some bread he'd saved, cigarettes to trade and shoes suitable for a long march. When the SS herded them out he had decided it was best to be at the head of the column. He knew that wherever they went, space would be limited. Those at the tail end of the march could end up sleeping out in the ice.

He described the deep snow and the biting cold, much as I remembered it. He estimated that 10,000 people were marched out of Auschwitz III, plus 30,000 from Auschwitz Main. They had begun the thirty-eight mile hike to Gleiwitz at gunpoint on that dreadful day.

He said that for the vast majority of the inmates, at that time of the year, with their clothing, their health and the emaciation they had suffered, it was undoable. 'They fell like flies,' he said, 'anyone who fell was shot.'

'Doesn't he look sad?' Susanne said when the excerpt stopped. 'He relived the whole story.'

They wanted my reaction straight away but I couldn't put it into words. I was so glad he remembered me and that I had played a part in his survival.

'I hadn't heard this story,' Susanne said. 'It was wonderful.'

I realised then it was a revelation for her too. She had done what she could but she had never really known how the smuggled cigarettes had helped her brother to stay alive.

'I couldn't do much during the war,' she told me, 'but I was glad it helped.'

She paused for a second then wished me a very long life and much happiness, which at my age is something.

I told her of my failed attempts to find her again after the war, to make my peace when I was more stable. 'I wish I had kept in touch,' I said.

'Yes,' she replied. 'It would have been nice, when we were younger.'

Chapter 22

The first broadcasts of my story made waves, all right. People I hadn't heard of for decades got in touch. The call that pleased me most came from Henry Kamm, a former *New York Times* correspondent who won the Pulitzer Prize and now lives in a converted mill in the south of France. He logged on to his computer as he does every morning, clicked on the BBC World Service news bulletin and spotted Rob's item about a British POW and Auschwitz. He pricked up his ears when he heard mention of a Jewish prisoner called Ernst and realised it was his life-long friend Ernie Lobet. I was overjoyed to hear from him and his kind words about the way I had tried to help Ernst raised my spirits tremendously. Soon after that a package arrived from France and I opened it to find copies of his books inside. I flicked through the pages and there at the front I found a touching handwritten dedication to me. I won't repeat it but it's something I will treasure for the rest of my days.

The phone has never stopped ringing since then. I was invited to Downing Street twice, taken to lunch at the House of Lords and I have addressed crowded meetings at both the Cambridge Union, and the Oxford University's Chabad Society for Jewish students.

There were countless radio, TV and newspaper interviews in the months that followed and it was all much more than I had bargained for. I was honoured by the International Raoul Wallenberg Foundation, who got in touch to say they wanted to present me with a diploma in recognition of what I had done and they were sending the artist Felix de la Concha to paint me. Audrey was quick off the mark that time, wanting to know who was supplying the undercoat.

I spoke to school groups and addressed the appeal dinner of the Holocaust Educational Trust at a swanky London venue a week after a specialist had told me bluntly, very bluntly, that I was going to lose the sight in my good eye. So, on doctor's orders, I stepped up onto the podium in my blazer and tie sporting a fine pair of dark shades to protect my remaining eye from the spotlights. Rob said I looked like an elderly Jack Nicholson on a bad day. He told me that the speech had to be tight as time was limited and I should get straight to the point. When I stood up and began my talk with the events in Egypt he guessed it would be a long night. In the end I only ran over by ten minutes, which is not bad for me. Now I can talk about it all, I feel I have to tell the whole story.

As it turned out the shades were unnecessary; a few weeks later I got a second opinion and I was told my good eye should last a lifetime. What more can you ask at my age?

It was a whirl of activity. Rob had persuaded me to work on the book by then and he was putting me through the mill pretty regularly, delving into corners of my memory that I had been reluctant to explore. It was hard going, both cathartic and painful in equal measure but the darkness is lifting on it and it's getting easier all the time.

As Rob's research continued it threw up some interesting questions about the nature of memory. He kept asking me if I was certain I had seen that *Arbeit Macht Frei* sign at the gates to Auschwitz III-Monowitz. I was, but he said some experts had questioned it and nothing survives at the site today to testify one way or the other. The sign everyone knows these days is at the gates of the main camp, Auschwitz I. After more than sixty years it is that one which is emblazoned on the collective memory although many camps had them. Rob said the most influential account of life in the camp – that of the survivor and writer Primo Levi – mentioned the sign at Auschwitz III more than once but the head of Research at the Auschwitz archive wasn't convinced. That left enough of a question in his mind for him to come back to me several times to double-check and of course there aren't many people left to ask. Then something odd happened. I met another survivor of that same camp living in the UK. He was a wonderful man named Freddie Knoller and I must have worked alongside him in IG Farben without ever knowing it. Rob chatted to him as well and he was not in any doubt about that dreadful sign. I had only seen it a couple of times, fleetingly, but he had marched through that gateway every single day.

From the start I wanted to understand the rest of Ernie's life story. I wanted to know what happened to him after Auschwitz and about his time in America. Rob had shown me a small chunk of the long Shoah Foundation video but only the section where Ernie talked about me, the cigarettes and the start of the death march. He said he wanted to get to the end of all the interviews before showing me the whole of Ernie's life story. I would have to wait a little longer.

The research began and then one day in the summer 2010 Rob drove up to Derbyshire with some more astounding news. This time it was not about Auschwitz but about something earlier, the torpedoing of the ship that I dived off in the Mediterranean back in 1941.

He said the records showed that the Italians had lost a lot of merchant ships in the Med during those months but only one vessel fitted the bill, the others were either in the wrong place or the dates didn't match.

Rob was convinced that the ship I had been loaded onto had been the *Sebastiano Venier*, also known as the *Jason*. He got out the maps and the records on the dining-room table and went through them all and it had to be the one. That changed quite a lot for me.

On 9 December 1941, the *Sebastiano Venier* was hit by a torpedo fired from one of our subs, HMS *Porpoise*, commanded by Lieutenant Commander Pizey. Hundreds of allied soldiers, many of them New Zealanders, were killed. Nowadays they'd probably call it friendly fire, and it would rank amongst the worst examples in history, but back then the calculation had been much simpler: wars weren't won by captives and enemy shipping was helping resupply Rommel. No matter how many prisoners died the ships had to be sunk to save the lives of those still fighting. The greater good depended on it whatever the cost. The price was paid by men like us.

That was the bad news. The carnage on board, especially in the hold where the torpedo had struck, had been appalling but, Rob had discovered, not all the prisoners on the ship had perished, and in fact most had survived the attack. I couldn't believe it, surely that wasn't possible.

I had made it up on deck soon after the torpedo struck and went straight over the side without a thought, kicking as hard as I could to get away from the stricken vessel. I had seen the ship receding slowly into the distance and tilting ever deeper towards the bow as it went and then I lost sight of it. I was convinced that boat had gone down with all those poor lads trapped inside it.

I remembered the sea had soon got rougher and I could barely see anything in the waves. Then the Italian subchaser was on top of us, slicing through the few survivors in the water and tossing depth charges around. I could still see the ship's name in my mind's eye, the *Centurion* or something like it. Looking at the records, Rob said that vessel was almost certainly the *Centauro* – an Italian Spica Class boat – and it was carrying a captured New Zealand general who lived to describe what he had seen.

There had been a number of people in the sea at that point but as time passed they had all gone under. There was no one in the water after that from what I could see around me. So how was it possible that anyone had survived, I asked? It was simple, Rob replied, the *Sebastiano Venier* didn't go down, in fact it became famous for staying afloat. I couldn't comprehend what he was saying at first. I was convinced the ship was just minutes away from sinking when I dived off. It had been another of those automatic responses; I didn't have to think. Now I was hearing of an even more remarkable drama that unfolded on board the ship whilst I was in the water being blasted by depth charges.

The *Sebastiano Venier*'s outward voyage, taking supplies to Benghazi, had been a terrible passage for the crew and theirs was the only ship of five to get through. Air attacks from Malta and the guns of the Royal Navy saw to the rest. The experience had shredded the crew's nerves. The Italian captain in particular had been nervous and jittery as they put to sea again and they all knew what awaited them on the return leg, even if the lads imprisoned down in the hold didn't. They made it as far as the southern coast of Greece when, according to the surviving accounts, the captain spotted the periscope of an allied sub poking through the waves. He panicked and concluded rashly that the game was up. He feared that the moment a torpedo struck, the 2,000 or so allied prisoners would fight their way on deck and overwhelm the few lifeboats on board. He ordered the crew to abandon ship before the first torpedo struck in order to save his own skin. That decision rebounded, plunging him into ignominy and his fate was sealed.

The *Sebastiano Venier* was about three and a half miles west of Methoni at the south western tip of Greece when the third torpedo fired by HMS *Porpoise* hit hold number one at the front of the ship, killing many of the men trapped there instantly.

Some of those I had left behind did what I had already done and dived into the waves, convinced that the ship was going down, but few of those survived. The vessel was turning to starboard by then and many of the men who jumped off the port side were caught in the wash as the stern swung around, and were pulled into the ship's propellers and cut to pieces.

The man who saved the ship and the remaining prisoners was a mysterious German who has never been identified to this day. He appeared like the strangest sort of guardian angel, brandishing a Luger pistol and a heavy spanner. He restored order and got the few Italian engineers who had been left behind by their superiors to fall in line and then, working through an allied NCO, he convinced the prisoners to calm down and stay on board. He told them they might be able to save the ship if they worked together and that the sea was now their greatest enemy. He ordered the men to the rear of the vessel, telling them that their weight would help relieve the strain – however fractionally – on the forward bulkhead; he said their lives depended upon it. He gave instructions for first-aid posts to be set up to treat the injured and got the engines going again but very slowly. I couldn't believe what I was hearing; it was a fascinating story and one I would love to have witnessed.

I would have been in the water about twenty minutes at that point and I had already been carried far away. With the water-logged bow of the ship acting as a drag the mystery German got the boat going astern and very slowly he edged it the remaining miles towards the shore. Several hours later, he beached it on the rocks to the grinding sound of steel. There were hearty Allied cheers for the German sailor who had put enmity aside to get as many men as possible to safety.

The lifeboats with the captain and crew inside had also made it slowly towards land and they got to the shore only to see the holed vessel limping towards them and refusing to go down. If the ship had sunk, few on his side would have faulted the captain for sacrificing the prisoners to save himself. As it was, with the boat limping towards land, he was damned and he must have known it. He was arrested, so the story goes, court-martialled and executed for his decision to abandon ship so soon.

The German, who vanished as quickly as he appeared, was a different animal altogether; he was probably a marine engineer but his consideration for the wounded prisoners was never forgotten and those who encountered him spoke of a man of great courage and humanity who, enemy or not, had saved hundreds of allied lives, though more died trying to get ashore from the beached ship.

I didn't know about any of this because I was on the loose for some time before I was recaptured and I never came across the other survivors, though some it turned out had also passed through Dysentery Acre.

I listened to what Rob was telling me but I was still wrestling with my own memory. It was a fantastic story. Nothing could ever be certain after such a long time, he said, but it was very hard to see how it could have been any other ship. I was staggered. It had been an appalling episode for me but like so much else it was swamped by what followed. Knowing so many men had survived that disaster was a relief. For almost seventy years I had assumed that I was the sole survivor. And then the penny dropped.

'I had no need to jump in the sea at all.'

'It looks like it,' Rob replied.

'Well what a silly-arse,' I said.

Chapter 23

15 November 2010

The day began damp and grey but by mid-morning I looked out to see the cloud base had lifted, leaving patches of mist below Win Hill, the peak at the other side of the valley from the house. It was named, legend has it, by the victorious side in an ancient battle. The vanquished army had taken up position on another nearby summit now known as Lose Hill. Not everything in the Peak District is so polarised. It's a friendly part of the world this, now I have mastered the dialect. Add to that a warm bed and three square meals a day and I reckon I've finally cracked it.

Rob arrived a little late and by then the sun had started to burn off the clouds and there were patches of blue sky over Hope Valley. He was bringing with him something I had waited twelve months to see: the full life story of Ernie Lobet – Ernst as I had known him – told in a video interview over four and a half hours long. I climbed the spiral stairs to the mezzanine floor, anxious to hear what became of the man I had known all those years ago. We settled down around the TV screen, Rob pressed play and Ernie began at the beginning and the beginning for him was a spacious eight-room apartment in what was, before the war, the beautiful German city of Breslau. The Lobethals were a prominent Jewish family. Ernie's father was the chief executive of a sizeable rope-making factory and life was good. They even had a Nobel Prize winner in the family in the shape of his great-uncle, Paul Ehrlich, who had developed a treatment for syphilis around the turn of the century.

Ernie described going to the Baltic Sea for a short holiday with their nanny in1929 when he was four years old, then coming back to find that their father had left them. I could tell it was a painful memory for him. His father had converted the assets of the firm into cash and fled to South Africa with another woman; there was a scandal and the story was all over the papers, he said.

His mother Frieda and grandmother Rosa were left struggling with no idea where he'd gone. They moved into a much smaller apartment and eventually his mother tracked her husband down, sued him and won. It was, Ernie said, a pyrrhic victory because she never saw a penny.

Their troubles then descended on them in legions. His mother contracted tuberculosis and was sent to hospital. Children were not allowed to visit TB patients in those days so he saw her no more than twice before the disease killed her in 1932. She died, he said, of a broken heart. A family that had had so much saw it all slipping away and this was only the beginning.

'He is absolutely gorgeous isn't he?' Audrey said, picking up on the compassion in his words as he spoke of his family. His grandmother Rosa struggled to bring up Ernie and Susanne alone. She was a remarkable women, but her family had been wealthy and she'd had servants most of her life. Now suddenly she was elderly and saddled with two children that she was ill equipped to raise.

'She was full of love and she would take off her shirt for her grandchildren,' he said struggling with the potency of the memory as if it had caught him unawares.

Eventually his grandmother gave in to pressure from the extended family and placed the two children in a Jewish orphanage. 'It was a terrible, terrible place,' Ernie said. He hated every moment of it and he became in his own words 'a very destructive influence'. Being small and skinny he was forced to eat more than the others and had to find ways of getting rid of the food. He hid piles of potatoes and gravy in a handkerchief and placed it in his pocket hoping to dump it later. He smiled as he described the sauce trickling down his legs as he ran to get rid of it after lunch.

Something strange was happening as he spoke. I felt I was really getting to know him for the first time and I liked what I saw. I think he was a more sensitive man than me but even relating that terrible childhood memory he managed to laugh.

He ran away from the orphanage several times and was eventually sent to live with foster parents. He said leaving that place was the happiest day of his early life. With his new guardians he had freedom to come and go as he pleased but the Germany he had known was twisting rapidly out of shape around him. He was eight when Hitler came to power in 1933 and two years later the Nuremberg Laws forbade marriage or sexual relations between Jews and non-Jewish Germans, accelerating the slide into the abyss.

As a thirteen-year-old he remembered the bicycle his grandmother worked slavishly knitting hats to buy him for his Bar Mitzvah. The ban on Jews working in universities and the professions had little direct impact on him as a boy but Kristallnacht – the night of broken glass – did. He recalled his fifteen-minute walk to school that day in November 1938, past smashed shop windows and ransacked properties. When he got to the beautiful synagogue in Breslau it was already in flames and the word spread that the Nazis were rounding up adult male Jews.

There was no more school after that. The desperate talk amongst the adults around him was of ways to emigrate, to get away. Susanne had won a place on the *Kindertransport* to England, but Ernie was left behind. He ended up working on a kibbutz-style project designed to encourage Jews to go back to the land and prepare them for a future life in Israel. They were tolerated for a while by the Nazis but eventually disbanded in the early years of the war.

Ernie, still only fifteen, came back home to look after his sick and aged grandmother who was by now totally dependent on him. They lived crammed into one room in a third-floor apartment as the rules constricting Jewish lives got tighter and tighter. Even the quantity of gas and electricity was restricted, forcing them to cook on a burner fuelled by kerosene from a friendly merchant. Ernie evaded the round-ups a little longer and got a job with a tyre remoulding company so he could support his grandmother.

Watching him tell his story, I was amazed how long he had managed to remain free. I had always feared he had endured far longer in the camps. It was a blessing of sorts, I told myself, but I knew – we all knew – where his story was going. Neighbours and a shopkeeper helped them secretly with extra food but the net was closing fast. German troops returning from active service were already bringing home accounts of what they had done with the Polish Jews: the round-ups, the ghettos, the random murders. The stories spread quickly but they were so gruesome no one wanted to believe them, it was a glimpse of things to come.

Ernie's grandmother had been spared so far, though her sisters had already been sent away. Then, in January 1943, Ernie's name appeared on one of the last lists of Jews to be deported from the city and he was told to prepare to be transported to the east. He expected it to be hard work, perhaps they would have to build roads or something like that, but no one knew exactly what lay ahead. He packed a rucksack, and what warm winter clothing he had and waited.

It was late in the afternoon when the men in leather coats came for him. They were Gestapo officers and they sounded civil at first, until his grandmother begged them to leave Ernie behind. 'My grandmother was standing there and she looked so pitiful,' he said, shaking his head wildly and biting his lip to fight back the tears. 'She was so helpless without me and she knew she couldn't cope. She begged and she begged them. "Can't you leave him?" she said. "He is my sole support." She didn't understand. Then they got rough.

"Get ready now," they said, and I knew I would never, never see her again. She was such a good woman."'

It was hard to watch him going through it all again. Even sitting in the comfort of my own home I could put myself in his place as he relived that awful parting and I could feel it as he did. Now Susanne had gone his grandmother was the only family he had and good God what a terrible thing the old lady had to face. She was so frail.

I began to understand why Ernie was telling his story. He was committing it to record so that others in the future would know that he, Ernie Lobet, once had a grandmother named Rosa who lived and was loved by her family. He too was bearing witness. He discovered later that she died in the Theresienstadt concentration camp.

I don't need to describe Ernie's transport in the cattle trucks, his arrival at Auschwitz or the separation of those who were gassed immediately from those who could be worked to death more slowly. Once inside Auschwitz III-Monowitz, he described that moment of absolute devastation when the new arrivals who came with women and children realised that those they loved had probably been killed and burnt already. Ernie was alone so he was spared the pain of seeing others he cared for suffer.

Needless to say, he had many strokes of luck that helped him to survive Auschwitz. You had to find a niche or some way to supplement the meagre diet or you died, he explained. Ernie began work digging the foundations for a building; he could handle a spade, most of the others had barely seen one before, but he was as miserable as they were. Then he got a break. One of the guards ordered him to sweep the construction hut they used to shelter in. It had an oven inside and he was told to keep the fire going. Next they ordered him to keep a lookout for the sergeant so that most of the guards could stay inside and out of the cold. That meant that when Ernie came in to stoke the fire he could warm himself up a bit. It got him through the worst weeks of that winter.

I had always known he was a clever chap and he was lucky all right, I could see that. He explained how he'd managed to hold onto a hundred marks, which he had hidden behind his belt when he arrived. It must have been a gamble trying to decide what to do with it but he opted in the end to give it to the Block Senior in return for half a loaf of bread. It was an expensive meal but on the strength of it he was asked to become a camp runner carrying messages for the man. That meant he got a little extra soup and the chance to conserve energy. He could see from those around him that exhaustion was a killer.

The ones who worked outside began wasting away very quickly. Hundreds died in front of him and he knew it was impossible, absolutely impossible, to survive the camp if you didn't find a little extra something to keep you alive. Where people worked also determined whether they lived or died. Ernie was lucky again and ended up working indoors with the German civilians which gave him a fighting chance, but no more than that.

As the story unfolded I heard his account of the cigarettes again and his meeting with me. It was a joy to be reminded of those few special moments but it was the rest I wanted to see.

Friendships among the prisoners weren't necessarily an advantage. 'Survival you had to do on your own,' Ernie said. How true that was, I thought. It was also the reason I'd been such a solitary person during the years of my captivity.

One friend did stand out for Ernie and he was a man named Makki or Maggi, it was hard to hear exactly which. Ernie knew him from the hachshara, the kibbutz-style project he had attended years earlier where they had both learnt to till and sow the land. Ernie had given Makki – as I will call him – some of the cigarettes I had smuggled to him, so I felt a connection to this man.

What I really wanted to know was what happened after Auschwitz but when Ernie turned to the death march his mood altered. Everything he had built up to give him a chance to survive was swept away but he was less malnourished than most, he had strong boots and cigarettes as currency. I had seen those frozen corpses myself, and tramped out of Auschwitz on that same icy road so I knew about those dreadful days. Ernie estimated that between forty and sixty thousand people had been marched out of the Auschwitz camps and that only about twenty thousand had arrived at the end of the march. That didn't mean they would live to see the end of the war, only that they had survived that particular ordeal.

Ernie knew straight away that he had to get to the front of the marching column because wherever they were going would be overcrowded. He was right. He was amongst the first to arrive at Gleiwitz concentration camp where he managed to get out of the snow and got a bunk for the night. Those who came later had to sleep on the hard, icy floor.

Rob had warned me obliquely to prepare for a gruelling story to come and I could not imagine how Ernie had survived. I had been forced to march right across central Europe but I knew that would have been impossible for them. It had almost finished me off and I had started in far better shape.

Ernie was in Gleiwitz for three days but they knew the Soviets were advancing rapidly. Wild rumours were flying around about what the guards would do with them next. Some said they were going to go to Buchenwald or Mauthausen concentration camps, others that Switzerland or Sweden had agreed to accept them. 'Anything would be believed,' Ernie said. 'Another favourite rumour said we were going to work in Germany in a jam factory. Jam had sugar in it and everybody was hungry.' I could imagine how tantalising that idea was; there was constant talk of food in our camp but for really starving men like them it must have been torture. The lawyers amongst the prisoners suggested there would be an amnesty for them. 'As if you could have an amnesty for people who had never been condemned,' Ernie added.

Finally they were told to get ready for a transport and then loaded into cattle trucks with no roofs. 'There must have been about eighty in that car,' he said, his eyes searching the floor. The snow was still falling when they set off and Ernie quickly lost track of time. 'I was standing most of the way but then a lot started to die and we threw them out and that created room so that we could sit. I don't know how many days we were in there. I had some bread left but we had no water.'

It was so frustrating hearing it all and not being able to help. I was muttering advice to him under my breath and it was as if he had heard me.

'One guy had a canteen,' he said 'and somebody produced some string and we tied it on and dangled it down from the train and as we moved, it scooped up the snow. When it was full we pulled it up and we melted it in our mouths. That was how we survived.'

It took him four days to reach Mauthausen in Austria. The terrible reputation of that stone-quarrying camp had reached them even in Auschwitz. 'We thought this would be our death but we were too tired, too weary to care,' he said. 'Some bread was thrown to us and we all made a beeline for it but I didn't get any; nobody would share. Anyone who was lucky enough to get some devoured it before the others could.'

Soon the word spread that Mauthausen was totally full and they were going to be shunted off somewhere else. Ernie repositioned himself in his chair as he spoke. I could tell he was pacing himself, his face was drawn but his manner was still so matter of fact. The train had set off again and it was as if Ernie couldn't bring himself to say what happened next. He took a deep breath, the corners of his eyes were red and he was shaking his head in disbelief. He tried to force a smile then he blurted it out. 'I lost my eyesight,' he said. 'I had my eyes wide open and I was looking out and it was all black.' His lip quivered as he spoke. 'It was all black,' he repeated. There he was in the back of an open cattle truck in the snow with all those dying people and he was blind and helpless.

He was struggling now as I had never seen him before, staring into the distance and shaking his head, his voice cracking as he spoke. 'It was so terrible,' he said, struggling to hold back the tears. 'The train rolled on and stopped and then rolled on again and it didn't seem to make any difference. The snow was still falling.' He paused and blew his nose. It was as if Ernie was ageing before us. The smiling face from the photographs had gone. The creases that normally ran from the side of his nose to the corner of his mouth cut deeper into his face.

He must have been totally dependent on his friend Makki who told him that they'd left Austria behind and the places they were passing through now had Czech names. Ernie still couldn't see anything.

As they rattled across the country, Makki told him that the news about them must have spread because, as they passed under bridges, local Czechs threw loaves of bread into the trucks to try and keep them alive. 'If you were standing on an overpass the sight must have been something to behold,' Ernie said. 'I don't know how many cattle cars there were but they were all open and inside you had these zebra-clad skeletons huddled together, listless like cows being led to the slaughterhouse.' They had never received as much as a slice of bread when they passed through Austria and it was the same when they crossed back into Germany but the Czechs had done what they could. It reminded me of the loaf thrown to us as we marched wearily through that same country around that time.

Ernie was now in a permanent fog and past caring; without Makki he would be helpless and he must have felt his life ebbing away in the darkness. He must have known that a blind slave labourer was no use to anyone and he would be shot as soon as it was noticed. After at least seven days in those open cattle trucks they arrived at place near Nordhausen in central Germany where they were ordered out of the trucks and into another grim concentration camp. Its name was Dora-Mittelbau and Ernie would never forget it.

He got some soup to eat and his eyesight returned before his affliction was spotted. He learnt quickly that the camp supplied labour to a secret underground factory where they were building Hitler's *Vergeltungswaffe* – the retaliation weapon we knew as the V2 rocket. It was the dictator's last desperate card.

Ernie was given a new camp number, this time thankfully not tattooed on his skin. His clothes, including a sweater that had kept him alive, were taken away and he was assigned to a barracks, where they slept two to a bunk. He had to start again at the bottom of the ladder with no source of extra food and he had been in the camps long enough to know that without that he wouldn't survive.

They were sent into the tunnels where the rockets were being built and Ernie was assigned to a work *Kommando* hauling bricks to Italian civilian bricklayers. He never saw a single rocket in his part of those caves and he couldn't care less. By then the Americans were preparing to cross the Rhine and the Russians had surrounded Ernie's home town, Breslau, but he was beginning to doubt whether the allies would arrive in time to save him. I recalled my own journey home and that moment when the treacherous river had seemed to lure me in to wash away my suffering and I wondered where Ernie had found the strength to hold on.

'The work was brutal and the food consisted of one litre of soup,' he said. He told his friend Makki they had to get out or they would certainly die. Nothing could be worse than where they were in those awful tunnels at Dora-Mittelbau. They heard that a party was being selected to go somewhere else to work. They both knew it was their only chance and they volunteered without knowing what it would involve.

Ernie realised that whatever lay ahead, they had a better chance if they said they had a specialism, real or imagined. He and Makki joined the long line of people wanting to get out and eventually they came face to face with an SS man who was deciding who stayed and who went.

Ernie stepped forward and the SS man demanded to know his profession. 'Locksmith,' Ernie said, though what he knew about that, he could write on his thumbnail. He was waved on to the transport. Makki was right behind him and he could hardly say locksmith as well, so when the SS man demanded his profession he answered, 'Electrician.'

'No, we need you here,' the soldier barked and Makki wasn't chosen. 'I was heartbroken,' Ernie said biting his lip and struggling with the weight of his own words. Then he gave up trying to contain himself, his face crumpled and he cried out loud covering his eyes with his hand. 'I wanted him to come,' he said his voice distorting, 'I never saw him again and he died and only because he said "electrician".' Ernie's chest jerked violently as he sobbed.

I felt uncomfortable watching his moment of private grief; it was like we had no right to be there. He was telling that story fifty years later and he was still heartbroken for his friend. They say around 20,000 prisoners died at that awful place and Makki was probably one of them. As he had done with his grandmother Ernie was testifying for his friend; that life, like all the others, mattered. They had pulled each other though Auschwitz and the death march and Ernie had helped him with the cigarettes I had smuggled to him but it was not enough.

Millions had died by then and there was little any of them could do to save themselves. Their reserves of courage and initiative had not delivered them. I knew from my own experience of war and captivity that the ones who came through owed their lives largely to chance. Ernie had used his breaks well but luck had played a large part in his survival.

I could tell from Ernie's delivery that some of his spirit had gone now; he had crossed a threshold. It was as if losing his friend tarnished his own remarkable endurance story; his speech became slower, like he was ticking off the details to get to the end.

The transport left with Ernie on it but the skeletal volunteers were only taken as far as Nordhausen, a camp at the other end of the same miserable tunnel complex, and he wasn't much better off. They slept on rows of bunks crammed inside a series of army garages. He guessed there were about 6,000 inmates held in that camp at the time, all trapped within yet another electric fence. The food was just as awful as in the other camps.

It was March, the days were melting into each other and he was losing track of time. He knew by then that the war was going to end but he was wasting away. The prisoners around him were dying rapidly and he feared he wouldn't live to see his liberation. Of the 6,000 in that camp when he arrived only 1,500 were still alive a few weeks later.

Each day Ernie was ferried into the tunnel in a small train to shift stones, but the work was heavy and slow, they were all weak and even the guards didn't really care any more. The 1,500 prisoners left towards the end could barely do the work of a hundred healthy men, he said. Then at the end of March the work stopped altogether; it no longer made sense.

The days passed as they waited for the Americans but they never came. The allied bombers were always high up above but heading for targets further a field. Then one day in early April Ernie heard air-raid sirens, though it made little difference to him now, there was nowhere to hide anyway. He heard bombs falling on to the camp, hitting some of the barracks buildings which burst into flames. He heard screaming and saw prisoners running around on fire and he realised they were dropping incendiaries; the burning gel from the bombs was sticking to them. Then he noticed that some of the blasts had damaged the fence around the camp and although the SS were in shelters it looked like quite a lot of them had been killed too. It was still too dangerous to escape.

Ernie's barracks was one of those still standing, so prisoners from the other blocks came in to shelter and they `all huddled together for a night without food, expecting the worst. The next morning they heard sirens again and the prisoners began to panic;

people were racing in all directions. As soon as he got out of the barracks Ernie saw the electrified fence was hanging loose and there was a gaping hole in it. All the SS men he could see were running away as quickly as they could. He saw some of the inmates climbing over the barbed wire and he followed them and once on the other side he began to run.

Then he heard the low drone of planes overhead and bombs being released and still he kept running across the fields as they exploded around him. He turned to see that the camp had been hit. The pilots far above can have had no idea that these military buildings had been turned into a concentration camp not long before. He kept on going until he felt like he had been running forever and then he dropped into a deep furrow near the edge of a forest to catch his breath.

Looking around, he spotted the body of a dead civilian and he guessed from his clothes that he was an Italian who had been killed the night before. The body was dressed in an old army jacket, nondescript trousers and a 'grotesque hat' with a visor. Ernie was looking down at it when he realised for the first time that he was free at last.

He rolled the dead man over and struggled to get the clothes off him. 'There is nothing worse than undressing a dead body,' he said. Rigor mortis had already set in but he managed to tear off the large trousers and jacket from the corpse and swapped them for his own zebra uniform. He was a civilian again.

As Ernie spoke those words, a smile broke out across his face for the first time in ages. I couldn't help it, I felt myself smiling with him; I knew what that moment must have felt like.

Now, wearing the stranger's clothes, he looked around and saw people in the distance but no one was taking any notice of him. The wind was blowing papers around from bundles lying in the field. He thought they would make good toilet paper and picking one up, he saw that it was a leaflet dropped from a plane. He stood in the open and read the words, 'Germans, throw away your weapons, the war is over. Surrender. Your Fuhrer has deserted you.' It was, he said, the most wonderful message he had ever received.

I too had crossed Europe around that time on foot. I knew he was still far from safe and I suspected there would be a couple more twists before Ernie's story was done and I was right. He walked on through the forest until he came to a country road crammed with German civilians pushing their belongings on prams and anything else with wheels. He guessed they had been bombed out of their homes and he noticed straightaway there were no youthful people amongst them, just old men and women plus mothers with children.

Then he spotted a robust peasant woman pushing her belongings on a wagon of some sort. When she saw his clothes she called him across, thinking he was an Italian. He realised the danger instantly, he couldn't speak the language but guessed she probably couldn't either. He had heard Italian spoken in the camps and spluttered something like, 'Nonparlo.' She looked at him suspiciously then gestured to him to push the cart and as he took her place, he noticed an enormous loaf of bread sitting on top of her belongings.

Ernie was smiling again describing the size of the bread, holding his hands wide apart like a crazy angler telling of the fish of his dreams. I glanced around the room and saw that Audrey and Rob were grinning with him as they watched him tell this story; we could all guess what was coming. He didn't keep us waiting. He told how he pushed the cart on for a few minutes until the forest thickened and then he made a dive for the bread, ran for the trees and was gone before she knew what had happened.

He heard her shouting '*Dieb! Dieb!*'– 'Thief! Thief! Get him!' No one was prepared to chase him through the woods for a loaf of bread, so when he was sure it was safe enough to stop, he sat down and ate the whole lot in one go.

It began to feel like his amazing story was coming to an end now, he was smiling a lot more and his head was tilted to the side as he remembered with some relief the closing days of the war after all he'd been through. Along the way he met Peter, a man he knew from the camps, who had also escaped, acquired civilian clothing and was making his way along the same country road.

Ernie was still wearing the cap he had taken from the dead Italian and he knew if anyone told him to remove it he was done for, his shaven head would give him away. Peter and he decided to head west to meet the Americans but without any visible sun, neither was sure which direction that was. Eventually they decided the civilians were probably heading in the right direction so they followed the line of the road whilst remaining under the cover of the forest.

'Halt!' They stopped dead in their tracks. The order had come from a German soldier who stepped out of the trees. He demanded to know who they were and where they were going and he said they couldn't go much further as the Americans were coming. They knew they looked emaciated, they were wearing ridiculous outfits and they had no hair. The only advantage they had was that they both spoke fluent German.

They told him they were civilian workers from Nordhausen where they had lost all their clothes in the bombing; what they were wearing was all they had. They had been sent to repair military vehicles at a town up ahead. It was in Ernie's words a 'cockamamie story'. Whether he believed them or not, the soldier said he would take them to his senior officer so they had no choice but to go with him. As they marched along he turned to them and asked if they could shoot. 'Of course,' Ernie replied, no doubt wondering where it would lead.

They knew the soldier didn't quite trust them; they spoke German but they were so thin by then they didn't look like Germans at all. As they got closer to the base, Ernie decided they would have to kill the soldier to save themselves but he couldn't speak to his friend as the armed man was marching behind them.

Nothing came of it. At least the soldier was Wehrmacht and not SS so that was something but the game would be up as soon as they were ordered to remove their hats.

They arrived at a command post where they were presented to a lieutenant with one arm. The soldier repeated their cover story for them but the officer interrupted before he could finish. 'Two more men, wonderful,' he said. 'I can use two more men.' He ordered the soldier to get uniforms and guns.

It dawned on Ernie that after years in concentration camps he was going to end the war in a German army uniform, with orders to shoot at his liberators and friends. Before the clothes and weapons arrived the officer asked if they had eaten, they said no and he sent them off to get some soup. They were tucking into their food half an hour later, wondering what to do next, when a soldier ran in shouting, '*Feind-alarm, Feind-alarm*' – enemy alarm. It meant the Americans were almost on top of them.

There was chaos; soldiers were running everywhere, revving up motorcycles and cars outside in the courtyard as the unit prepared to make its escape. Ten minutes later Ernie and Peter were still sitting there huddled over their soup without a single German soldier in sight. He was a master storyteller and not for the first time I was laughing with him as he described the scene.

They stepped outside not knowing where to go and then they saw the first tanks coming towards them, each with a white star on its side. Ernie's face was animated again as he spoke and he was making large sweeping gestures with his hands as he described the enormous column and seeing those soldiers in strange uniforms everywhere. He heard someone blow a whistle, the column came to a halt and a soldier opened the hatch on the tank's turret, looked down at him and said, 'Polski?' It was the first black man he had ever seen and he was asking if Ernie was Polish.

'No,' he replied, '*Konzentrationslager*' [Concentration camp]. The American's face showed he had no idea what he meant. This was the moment of liberation Ernie had dreamt of endlessly but the soldier was looking for a different sort of release. 'Do you have any Cognac?' he asked. The soldier must have been disappointed with their reply and the column moved off, leaving them standing there.

Ernie's face relaxed into a broad smile as he recalled the encounter. I felt, watching him, like I'd lived through it with him and now I was smiling too.

The rest of Ernie's story was delivered in a different gear; he was on the home straight. He got to Paris and lived by selling cigarettes on the streets, learnt French at the Alliance Française and eventually got to America on board the SS *Marine Flasher*, an immigrant ship. He cried when he sailed past the Statue of Liberty and set foot in New York on Labour Day 1947. After all that, poor Ernie was drafted into the US army not long after arriving in America and sent to fight in the Korean War, where he took part in the Incheon landing. In the years that followed he sold vacuum cleaners in Harlem and studied hard. Like me, he became an engineer and years later, he retrained as a lawyer. I could see it had been a struggle but it was his version of the American dream and though Korea must have been a shock, he took it in his stride. I couldn't believe it. It was an incredible turnaround for the lad I had known in Auschwitz.

I was astounded when I was told how similar our post-war lives had been, engineering was just the start. He liked to drive fast and developed a love of British sports cars, starting with his Austin-Healey and moving on to a Jaguar like mine. He refused to dwell on the past or burden anyone with his own suffering and I am told he never really talked about Auschwitz until very late in his life.

He was a man of good cheer, I am told, and I am sure we would have had a lot to talk about without ever mentioning those terrible years. Ernie's lifelong friend Henry Kamm said of him, that he came to America with nothing except the clothes on his back and out of his own intelligence, energy, willpower and ambition he created a life for himself and a very enviable life it was. Henry said Ernie left behind a great number of friends when he died.

When Ernie was asked at the end of his story what advice he would give future generations he said: 'For evil to succeed all that was needed was for the righteous to do nothing.' I was thrilled to hear his words. From the moment we began working on the book I had repeated the same maxim endlessly to Rob like only a man in his nineties can and now there it was, the same sentiment on Ernie's lips. I was struggling to contain myself as he went on. It was too good to be true. 'You cannot let things go,' he said. 'You have to fight for what you believe and you can't be passive, you cannot let somebody else do it for you. If you have to be aggressive to reach your goal and take a stand, then do it.' With that Ernie – the friend I helped but had never really known – shrugged his shoulders, smiled and thanked his interviewer. His story was over and so was mine.

Behind the house the winter sun was dropping in the sky, casting long shadows and turning Win Hill the colour of rust.

'Ernie got it,' I said afterwards. 'His experience taught him that you've got to fight for what's right. It gets you into a lot of trouble but he came to the same conclusion as me.' People think it could never happen again and particularly that it could never happen here. Don't you believe it; it doesn't take much.

I will always regret not tracking Ernst down when he was alive and if I had known he was in America I would have gone and found him without doubt.

The Great Architect had turned his back on Auschwitz, I am convinced of that, but I knew when I talked to Ernie the day was a little brighter and that's something you never forget. Now as an old man there is at least one face in that crowd that I can reflect on and say to myself: I did what I could.

I had always remained positive even as a POW and in a strange way I had convinced myself, rightly or not, that I was still the master of my own fate, that I was taking the initiative. Ernie and

Makki had used their intelligence and made the very best of their chances and still, on the flip of a coin – the choice of a word, 'electrician' or 'locksmith' – Ernie survived and his friend had died.

No one can claim a monopoly on another's salvation; Ernie Lobet was the hero of his story, but I am proud to have played a small part in helping one man through the obscenity of Auschwitz. After that it was up to him.

A part of me died in there but I stayed angry even when there was little I could do. I admit I have left it late but now people are prepared to listen and I want my story to do some good, that's all I ever really wanted.

I can still pack a bit more in even at my age but I have had a very good life and I've lived it to the full. And, as I like to say, I've filled the book.

Acknowledgements

I would like to thank Audrey for her endless patience, love and support over the many years we have spent together; for her understanding and above all for keeping my feet firmly on the ground and putting up with me in both good and hard times. She is my harshest critic and greatest friend. I am most grateful to Sir Martin Gilbert for finding the time in a very busy schedule to offer his generous feedback on the manuscript which was most gratefully received. Thanks to Lord Janner, Karen Pollock and the team at the Holocaust Educational Trust for their on-going help and support. Their work is beyond value. Thanks to Gordon and Sarah Brown for inviting me to Downing Street and to Iain Duncan Smith, Michael Gove and Ed Balls for their interest in the story. I would like to add a special tribute to the work of the Red Cross whose food parcels gave the POWs hope and lifesaving nutrition in equal measure.

Denis Avey

I would like to add my thanks to Audrey for her patience and hospitality during the endless days of interviewing, for her warmth, openness and a boundless sense of fun. What I have unleashed has not always been easy for her to deal with but she has been wonderful throughout. She managed it with a great sense of humour and entertained us all through many wonderful evenings of honest discussion and laughter over a sherbet or two. Long may it continue.

Can I also thank Regi and the children Jan and Anja for supporting me through a momentous year. It was hard going and you were wonderful – as you always are – especially when I am under great pressure. Thanks also to Mark James, Simon Enright, Jonathan Chapman, Saleem Patka, Wanda Petrusewicz, Richard Jackson and Andrew Whitehead at the BBC for smoothing the way for me to cut my hours to work on the book, and at a time when the BBC World Service – the jewel in the crown – is suffering so badly from budget cuts. A special mention to Patrick Howse, who grasped the significance of Denis' testimony from the outset, for his hard work and friendship. He is a man of boundless enthusiasm who embodies the best ideals of the corporation. Likewise thanks to David Edmonds for his wise counsel and to Kevin Bakhurst at the BBC News Channel and to Jeremy Skeet and Kirsty Reid at Bush House for their enthusiasm for the story. Thanks also to Joanne McNally for putting me onto the story of the POW camps near Auschwitz many years ago.

Above all I would like to pay tribute to my friend and mentor James Long for his constant advice and guidance, leading me through the world of publishing, assisting with research, and helping me edit and structure the manuscript. Always dependable, he was a source of great inspiration and energy and calmed my nerves on many occasions. Whether it be assisting in an unsuccessful attempt to break into a hotel after a late night locked-out or fixing an 'aga' whilst going on about cars, he was always there. When a 'desperado' was called for James was on hand. I couldn't have done it without him.

Rob Broomby

Together we would both like to express our deepest gratitude to Susanne Timms, a truly remarkable woman, who along with Peter James and Lynn Amari offered their trust, friendship and encouragement. They provided the missing link in the story and they have brought great comfort. Their input cannot be measured. We only wish we had all had the chance to get to know each other much sooner.

Thanks also to Shirley Spector for her kind words – I hope one day we will all meet – and to Henry Kamm – a new friend – for his wisdom and advice, above all for getting in touch in the first place and for taking a stranger into his home and making him welcome. A mention too for the Warwick family for their part in solving the mystery and to Michael Wood who opened the door at the right moment and saved the day; without him all would have been lost. A very special acknowledgement is due of course to the University of Southern California Shoah Foundation Institute for Visual History and Education Archive for its marvellous work, without which so many stories would have been lost forever and for its kind permission to use the Ernie Lobet testimony (No 4365) without which parts of this particular story may never have come to light. Likewise to the staff of the Auschwitz archive for their input and to Freddie Knoller for his comments.

We are both immensely grateful to Rupert Lancaster at Hodder & Stoughton for his foresight, wisdom and confidence in the book from the beginning and of course to our agent Jane Turnbull who has smoothed the way allowing it all to happen so rapidly.

Rob Broomby and Denis Avey

PICTURE ACKNOWLEDGEMENTS

Author's collection: pages 1, 2, 4, 6. Courtesy of BBC News: 7 below left. © Getty Images: 3 above left. © Imperial War Museum London: 3 above right (H23490), below left (E1383), below right (E5512). © Dave Poole: 8 below. Courtesy of The State Museum Auschwitz-Birkenau in Oswiecim: 4 centre, 5. Courtesy of Suzanne Timms: 7 above left and right. © Yakir Zur: 8 above. Image taken from the videotaped interview of Ernest Lobet provided by the University of Southern California Shoah Foundation Institute for Visual History and Education, www.college.usc.edu/vhi: 7 below right.

Notes on Sources

Since this book was first published in March 2011 it has become an international best-seller, translated into nine languages. Whether in Holland or Italy or New Zealand, readers have been enthralled not only by the Auschwitz material, but also by its account of one man's extraordinary war. Originally conceived as a personal memoir, the intense interest it has generated means it is now seen as an important testimony.

At an early stage in the preparation of the book, we (Rob Broomby and James Long)[1] began to work together to explore and research Denis Avey's memories, many of which had been locked away in his head for nearly seventy years. These interviews for the book were conducted in person, with follow-up conversations on the phone, between March and December 2010. We were dealing with events that took place seventy years ago, when Denis was in his early twenties, and, if necessary, we returned to anything that was unclear over and over again until we were satisfied,

---

1 James Long worked at the BBC for many years as a radio and TV news correspondent on economic and political affairs, also specialising in complex investigations into business scandals, before becoming managing editor then editor-in-chief of a European TV station. He became a full-time writer in 1990 and has since published many books. His non-fiction book, *The Plot Against Pepys*, co-written with Ben Long, was published by Faber in 2007. It received critical acclaim for the forensic and detailed nature of its research, revealing much new material on Pepys's imprisonment for treason. In other fields, he has a great deal of experience in interviewing older people about their life stories. He now spends a significant proportion of his working life in the voluntary sector as a trustee of a major charitable trust.

carefully rechecking times, names and places. We also consulted archives and other published works. (See the Acknowledgements and Bibliography in this book for more details.)

Readers can see Denis Avey talking about his experiences at http://youtu.be/IHRURFAJ1Ek, and there is a short extract from Ernest (Ernst) Lobethal's Shoah Foundation testimony concerning Denis at http://youtu.be/eXNarZYRwJk.)

p.1 'I was there because of something I did in the war': As with so many others, it took Denis a long time before he could talk about his time at Auschwitz. See Joseph Robert White, *Holocaust and Genocide Studies* (Vol. 15 No 2, Fall 2001, page 284):

> Save those who testified at Nuremberg, the veterans had few opportunities to place their experiences in perspective. Most ageing veterans kept silence until British filmmaker Maurice Hatton produced in the 1990s a documentary about their experiences, *Satan at His Best*.

In the same article (page 285), E715 survivor Eric Doyle is quoted saying, 'Their [the inmates'] condition and treatment was so bad that it was impossible to explain it to people in England . . . '(See also Stephen Davies and Nick Hunt, 'Silent Veterans Trapped in the Ruins of a Dead War', *Times Higher Education Supplement*, 11 July 1997, page 19a)

p.55 'And that was the battle of Beda Fomm': What is remarkable about Denis is that he remembers so much detail. That gave us plenty to work with when piecing together his military exploits in the Libyan desert before his capture. Military records and later histories tend to concentrate their attention on officers rather than enlisted men, who were rarely given an overall view of strategy at the time. Denis's memories of the battles of Beda Fomm and Sidi Rezegh were very clear, fitting later accounts and the Rifle

Brigade archives. However, he was less certain about the dates of his desert illnesses and his trip to South Africa. After studying the War Diary of the Second Battalion of the Rifle Brigade, it proved possible to identify other key events and 2RB actions of which he had no personal memory at all and this helped us to fit those periods of absence precisely into the published timeline of history. (See also National Archives WO 169/362; WO 201/887.)

p.113 'they threw his body into the pit below': This incident concerns Battery Sergeant Major Charles Coward, who was the senior British NCO at E715 for most of Denis Avey's time there, and who occupied a very difficult position in the camp. He walked a fine line between looking after the British POWs' interests and cooperating with the Wehrmacht sufficiently closely to secure those interests. A thoroughly researched piece by Joseph Robert White in Volume 15 of *Holocaust and Genocide Studies* explores and questions Coward's role in detail, concluding that Coward's activities have divided witnesses deeply. Denis felt unqualified to comment in this book on Coward's more controversial claims because he had no direct knowledge of them.

p.122 'I met Hans whilst working on the first floor of a brick building': We continue to search for a precise identity for 'Hans', the nickname used for the Dutch Jew with whom Denis changed places. Since the book has become a best-seller in Holland, several Dutch readers have suggested who Hans might have been, but we know little about him and not enough so far to identify him among so many who died.

p.131 'When night fell, we were marched to our respective camps; the Jews to Auschwitz III, sometimes called Monowitz': In 2001, when interviewed for the Imperial War Museum, (see note to p.208, below) and on some later occasions, Denis called the camp he entered during the swap Auschwitz-Birkenau rather than Auschwitz

III-Monowitz. In the modern day, the layout, naming and functions of the many parts of the death camps are clear to us. We can see where the IG Farben factory site began and ended, where Birkenau and its crematoria lay and where the Monowitz camp was. At the time, the POWs who were sent to the E715 camp in a place whose name the world had not yet learnt, knew very little of such detail. Lyn Smith, who conducted the Imperial War Museum interview in 2001, referred to the whole complex of camps and sub-camps as Auschwitz-Birkenau. She informed us that:

> Many camp survivors also get confused about names, locations and . . . no wonder: it is only with the emergence of the history, especially since the Eichmann trial in 1961, that there has been massive interest in the Holocaust, and the full history and organisation has become known. These people would have been in the midst of a chaotic, bewildering, confusing situation – designed as such by the Nazis. It is also the same case with other war veterans I have found.

Interviewed by the *Jewish Chronicle* (17 November 2011) she said: 'People do sometimes make mistakes with names, particularly when it's spontaneous and in the middle of an interview – this is to be expected.' Even if Denis was not sure of the correct name for the camp he entered, he soon showed us that he knew exactly how he got there. Using scale maps and wartime aerial photographs, we walked him step by step through his journey and it became absolutely clear that the swap had taken him into Auschwitz III-Monowitz. It has been suggested that he should not have been in any doubt because the E715 POW camp and Auschwitz III-Monowitz were so close to each other. The route from the E715 entrance gate to the Auschwitz III-Monowitz entrance gate is 800 metres long. We have been there and measured it on the ground. In between the two camps there were various wartime installations, including anti-aircraft gun emplacements, so there was no unobstructed view. POWs and Jewish prisoners working in

IG Farben were marched to and from their camps in different directions and at slightly different times. POWs were aware that Auschwitz III-Monowitz (also known as Buna Camp, Lager IV, Monowitz-Dorfrand, Buna-Monowitz and several other names) was one of several Jewish camps. In snatched conversations with Jewish prisoners, which could rarely extend to more than a few words because of the ever-present danger of the prisoners being shot, Denis Avey and other POWs heard frequently of Jewish prisoners having 'gone up the chimney' overnight. They did not and could not then know, as the world knows now, where all 'the chimneys' were, and precisely how the death camps were organised. It is an unfortunate misunderstanding of wartime conditions to suppose that prisoners had full knowledge of their surroundings.

The potential for confusion over names and places was emphasised in a letter to the British publishers of this book in February 2012. Holocaust survivor Sam Pivnik, said he was initially sceptical about some of Denis Avey's account until he read it himself:

> When I was first told of Avey's story I thought it took place in Auschwitz 1 or Auschwitz 2 (Birkenau). Since I read the book I now know the events took place in Buna, which is a camp I had no knowledge of.

p.140 'I saw the sign bearing the cruel promise "Arbeit Macht Frei"': Some claim that there was never such a sign at Auschwitz III-Monowitz and the only one in the vicinity was the well-known (and photographed) example at Auschwitz I. During the research, we had gone back over that issue many times with Denis until we came to recognise his unshakable certainty on the subject. The Auschwitz III-Monowitz camp was destroyed after the Russians arrived and no known photos exist of that gate. When we visited Auschwitz to inspect the site of E715, Auschwitz III-Monowitz and IG Farben, we discussed the sign with Piotr Setkiewicz, Head of Research at Auschwitz, who expressed the opinion that there was no evidence for its existence. However, Primo Levi's two-volume account of his time in the Auschwitz III-Monowitz camp, *If This is a Man* and *The Truce*, include three specific and vivid references to an 'Arbeit Macht Frei' sign at the Auschwitz III-Monowitz gate. The third reference, near the beginning of *The Truce*, describes the view of the camp as he left in a cart, sick, seeing the huts, the roll-call square with its gallows and '. . . the gate to slavery, on which one could still read the three, now hollow, words of derision: "Arbeit Macht Frei", "Work Gives Freedom".'

Rob Broomby also met Monowitz survivor Freddy Knoller, who told him emphatically that the sign had indeed existed at the Auschwitz III-Monowitz gate and that he had marched under it twice a day for a year. Another memoir, Auschwitz III-Monowitz survivor Louis de Wijze's *Only My Life*, also describes the sign (page 28): '"Arbeit Macht Frei", labour liberates, reads the curse above our heads as we march through the gate.' Joseph Borkin, in *The Crime and Punishment of I.G. Farben*, states that the sign was at the Auschwitz III-Monowitz gate, as does Diarmuid Jeffreys in his book, *Hell's Cartel*.

p.148 'We shuffled out onto the Appelplatz where we were counted': Denis's recollection was that he had a number on his borrowed uniform, as did some of the other prisoners in Auschwitz III-Monowitz and that this was sufficient to satisfy any checks with no need to show a tattoo. One of the Jewish survivors of the camp, who settled in Britain after the war, Rudy Kennedy, also testified to having his number on his uniform: 'I had my number on my tunic with the double triangle that showed that I was a Jew' (Rudy Kennedy/Karmeinsky Shoah foundation details, Testimony No. 35935).

p.152 'The swap took weeks of meticulous planning and observation': Denis spent a great deal of time observing the interaction between the 'stripeys' and their Kapos, working out who might be open to bribery to bring about the swap. The people who had to know about it were Denis's bunk mates Jimmy Fleet and Bill Hedges, plus the two Jewish prisoners who flanked him in the marching column and concealed him between them in the hut overnight, as well as the Kapo in charge of that work detail and, of course, the Jewish prisoner with whom he swapped. Was there a seventh insider who helped with these arrangements by organising the bribes? That question has been impossible to resolve with certainty and that is why it was omitted from the final text of the book.

There is one possibility that may explain this and we are still investigating it. Ernst had a close friend with him in Monowitz, 'Makki', whom he believed later died in the caves of Dora-Mittelbau (see pages 246-251). In July 2011, three months after publication, we discovered that Makki's full name was Max Fried. We know that Makki also received cigarettes from Denis via Ernst. Cigarettes, the gold currency of the camps, were the bribes that made the swap work. Remarkably, Max Fried's name appears as an early entry in an address book Denis had on his return from the war. It is written under an entry for a Red Cross official who was a contact point for returning prisoners trying to find each other and was clearly penned at the same time. Denis cannot remember why Max's name is there but clearly it mattered to him at the time.

This is no small thing. Denis was punctilious about not revealing real names in the camp. Ernst only knew Denis as 'Ginger' and the only reason that Denis risked asking for Ernst's real first name was because he needed it to be able to contact Ernst's sister in England. The fact that Denis was apparently seeking Max Fried in 1945/6 may indicate that it was Max, Ernst's close friend, who helped facilitate the swap.

p.145 'With the barracks lost in darkness it was easier to talk': It became clear during our questioning that Denis and other E715 prisoners had heard rumours of prisoners from the Allied forces being held elsewhere in Auschwitz with the Jews. We now know that such prisoners did exist – one was Karel Sperber, a ship's doctor held in Auschwitz III-Monowitz after capture from a British merchant navy vessel. There was also a New Zealand soldier (and while New Zealanders understandably show irritation at being mistaken for Australians, it is a mistake often made) who was working in the Auschwitz furnaces. Colin Rushton's book, *Spectator in Hell*, contains an account (pages 172-173) by a British soldier in the Green Howards, Terry Gorman, who 'had more than one job at Auschwitz, including the supply of firebricks from Auschwitz to the Birkenau crematoria . . . A New Zealand soldier helped Terry in this job . . . ' Rushton goes on to say, quoting Gorman, that their 'main job at Auschwitz was in the boiler room or *kesselhaus* . . . ' One of Denis's objectives on entering the Monowitz camp was to find out more about any such prisoners. In the IWM interview he says, talking of his temporary bunkmate in Auschwitz III-Monowitz, 'Now, he told me of an Australian POW that was working in Birkenau . . .' This, we believe, was probably the New Zealand soldier described by Gorman. Much later, after 1995, Denis heard about a book by an Australian, Donald Watt, called *Stoker*, which has since been discredited and he went to some lengths to get it. He read the book and wondered if Watt might have been the prisoner he had heard about in the camp years before. He told Lyn Smith in the 2001 interview of his subsequent unsuccessful efforts to contact Watt and then related to her the details of Watt's activities as told in the book. He concludes in the IWM interview, 'The book is real bad reading, real bad reading. A lot wouldn't believe it.' The man who attracted Denis's interest in 1944 was not Donald Watt.

p.186 'No one at home understood what us soldiers had been through': Prisoners of war found that few people wanted to listen to their experiences when they returned. See Colin Rushton, *Spectator in Hell* (page 250 onwards). Survivors were usually advised to 'forget about it' by the authorities and by those who wanted to focus on the victory and not on the terrible revelations from the extermination camps. There was a further problem. Accounts such as that of Arthur Evans in *Sojourn in Silesia* (page 62) show that prisoners like

Denis were often treated by their countrymen as having failed in their duty by being captured. The E715 prisoners were seen by some as having helped Hitler's war effort through their work in the IG Farben factory, adding to the strain of return. That is why the acts of sabotage they were able to perform always mattered so much to them. (It is interesting to note that POWs like Denis, who had a technical education before they joined up, took particular pride in knowing the most effective means of conducting such sabotage.)

There is a recurrent pattern of such prisoners only starting to confront all these memories late in life:

> Upon demobilisation, the British Government implored veterans to get on with their lives and to forget the past, something they took as an order. While avoidance worked well in the short run, problems surfaced for many at retirement age, when work and rearing families no longer occupied their time. One veteran who died (of a brain tumour) in 1992 spent his last days in anguish over E715, Auschwitz and the evacuation march of 1945. (White, *ibid*)

p.188 'Looking back I was in terrible state. PTSD they call it now': The symptoms of Post Traumatic Stress Disorder affected many 'other ranks' returning from POW camps, but were not then fully understood. Captured officers generally had a more dignified time and it is their camps that have inspired the film and television images familiar to us today. Camps for ordinary soldiers were far more uncomfortable. The labour camps were even worse and E715 at Auschwitz (where Denis was incarcerated) was at a further extreme. Ordinary soldiers such as Denis were forced to witness the frequent brutal killings of Jewish prisoners working alongside them. Research showed that months of malnutrition in these camps made Post Traumatic Stress Disorder even worse:

> American psychological studies after the war established that prolonged malnourishment tends to exacerbate the incidence of

post-traumatic stress disorder (PTSD), misleadingly labelled 'combat fatigue' during World War II. (*Holocaust and Genocide Studies*, Vol. 15 No 2, Fall 2001, page 85)

p.196 'Some of the Allied survivors of E715 swore affidavits during 1947': For a period of eighteen months in the early post-war years, at the time when the American prosecutors were assembling their case and beginning the trial of key IG Farben executives, Denis was hospitalised in England, dangerously ill with systemic TB. After a series of disabling operations, he endured a slow and difficult recovery in a sanatorium.

p.208 'The Imperial War Museum sent someone to talk to me': Holocaust historian Lyn Smith recorded five hours of interview with him in 2001 for the IWM's sound archive. According to Ms Smith, Denis became very emotional at times and the narrative, not surprisingly, was less than clear. As Lyn Smith commented in 2011, 'He didn't want to re-enter the nights spent in the Jewish camp at this stage, apart from a few details he gave me which upset him. I had pushed him far enough at that first meeting . . . his emotional state at speaking of the whole experience in Auschwitz was obviously heightened.' She went on to say that, 'He had never spoken about any of these things before and I caught him on the hop. I don't suppose he thought for a moment he was going to talk about the things he did with me.' She described him as 'A very upright person. I wouldn't doubt him for a moment.'

(Denis's somewhat unclear account of the swap in the 2001 interview was not included in the brief summary on the Imperial War Museum's computerised indexing system, which has led to some confusion about when Denis first talked of the swap.)

Following the 2001 IWM interview, Denis wrote a letter to the Museum thanking them for '. . . helping me to exorcise this "mental clamp" that has held me all these years'.

p.236 'the ship I had been loaded onto had been the *Sebastiano Vernier*': The torpedoing of the ship that was taking Denis to captivity in Italy was a mystery for quite some time. We could work out the date with some precision – Denis was wounded at the bloody battle of Sidi Rezegh in the third week of November 1941. The ship sailed from Benghazi just before the port was captured by allied forces nearly a month later. The torpedoing had to have taken place close to the west coast of southern Greece, because after clinging to his crate for around twenty-four hours, he was washed up there.

The logs of the Allied submarines operating in the area showed that no ship was sunk in the right place at the right time. Another returning fragment of Denis's memory solved the mystery. As the book explains, he remembered that, soon after he dived in, an Italian sub-chaser came charging through the water very close to him, dropping depth charges. He had glimpsed its name, high up on its side, as it carved past him and he remembered that name as something like 'Centurion'. A search of Axis naval records showed that the sub-chaser *Centauro* was based in the area at exactly that time and then it all fell into place because eyewitness accounts and naval records showed that the *Centauro* was the escort when the *Sebastiano Venier* was torpedoed but, remarkably, was saved from sinking. After further scouring of records, we then located the infamous holding camp, 'Dysentery Acre', to which Denis was taken on recapture. It was a short distance north of Methoni, near where he had washed ashore – the final piece of the puzzle. (See also National Archives, ADM 223/48; http://www.naval-history.net; http://www.secondworldwar.org.uk/britsubporpoise.html; http://uboat.net/allies/warships/ship/3412.html.)

The affidavits of other E715 prisoners are held at the Imperial War Museum and copies of those used by Duncan Little for his book *Allies in Auschwitz* can also be accessed at the Wiener Library, 4 Devonshire Street, London W1W 5BH (www.wienerlibrary.co.uk).

p.257 'I am told he never really talked about Auschwitz ': Avner Shalev, the Chairman of Israel's Yad Vashem Directorate wrote to Denis in November 2010 saying they wished 'to express their appreciation and thanks to Denis Avey for his help to a Jewish inmate, Ernst Lobethal in Auschwitz III-Monowitz'. Yad Vashem said, 'The decision to issue a letter of appreciation was taken by the Commission for the Designation of the Righteous. The record of the humane conduct of Denis Avey will be preserved in our archive for the benefit of future generations.'

Bibliography

Baxter, Ian, *The Commandant: Rudolf Höss, the creator of Auschwitz* (Maverick House, 2008)

Borkin, Joseph, *The Crime and Punishment of I.G. Farben: The birth, growth and corruption of a giant corporation* (André Deutsch, 1979)

Castle, John, *The Password is Courage* (Souvenir Press, 1954)

deWijze, Louis, *Only My Life: A survivor's story* (St Martin's Press, 1996)

Edge, Spencer and Henderson, Jim, *No Honour, No Glory* (Collins, 1983)

Evans, Arthur Charles, *Sojourn in Silesia* (Ashford Writers, 1995)

Hargest, Brigadier James, *Farewell Campo 12* (Michael Joseph, 1945)

Hayes, Peter, *Industry and Ideology: IG Farben in the Nazi Era* (Cambridge University Press, 1988)

Hoess, Rudolf, *Commandant of Auschwitz: The autobiography of Rudolf Hoess* (Pan Books, 1961)

Jeffreys, Diarmuid, *Hell's Cartel: IG Farben and the making of Hitler's war machine* (Bloomsbury, 2008)

Knoller, Freddie with Landaw, John, *Living with the Enemy: My secret life on the run from the Nazis* (Metro, 2005)

Latimer, Jon, *Operation Compass 1940: Wavell's Whirlwind Offensive* (Greenwood Press, 2004)

Levi, Primo, *If This is a Man / The Truce* (Penguin Books, 1979)

Little, Duncan, *Allies in Auschwitz: The Untold Story of British POWs Held Captive in the Nazis' Most Infamous Death Camp* (Clairview, 2009)

Longden, Sean, *Hitler's British Slaves: British and Commonwealth POWs in German industry 1939–1945* (Arris Books, 2005)

Lyman, Robert, *The Longest Siege: Tobruk – the Battle that saved North Africa* (Pan Books, 2010)

Macksey, Kenneth, *Beda Fomm: The classic victory* (Ballantine Books Inc., 1972)

Moorehead, Alan, *The Desert War: The classic trilogy on the North Africa Campaign*, 1940–43 (Aurum, 2009)

Neillands, Robin, *The Desert Rats: The Armoured Division 1940–1945* (Aurum, 2005)

Playfair, Major-General I. S. O., *History of the Second World War: the Mediterranean and Middle East. Volume 1: The Early Successes against Italy* (Naval and Military Press, 2004)

The Rifle Brigade 1939–1945. Volume 1 (The Rifle Brigade Club and Association, 1946)

The Rifle Brigade Association Journal (sundry volumes)

The Rifle Brigade Chronicle (contemporary issues, published irregularly for their troops in the field, 1939–1942)

Rushton, Colin, *Spectator in Hell: A British soldier's extraordinary story* (Pharaoh Press, 1998)

Setkiewicz, Piotr, *The Histories of Auschwitz IG Farben Werk Camps 1941–45* (Auschwitz-Birkenau State Museum, 2008)

Steinberg, Paul, *Speak You Also: A Survivor's Reckoning* (Allen Lane, 2001)

White, Joseph Robert, '"Even in Auschwitz . . . Humanity Could Prevail": British POWs and Jewish Concentration-Camp Inmates at IG Auschwitz, 1943–1945', *Holocaust and Genocide Studies*, Vol. 15, Number 2 (Oxford University Press/US Holocaust Memorial Museum, Fall 2001, pp. 266–295)

Wiesel, Elie, *Night* (Bantam Books, 1982)

Index

The Holocaust Educational Trust

Founded by Lord Janner of Braunstone and the late Lord Merlyn-Rees, the Holocaust Educational Trust (HET) was formed in 1988. HET was developed by MPs and Peers as a result of a renewed interest and a need for knowledge about the Holocaust, during the passage of the War Crimes Act in the late 1980s.

Our aim is to raise awareness and understanding of the Holocaust and its relevance today in schools and amongst the wider public. We believe the Holocaust must have a permanent place in our nation's collective memory.

One of HET's first achievements was to ensure that the Holocaust was included in the National Curriculum in 1991 – for Key Stage 3 students (11–14 year olds). We also successfully campaigned to have the assets of Holocaust victims and survivors released and returned to their rightful owners.

Having played a crucial role in the establishment, delivery and development of Holocaust Memorial Day in the UK, HET continues to play a key role in the delivery of the day.

We work in schools and higher education institutions, providing teacher training workshops and lectures, as well as teaching aids and resource materials.

The Holocaust Educational Trust's Lessons from Auschwitz Project for post-16 students and teachers is now in its thirteenth year and has taken more than 12,000 students and teachers from across the UK to Auschwitz-Birkenau.

You can find out more about the Holocaust Educational Trust at www.het.org.uk